Art and Social Life

Art and Social Life

G.V. Plekhanov

AAKAR

Art and Social Life
G.V. Plekhanov

First Published 1912
First Aakar Edition 2011
Reprinted 2023

ISBN 978-93-5002-175-0

Published by
AAKAR BOOKS
28 E Pocket IV, Mayur Vihar Phase I
Delhi 110 091, India
www.aakarbooks.com

Printed at
D.K. Fine Art Press, Delhi

CONTENTS

GEORGI VALENTINOVICH PLEKHANOV

G. V. PLEKHANOV was born in 1856, the son of a small landowner in the Province of Tambov. He was educated at the Voronezh Military Gymnasium, but later forsook the military career that had been intended for him. The following dates in his life may be of interest to the reader:

1873. Entered the Konstantinov Military College.

1874. Transferred to the St. Petersburg Mining Institute.

1876. As a Narodnik student took a leading part in the anti-Tsarist demonstration of students and workers at St. Petersburg in December. Forced to take refuge abroad.

1877. Returned to Russia to conduct revolutionary propaganda among the workers.

1880. Again forced into exile, which was to last for 37 years.

1883. Assisted in founding The Emancipation of Labour Group —the first Marxist Russian Social-Democratic Organisation. Published his *Socialism and the Political Struggle* directed against the programme of the Narodnaya Volya (terrorist faction of the Narodniks).

1885. *Our Differences*: directed against the Narodniks and their theory of the peasant commune as a basis for socialism in Russia.

1889. Participated in the formation of the Second International.

1895. *On the Development of the Monist View of History*: the first comprehensive exposition of Marxist philosophy to be made in the Russian language. (Published in English under the title of *In Defence of Materialism*. Translated by Andrew Rothstein. London, 1947, Lawrence & Wishart.)

1899. The first of his *Letters without Address* published.

1900. Joins the editorial board of Lenin's *Iskra*.

1903. Supports the Bolsheviks at the Second Congress of the Russian Social-Democratic Labour Party: but breaks with them a few months later.

1905. Supported the Mensheviks on the issue of armed proletarian insurrection. His *French Dramatic Literature and French Eighteenth Century Painting from the Sociological Standpoint* published in *Pravda*.

1912. *Art and Social Life* published in *Sovremennik*.

1914. Calls for unity between the capitalist and working classes of Russia to continue the war to a victorious conclusion.

1917. Returns to Russia. Opposes the campaign for Soviet power, but after October refuses to advocate resort to arms against the workers. Measures for his safety and well-being assured by the Soviet Government.

1918. Death at a sanatorium in Finland. Burial at Petrograd near the grave of the great revolutionary philosopher and critic, Belinsky.

INTRODUCTION

THE name of Plekhanov is well-known in Britain as that of an outstanding Marxist, though few of his philosophical and political works have been translated into English. His writings were of fundamental importance in Russia. They played a major part in defeating idealist and Utopian theories of socialism and provided a basis in Marxist theory for the early Russian Social-Democratic movement. More than this, they made a considerable original contribution to Marxist thought throughout the world.

So far Plekhanov has scarcely been known in this country as a literary and art critic. In this field, however, he did important pioneer work, contributing much that is original and invaluable for the Marxist theory of literature. The purpose of this book is to acquaint the English reader with some of these writings. Those translated here have been selected as representing the most fundamental of the Marxist research which he conducted into the origins of art and the relationship of art and literature to society.

Plekhanov was the first Russian to apply the Marxist method to the study of aesthetics and the origins of art, to literature and to literary criticism. He first turned his attention to literary criticism in the 'eighties, when he was concerned to expose the mistakes of Narodnik[1] ideology. His articles on the works of such Narodnik writers as Uspensky, and others of lesser stature, showed how their realistic portrayal of life in the Russian village in fact refuted their own political idealism.

It was the rise of a working-class in Russia that made possible Plekhanov's "scientific criticism," as he termed it—this new contribution to criticism, in which he differed from his great

[1] Narodniks: literally, populists, i.e. friends of the people. They believed that the peasant communes could become the basis for a socialist Russia. Consisting of young intellectuals from the professional classes and the gentry, they went out among the peasantry and sought to educate them and rouse them against the autocracy. They did not attach importance to the proletariat as a revolutionary class.

from his great predecessors, Belinsky, Chernyshevsky and Dobroliubov.[2] For although he carried forward the revolutionary democratic traditions of these great critics, their materialism, and emphasis on the social character of literature, he particularly opposed what he called Chernyshevsky's "criticism of enlightenment."

In referring to this "criticism of enlightenment" Plekhanov meant that, although a materialist, Chernyshevsky lacked an adequate understanding of the historical forces that could lead to the overthrow of the autocracy, and that he therefore based his criticism on "what ought to be if men would listen to the voice of reason."

In the early 'sixties, when Chernyshevsky was writing, the Russian working class to all intents and purposes was not yet in existence. A whole epoch, that of the development of industry, of a bourgeois class and a proletariat, lay ahead. The Russian peasantry and progressive intelligentsia, to whom Chernyshevsky turned, were by their nature incapable of achieving a socialist revolution. In this sense Chernyshevsky's views were Utopian. The proof of this was to be found in the failure of the Narodniks, in the later 'sixties and 'seventies, to rouse the peasants against the autocracy. Plekhanov, as a student, himself participated in this movment and drew valuable lessons from it.

It was the rise of the Russian working class, with which he had been in day-to-day contact during his revolutionary activities in St. Petersburg, that prepared the ground for Plekhanov's acceptance of Marxism.

Plekhanov developed the Marxist thesis that idealism is hostile to scientific aesthetics, that literature and art in their origin and development can only be truly understood in the light of the materialist conception of history. His scientific criticism placed in the forefront an analysis of the relationship between men's mode of life and their aesthetic

[2] *V. G. Belinsky* (1811-1848). The first great Russian literary critic, and the first to give an historical perspective of Russian literature, its achievements, potentialities and tasks. *N. G. Chernyshevsky* (1828-89). Developed the work of Belinsky in the period of the peasant revolts and "Emancipation" of 1861. Literary critic, economist, pedagogue, and revolutionary organiser. In 1862 exiled to Siberia, and kept there until 1881. *N. A. Dobroliubov* (1836-1861). Friend and collaborator of Chernyshevsky in the literary field.

tastes, between social classes and the creation of works of art.

In pursuing these themes he was animated by the desire to make literature the property of the working class and to develop literary criticism as a weapon of the working-class struggle for emancipation. In an article addressed to the working-class reader Plekhanov wrote: "You must have *your* poetry, *your* songs, *your* verse. In them you must seek the expression of your own grief, your own hopes and aspirations."[3] He developed this idea further in a number of his critical articles, one of the most outstanding of which is that on Gorky's play, *The Enemies*.[4]

In the early days of his exile Plekhanov was forced to live from hand to mouth. Yet he not only mastered in a few years the Marxist classics and a large number of works bearing on history and economics by bourgeois writers, but also undertook the study of such varied scientific subjects as zoology, anatomy, geology and anthropology. His knowledge in the latter field is revealed with telling effect in his *Letters without Address*, where he deals primarily with the subject of primitive art.

Here Plekhanov gives us a deep analysis of the sources and laws of development of art. He shows art as springing, in the first place, from the material, economic and social requirements of man. Man's primary attitude to reality was "utilitarian"; his skill and creative activity arose from his attempts to utilise and shape the objects around him to serve as weapons, tools, vessels and so on. It was only secondarily that the aesthetic aspect entered in, that men began to ornament themselves and the things they made; and in the most primitive societies, this art was always directly related to a useful social purpose. Again, Plekhanov proves that "labour is older than play." He is careful to show, however, that where the character of labour and the material needs of society do not determine the form and content of art *directly* they always do so *indirectly*, for example, through the primitive forms of religion to which they give rise. The development of the forces of production, which led to the division of labour, accentuated this in-

[3] *A Few Words to the Working-Class Reader* (1885).

[4] *The Psychology of the Working-Class Movement* (1907).

direct dependence of art on the material requirements of society and on social classes, but in no way altered the fact of its dependence.

Having clearly established the relationship of art to labour in primitive society, Plekhanov goes on to develop scientific criticism in relation to class society in historical times. In his article on French eighteenth century drama and painting, Plekhanov applies the materialist outlook on history to art in a class society, in order to show how, directly and indirectly, art and literature continue to be dependent upon the economic life of society. He vividly demonstrates how the creation of artistic works and their appreciation are in the final analysis dependent on the artist's and his public's class position in society—in other words on their relationship to the means of production. He shows how the development of art and literature, the changes in its content, and the differences of artistic taste and form from one period to another are not due to the whim of some accidental fashion. They are determined in the final count by the development of the class struggle, by the rise of new classes, by the decline of old ones, and by the needs and requirements of these classes at varying stages in their struggle for power.

In his article on *Art and Social Life* Plekhanov takes this analysis still further and traces for us how the art of a society dominated by a given class will decline when that class can no longer act as a progressive force.

In Plekhanov's view, the work of a writer is *progressive* when it is based upon the interests of a class that can at a given period lead the whole of society forward and thus constitutes the broadest means of ideological communication between the people. For his own time, as we have seen, Plekhanov already regarded this class as being the proletariat. The "narrowed confines" of bourgeois art in this same period he regarded as *unprogressive* or "devoid of content." For, as the bourgeois class is the ruling class and seeks to conserve its dominance at all costs, a decline in art takes place which finds expression in an attempt to escape from reality, in mysticism, formalism, naturalism and the practice of "art for art's sake."

As will be seen, one common factor unites the supporters of all these "isms": they turn their back on the

In his *Letters without Address* Plekhanov showed that, "in a work of art, form must, in the final analysis, correspond with content." In his *Art and Social Life* he brilliantly develops this thesis. He shows how artists who are dependent upon a doomed class are afraid to face reality and how they reveal their ideological bankruptcy in attributing primary importance to form rather than content. Placing an intrinsic value on line, colour, word and effect, rather than treating them as means of expression for the essential ideas and social movements of their time, which they ignored, these artists ceased to produce true works of art. Without any firm roots in reality the forms they used were unstable, disintegrated and degenerated. History has proved Plekhanov right. Most of these artists are already forgotten. Finally, Plekhanov convincingly demonstrates how art for art's sake, which the artist espouses in his revolt against society, becomes art for money's sake.

While Plekhanov made a tremendous contribution from the Marxist point of view to the study of the laws governing the development of art and literature, certain departures from his own declared acceptance of Marxist criteria are reflected in his literary work. These divergences are closely connected with his philosophical and political differences with the Bolsheviks. Perhaps the most important of them in the literary field is that connected with the function of literature. The development of his approach to this question is well illustrated in his attitude to Chernyshevsky.

We have already noted that Plekhanov criticised Chernyshevsky as an "enlightener"—as seeing the motive force of history in reason and morality, in the idea of "what ought to be if men would listen to the voice of reason." However, later Russian Marxists have pointed out that Plekhanov's criticism did not take into account the importance of the *revolutionary* character of Chernyshevsky's teaching. Chernyshevsky worked for the achievement of his aims through the organisation of the peasantry for the revolutionary overthrow of the autocracy. His writings, across the censorship, sought to influence the young people of his time to take up this work.

But Plekhanov did not appear to appreciate Chernyshevsky's view that it was the task of the writer to offer a solution to the problems of society, to point out the way forward to the reader and thus help to *change* society. In his criticism of Gorky's *Mother*,

portance of the *revolutionary* character of Chernyshevsky's teaching. Chernyshevsky worked for the achievement of his aims through the organisation of the peasantry for the revolutionary overthrow of the autocracy. His writings, across the censorship, sought to influence the young people of his time to take up this work.

But Plekhanov did not appear to appreciate Chernyshevsky's view that it was the task of the writer to offer a solution to the problems of society, to point out the way forward to the reader and thus help to *change* society. In his criticism of Gorky's *Mother,* Plekhanov attacked the author for acting as "a propagandist of Marxist views" and advised him that "to speak mainly in the language of logic was little suited to an author, a man who speaks mainly in the language of images."[5] Plekhanov went even further than this. He maintained that literary criticism, which he believed to be the rightful place for "the language of logic"[6] should be "as objective as physics." The critic must not praise those authors whose works express the social trends that please him while rejecting those which give expression to ones he finds unpleasant.[7] Plekhanov thus tended to confine literature and criticism to a passive and contemplative role, excluding the partisan, class outlook that Marxist thinkers and critics have considered essential. From the Bolshevik standpoint the most important answer to this was given by Lenin in his article *The Party Organisation and a Party Literature,* written in 1905.[8] In answer to the question, what is meant by a "party literature" Lenin wrote: "Not only that for the socialist proletariat literature cannot be an instrument for the profit of individuals or groups.... Literature must become a cog and screw of one single great social democratic mechanism, brought into action by the whole conscious vanguard of the whole working class." True, he makes the reservation that "comparisons are odious" and that any comparison of literature with a screw, of a living movement with a mechanism, must be odious too. "There is no question," he goes on, "but that in this matter a guarantee of greater scope for individual

[5] G. V. Plekhanov, *Works,* Moscow, 1925, Vol. XIV, p. 192.

[6] *Ibid.,* p. 183.

[7] *Ibid.,* p. 184.

[8] V. I. Lenin, *Works,* Vol. VIII, Moscow, 1931, p. 386.

initiative, individual tastes, scope for thought and fantasy, form and content is absolutely essential...." Nor does he suggest that literature can be transformed all at once to fulfil such a role. "Far be it from us to advocate some sort of uniform system or solution of the problem by means of a few decrees.... It is a question of the whole of our party, the whole conscious proletariat throughout Russia becoming aware of this new task, posing it clearly and tackling its solution on every possible occasion."[9] In a striking passage he then goes on to show why he considers that neutrality in the literary field must be false. "To live in society and be free from society is impossible. The freedom of the bourgeois writer... is only masked (or hypocritically masked) dependence on the money bag, on bribery, on maintenance. And we socialists are unmasking this hypocrisy, tearing down the false signs—not in order to arrive at a classless literature (this will be possible only in a socialist, classless society), but in order to oppose to hypocritically free literature, which is in fact tied to the bourgeoisie, a truly free literature, *openly* linked with the proletariat. It will be *free* because, not profit and career, but the idea of socialism and sympathy for labour will win ever new forces to its ranks."[10]

Among other difficulties in Plekhanov's work are those arising from his acceptance of certain Kantian and Darwinian concepts that conflict with a Marxist outlook. Such is his belief, deriving from Kant, that the individual is endowed with a "faculty" that he terms "the contemplative faculty" determining his appreciation of beauty. He makes it clear that he regards this faculty as in the nature of an instinct. Again, he relies on Darwin's "principle of antithesis" to explain a number of artistic phenomena.

Plekhanov's approach is often based on the sharp line he draws between social influences and "the contemplative faculty," between environment and instinct, between man's perception of reality and his "aesthetic sense."

This is not unconnected with his acceptance for some time of the "theory of hieroglyphics." According to this theory "forms and relationships of things in themselves

[9] V. I. Lenin, *Works*, Vol. VIII, Moscow, 1931, p. 388.

[10] *Ibid.*, p. 389.

cannot be such as they seem to us, i.e. as they appear to us 'translated' in our heads. Our images of the forms and relationships of things are no more than hieroglyphs."[11]

Lenin rejected this theory and advanced the theory of reflection, which regards the mind as directly reflecting the objects we see, their forms and relationships.[12] It was Plekhanov's denial of this direct reflection of reality in the human mind, his supposition that instead it indirectly received symbols of reality, that facilitated his acceptance of an absolute criterion of beauty—in other words his "contemplative faculty." This faculty was quite unrelated to social and class conditions. His acceptance of it helps to explain the contradiction between Plekhanov's objectivist attitude to aesthetics, art and literature and his view of the working class as the historically progressive class of his time.

In the foregoing an attempt has been made to indicate the inconsistencies to be found in the writings included in this collection. These reflect the more fundamental philosophical inconsistencies in his interpretation of Marxism which led him eventually to join with the Mensheviks.

In Lenin's view, they arose from his failure to understand the full dialectical content of Marxism, which requires the fullest study of any phenomenon in all its changing, contradictory aspects, both in its internal struggle, motion and development and in the light of the external influences bearing on it. This, it can be seen, is a problem of method that is of fundamental importance for Marxism. Plekhanov, in effect, tended to transfer to Russia an *application* of Marxist method already made in regard to certain western capitalist countries, instead of applying Marxist *method* afresh to an analysis of all the aspects of the situation peculiar to Russia. He believed that the proletariat must act as an auxiliary force in the Russian bourgeois revolution and not as an independent leading force. He had no faith in an alliance of proletariat and peasantry. No doubt his disillusionment with the

[11] G. V. Plekhanov, *Materialismus Militans, Works,* Moscow, 1926, Vol. XVII, p. 34.

[12] V. I. Lenin, *Materialism and Empirio-Criticism,* Chapter 4, § 6.

escapist and degrading literature imported from the other side of the Atlantic and by the cynical literature of gloom and despair published by "intellectual" writers. The cynicism, hopelessness and pessimism of such works are not new. Plekhanov wrote at a time, in the first decade of this century, when just such morbid and reactionary works were being produced by the Russian intelligentsia. The sham high-brow in his ivory tower was just as much a feature of pre-revolutionary Russian society as he is in Britain today. Plekhanov tells us why this was so; he explains how the high-brow artist and literateur, with his incomprehensible phrases, his symbols, his cubes, his introspection, gloom, thinly veiled pornography and other idiosyncrasies, far from standing above society and classes, as he affects to do, is really very mundanely subordinate to them in a retrogressive way. It is for these very reasons that Plekhanov's work is so interesting and important for us today.

The translators, wherever possible, have given the original text of English quotations by Plekhanov. Where German and French originals have been used by the author direct translations have been made from the original unless otherwise stated. Some additional footnotes to those of the author and the Russian editors have been introduced to assist the English reader in regard to personages with whom he may not be familiar. Most of the Russian verse quoted by Plekhanov has not been previously translated into English.

German and French originals have been used by the author direct translations have been made from the original unless otherwise stated. Some additional footnotes to those of the author and the Russian editors have been introduced to assist the English reader in regard to personages with whom he may not be familiar. Most of the Russian verse quoted by Plekhanov has not been previously translated into English.

LETTERS WITHOUT ADDRESS

FIRST LETTER[1]

HISTORICAL MATERIALISM AND ART

DEAR SIR,—We are going to have a discussion together about art. But in all research of any accuracy, no matter what its subject, it is essential to keep to a strictly defined terminology. We must, therefore, in the first place, say exactly what meaning we attach to the word *art*. On the other hand, there is no doubt that a definition of the subject that is in any way satisfactory can only emerge as a result of our research. In other words, we have to define something which we are not in a position to define. How are we to find a way out of this contradiction? I think that we may do so in this way: for the time being I shall adopt a temporary definition and afterwards I shall amplify and correct it as the problem is clarified in the light of our research.

What tentative definition, then, am I to adopt?

Leo Tolstoy, in his book, *What is Art?*, cites a number of definitions of art that in his view contradict each other, and finds none of them satisfactory. In actual fact, the definitions he quotes are by no means so widely divergent nor so mistaken as he thinks. But let us allow that they are all very bad ones and try and see whether we cannot accept his own definition of art.

[1] This letter first appeared in part only, in 1899, in the journal *Nachalo*. It was published under the title of "On Art—A Sociological Study" and the pseudonym, N. Andreyevich. The journal was closed down, however, when only the first half of the article had been printed. It appeared in full later in the same year in *Nauchnoye Obozrenie* (*The Scientific Review*), this time under the title of "Letters without Address—First Letter" and with a different pseudonym, A. Kirsanov. The second and third letters followed in the same journal in the year 1900, but at the time were published as two parts of the same letter. The last three letters, which were not published during the author's life-time, have been conventionally numbered four, five and six. For the convenience of the English reader each letter has been given a title indicative in some degree of its content. These headings are not Plekhanov's.—TRANS.

"Art," he says, "is one of the means whereby men communicate with one another. . . . And a special feature of this communication, which distinguishes it from communication by means of words, lies in the fact that by words one man conveys to another his *thoughts* [my italics], whereas by art men convey to each other their *feelings* [my italics again]."

As far as I am concerned, I shall for the moment confine myself to only one observation.

In Count Tolstoy's opinion, art expresses men's *feelings*, while words express their *thoughts*. This is not correct. Men use words not *only* for the expression of their thoughts, but for expressing their feelings as well. The proof is *poetry*, in which it is precisely *the word* which serves as medium.

Count Tolstoy says himself:

"To evoke inwardly a feeling one has once experienced and, having done so, to convey that feeling by means of movements, lines, colours and images expressed in words, so that others may experience the same feeling—this is the function of art."[1] From this it is clear that, as a special means of communication between men, words cannot be regarded as distinct from art.

Neither is it true that art *only* expresses men's feelings. No, it expresses both their feelings and *thoughts*, though it expresses them *in living images and not abstractly*. It is in this that its main distinguishing feature lies. In Count Tolstoy's opinion "art begins at the point where man, with a view to conveying to others the feeling he has experienced, evokes that feeling in himself anew and expresses it by certain external signs."[2] I consider, however, that art begins at the point where man evokes within himself anew feelings *and thoughts* experienced by him under the influence of his environment and *gives a certain expression to them in images*. It goes without saying that in the vast majority of instances he does this in order to convey to *other people* the thoughts and feelings he has recalled. Art is a *social* phenomenon.

The changes I wished to make in the definition of art given by Count Tolstoy are covered for the time being by the corrections I have indicated.

[1] From the essays of Count Tolstoy. The most recent of his published work, Moscow, 1898, p. 78.

[2] *Ibid.*, p. 77.

other people the thoughts and feelings he has recalled. Art is a *social* phenomenon.

The changes I wished to make in the definition of art given by Count Tolstoy are covered for the time being by the corrections I have indicated.

But I will ask you as well, sir, to take note of the following idea expressed by the author of *War and Peace*:

> Always, at all times and in every human society, there is a religious consciousness of what is bad and what is good common to all the people of that society, and it is this religious consciousness which determines the worth of the feelings conveyed by art.[4]

Our research is going to demonstrate, among other things, how far this idea is right; in any case it deserves the greatest attention, because it brings us face to face with the question of *the role of art in the history of the development of mankind.*

Now that we have some preliminary definition of art I must clarify the point of view from which I look at it.

Here I will say without equivocation that I view art as I do all social phenomena, from the standpoint of the materialist conception of history.

What is the materialist conception of history?

We know that in mathematics there exists a method of *proof by inversion.* I shall have to resort here to this method, which may be called *the method of explanation by inversion.* What I shall do will be first to recall the meaning of the *idealist* conception of history and then I shall show in what way the opposite, materialist conception of history differs from it.

The idealist conception of history, if we consider it in its pure form, consists in the conviction that the development of thought and knowledge is the ultimate cause of the historical movement of mankind. This view held complete sway in the eighteenth century, whence it was passed on to the nineteenth century. Saint-Simon and Auguste Comte[5] held firmly to it, although their views in some res-

[4] From the essays of Count Tolstoy. The most recent of his published work, Moscow, 1898, p. 85.

[5] *Henri de Saint-Simon* (1760-1825). One of the great French Utopian Socialist thinkers of the early 19th century who sought "the improvement of the lot of the poorest class" under the leader-

pects were in flat contradiction to the views of the philosophers of the preceding century. Saint-Simon, for example, poses the question as to how the social organisation of the Greeks arose.[6] And this is how he answers it: "The religious system (*le système religieux*) acted in their case as a basis for their political system....The latter was modelled on the former." And in proof of this he refers to the fact that the Greek Olympus was "a republican assembly" and that the constitutions of all the peoples of Greece, no matter how they might differ from one another, had one common feature in that they were all republican.[7] But this is not all. The religious system that lay at the basis of the Greek political system, itself arose, in Saint-Simon's view, from the totality of their *scientific* concepts, from their *scientific philosophical system.* The scientific concepts of the Greeks thus provided a most profound basis for their social life, and the development of those concepts was the mainspring of the historical development of this way of life, the main cause which conditioned the historical replacement of certain forms by others.

Similarly Auguste Comte thought that "the whole social mechanism is based, in the last analysis, on opinions."[8] This was simply a repetition of the Encyclopaedists' outlook, according to which *c'est l'opinion qui gouverne le monde* (the world is governed by opinion).

There is another variety of idealism which finds its most extreme expression in the absolute idealism of Hegel. How is the historical development of mankind to be explained from his point of view? I will clarify it by an example. Hegel poses the question: why did Greece fall? He points out a number of reasons for this phenomenon; but the most important of them, in his eyes, was the cir-

ship of the educated and industrial classes. *Auguste Comte* (1798-1857). Pupil of Saint-Simon, mathematician and philosopher. Leader of the *positivist* school of thought. Sought to found a science of *sociology* (the term was originated by him) based on three phases in the development of human knowledge: theological, metaphysical and positive.— TRANS.

[6] In Saint-Simon's eyes Greece had a special significance because, as he put it, "it is with the Greeks that human thought began to take a serious interest in social organisations."

[7] See his *Mémoire sur la science de l'homme*.

[8] *Cours de philosophie positive*, Paris, 1869, Vol. I, pp. 40-1.

cumstance that Greece gave expression to only one stage in the development of the Absolute Idea, and was bound to fall when that stage had been completed.

It is clear that although he knew that "the fall of Lacedaemon was due to an inequality of possessions," Hegel held the opinion that social relations and the whole course of the historical development of mankind are determined, in the last analysis, *by the laws of logic, by the course of development of thought.*

The materialist view of history is diametrically opposed to this. Whereas Saint-Simon, looking at history from the idealist point of view, thought that the social relations of the Greeks were to be explained by their religious outlook, I, as a supporter of the materialist viewpoint, will say that the Greek Olympus was a reflection of their social structure. And whereas Saint-Simon, in answer to the question as to whence the Greeks drew their religious ideas, replied that these ideas arose from their scientific philosophy of life, I think that the Greek scientific philosophy of life was itself conditioned in its historical development by the development of the productive forces at the disposal of the Hellenic peoples.[9]

Such is my view of history in general. Is it correct? This is not the point at which to prove it. At this point I shall ask you to *assume* that it is correct and, with me, to accept this assumption *as the point of departure for our research into art.* It goes without saying that this research into *the question of art in particular* will, at the same time, also be a verification of *my historical outlook in general.*

Indeed, should this whole outlook be mistaken, by taking it for our point of departure we shall explain very little about the evolution of art. But if we can satisfy ourselves that it helps us to explain this evolution better than other standpoints do, we shall then possess a new and powerful argument in its favour.

[9] A few years ago there was published in Paris, *Histoire de la Technologie* by A. Espinas, which represented an attempt to explain the development of the philosophy of the ancient Greeks by the development of their productive forces. This is an extremely important and interesting attempt, for which we owe a great debt of gratitude to Espinas, despite the fact that the results of his research are erroneous *in many particulars.*

biological materialism provides excellent material for the critique of one-sided historical ("economic") materialism.

I realise the full seriousness of this objection and intend, therefore, to dwell on it. I shall find this all the more useful in that, by answering it, I shall thereby answer a whole series of similar objections which can be borrowed from the sphere of the mental life of animals. First of all let us try as accurately as possible to define the conclusion we have to draw on the basis of the facts cited by Darwin. And to this end let us see what inferences he himself draws from them.

In the second chapter of the first part of his book on the descent of man we read:

> *Sense of Beauty.*—This sense has been declared to be peculiar to man. But when we behold male birds elaborately displaying their plumes and splendid colours before the females, while other birds not thus decorated make no such display, it is impossible to doubt that the females admire the beauty of their male partners. As women everywhere deck themselves with these plumes, the beauty of such ornaments cannot be disputed. The bower-birds by tastefully ornamenting their playing-passages with gaily-coloured objects, as do certain humming-birds their nests, offer additional evidence that they possess a sense of beauty. So with the song of birds, the sweet strains poured forth by the males during the season of love are certainly admired by the females, of which fact evidence will hereafter be given. If female birds had been incapable of appreciating the beautiful colours, the ornaments and voices of their male partners, all the labour and anxiety exhibited by them in displaying their charms before the females would have been thrown away; and this it is impossible to admit. Why certain bright colours and certain sounds should excite pleasure, when in harmony, cannot, I presume, be explained any more than why certain flavours and scents are agreeable; but assuredly the same colours and the same sounds are admired by us and by many of the lower animals.[1]

And so the facts cited by Darwin testify to the capability of the lower animals, as of man, to experience aesthetic pleasure, and to the fact that sometimes our aesthetic tastes coincide with the

[1] The Russian text quoted by Plekhanov is that published in St. Petersburg in 1899 (*Proiskhozhdeniye Cheloveka*), the translation being edited by the great Russian scientist Professor I. M. Sechenov. The appropriate quotations given here are from the first edition of Darwin's book, as published by Appleton & Company, New York, 1872. They differ in a number of instances, but not in essentials, from the Russian translation available to Plekhanov. The above quotation is from Part I, Chap. II, p. 61 of the 1872 publication. The second edition first appeared in London in 1874, and the similar passage to that quoted appears there in Part I, Chap. III, having been considerably altered in form.—Trans.

tastes of the lower animals.[1] But these facts do not provide us with an explanation of the *origin* of the tastes in question.

And if biology does not explain to us the origin of our aesthetic tastes, it will all the less be able to explain their *historical development*. But let Darwin speak again:

> The taste for the beautiful, at least as far as female beauty is concerned, is not of a special nature in the human mind; for it differs widely in the different races of man, as will hereafter be shown, and is not quite the same even in the different nations of the same race. Judging from the hideous ornaments and the equally hideous music admired by most savages, it might be urged that their aesthetic faculty was not so highly developed as in certain animals, for instance, in birds.[2]

If the concept of the beautiful is different for different nations of one and the same race, it is clear that the reasons for such differences are not to be sought in biology. Darwin himself tells us that our search must be directed to another quarter. In the second English edition of his book, in the paragraph I have just quoted, we come across these words, which are not to be found in the Russian edition, edited by I. M. Sechenov from the first English edition: "With cultivated men such (i.e. aesthetic) sensations are, however, intimately associated with complex ideas and trains of thought."[3]

This is an extremely important pointer. It directs us *from biology to sociology*, since it is obvious that, in Darwin's opinion, it is social causes which bring it about that the sensation of beauty *in civilised man* is associated with a great many complex ideas. But is Darwin right in thinking that such an association takes place only with civilised men? No, he is not. And it is very easy to satisfy ourselves of this. Let us take an example. We know that the skins, claws and teeth of animals play a very important part in the adornment of primitive peoples. How is this to be explained? By the combination of colours and lines in these objects? Not at all. For in adorning himself, for example, with the skin,

[1] In Wallace's opinion, Darwin very much exaggerated the significance of the aesthetic sense in relation to sexual selection among animals. Leaving it to the biologists to decide how far Wallace is correct, I shall assume that Darwin's view is unconditionally correct, and you will agree, Sir, that this assumption is the least favourable to my point of view.

[2] Darwin, *The Descent of Man*, Part I, Chap. 2.

[3] *The Descent of Man*, London, 1883, p. 92.

tivated men such (i.e. aesthetic) sensations are, however, intimately associated with complex ideas and trains of thought."[13]

This is an extremely important pointer. It directs us *from biology to sociology,* since it is obvious that, in Darwin's opinion, it is social causes which bring it about that the sensation of beauty *in civilised man* is associated with a great many complex ideas. But is Darwin right in thinking that such an association takes place only with civilised men? No, he is not. And it is very easy to satisfy ourselves of this. Let us take an example. We know that the skins, claws and teeth of animals play a very important part in the adornment of primitive peoples. How is this to be explained? By the combination of colours and lines in these objects? Not at all. For in adorning himself, for example, with the skin, claws and teeth of a tiger or the skin and horns of a bison, the savage is hinting at his own agility or strength: the man who has overcome something agile is himself agile; the man who has overcome something strong is himself strong. Moreover, it is possible that an element of superstition may be involved here. Schoolcraft tells us that the redskin tribes in the west of North America are exceptionally fond of adornments made from the claws of the grey bear, the fiercest of all the beasts of prey in those parts. The redskin warrior believes that the fierceness and bravery of the grey bear are communicated to those who adorn themselves with its claws. Thus these claws, Schoolcraft observes, serve him in part as an adornment, in part as an amulet.[14]

In this case, of course, one cannot suppose that the skins, claws and teeth originally appealed to the redskins solely by virtue of the combination of colours and lines peculiar to these objects.[15] No, the reverse is far more probable, i.e. that these objects were at first worn only as an outward sign of bravery, agility and strength and that it was only afterwards and in fact as a result of their being

[13] *The Descent of Man,* London, 1883, p. 92.

[14] Schoolcraft, *Historical and Statistical Information respecting the History, Condition and Prospects of the Indian Tribes of the United States,* Vol. III, p. 216.

[15] There are cases where similar objects have an appeal solely due to their colour, but of these I will write later.

an outward sign of bravery, agility and strength that they began to evoke aesthetic sensations and came to be classed as adornments. And so aesthetic sensations not only "*can*, with savages, be associated" with complex ideas, but *arise* sometimes precisely as a result of such ideas.

Another example: we know that the women of many African tribes wear iron rings on their arms and legs. The wives of rich men sometimes wear little short of a pood[16] of such ornaments.[17]

This is, of course, very inconvenient, but the inconvenience does not prevent their taking pleasure in wearing these fetters of slavery, as Schweinfurth puts it. Why is it that the negress finds pleasure in burdening herself with such fetters? Because, thanks to them, both she and others think she is beautiful. And why does she appear beautiful? This is the outcome of a fairly complex association of ideas.

It is among those tribes which, in Schweinfurth's words, are now passing through an *iron age*—i.e. for whom iron is a *precious metal*—that a passion for such ornaments develops. *That which is precious* seems *beautiful*, because the idea of *wealth* is associated with it. In putting on, shall we say, twenty pounds of iron rings, a woman of the *Dinka* tribe seems to herself and her fellows more beautiful than she was when she was wearing only two, i.e. when she was poorer. It is clear that here it is not a question of the beauty of the rings, but of the particular conception of wealth which is associated with them.

A third example: among the *Batoka* tribe on the upper Zambesi the man who has not had his upper incisors drawn is considered ugly. Where does this strange conception of beauty come from? It, too, developed as the result of a fairly complex association of ideas. The Batoka extract their upper incisors in their desire to resemble the *ruminant animals*. From our point of view this is a somewhat incomprehensible aspiration. But the Batoka are a pastoral tribe and look on their cows and bulls almost as gods.[18] Here again that which is precious is beautiful, and aesthe-

[16] 36 lb., avoirdupois.—TRANS.

[17] Schweinfurth, *Au Coeur de l'Afrique*, Paris, 1875, Vol. I, p. 148. See also Du Chaillu, *Voyage et Aventures dans l'Afrique Equatoriale*, Paris, 1863, p. 11.

[18] Schweinfurth, *op. cit.*, I, 148.

colours or the shape of objects, even with primitive peoples, are associated with extremely complex ideas and that, at the very least, many of these shapes and combinations appear to them beautiful only owing to such an association.

What evokes this association? And whence arise those complex ideas that are associated with the sensations evoked in us by the appearance of objects? It is obvious that it is not the *biologist*, but only the *sociologist* who can answer these problems. And if the materialist conception of history enables their solution better than any other conception of history, if we are convinced that the association indicated and the complex ideas we have mentioned are conditioned and created in the last analysis by the state of the productive forces of a given society and by its economics, then it must be admitted that Darwinism does not in the least contradict the materialist conception of history, which I have tried to outline above.

I cannot say much here about the relationship of Darwinism to this conception. But I will, nevertheless, say something.

Note the following quotation:

> "It may be well first to premise that I do not wish to maintain that any strictly social animal, if its intellectual faculties were to become as active and as highly developed as in man, would acquire exactly the same moral sense as ours. In the same manner as various animals have some sense of beauty, though they admire widely different objects, so they might have a sense of right and wrong, though led by it to follow widely different lines of conduct. If, for instance, to take an extreme case, men were reared under precisely the same conditions as hive-bees, there can hardly be a doubt that our unmarried females would, like the worker-bees, think it a sacred duty to kill their brothers, and mothers would strive to kill their fertile daughters; and no one would think of interfering. Nevertheless the bee, or any other social animal, would in our supposed case gain, as it appears to me, some feeling of right and wrong, or a conscience."[1]

What follows from this? It follows that there is nothing *absolute* in men's moral concepts; that they change together with the changes in those conditions under which men live. And what creates these conditions? What calls forth these changes? About this Darwin tells us nothing; and if we say and prove that their conditions are created by the state of the productive forces and change as a result of the development of these forces, we shall

[1] *The Descent of Man*, Part I, Chap. 3.

certainly not come into conflict with Darwin, but, on the contrary, we shall supplement what he has said and explain what he has left unexplained; and we shall do so by applying to the study of social phenomena the very same principle which proved of such tremendous service to Darwin in *biology*.

It is, on the whole, extremely odd to oppose Darwinism to the conception of history I am defending. Darwin's sphere was a completely different one. He examined the descent of man as a *zoological species*. The supporters of the materialist viewpoint seek to explain the *historical* fate of this species. Their sphere of research begins precisely where the Darwinist's sphere of research ends. Their work cannot be a substitute for what the Darwinists give us, and similarly the most brilliant discoveries of the Darwinists cannot replace the research of materialist historians, but can only prepare the ground for it, in the same way as the physicist prepares the ground for the chemist, his work in no way removing the necessity for research that is properly chemical.[1] The whole question may be summed up as follows. Darwin's theory was, in

[1] Here I must make a reservation. Whilst, in my opinion, the researches of Darwinian biologists prepare the ground for sociological research, this must be understood only in the sense that the successes of biology—*in so far as they are concerned with the process of the development of organic forms*—cannot but assist in the perfection of sociological scientific method *in so far as it is concerned in the development of social organisation and its products: human thoughts and feelings*. But I do not in the least share the social views of Darwinists like Haeckel. It has already been noted in our literature that Darwinian biologists, in their consideration of human society, do not in any way make use of Darwin's *method*, but merely idealise the instincts of animals (for the most part beasts of prey) which the great biologist studied. Darwin was by no means "sattelfest" (thoroughly grounded) in social questions; but those social views which he reached as the result of his theory have little resemblance to the conclusions drawn from it by the majority of Darwinists. Darwin thought that the development of social instincts was "extremely useful for the advancement of the species." This view cannot be shared by those Darwinists who preach *the social struggle of all against all*. True, Darwin says: "There should be open competition for all men; and the most able should not be prevented by laws and customs from succeeding best and reaching the largest number of offspring." But advocates of the social war of all against all should not base themselves on this statement. Let them remember the Saint-Simonists. The latter talked of social competition in the same way as Darwin; but in the name of competition they demanded social reforms such as Haeckel and his fellow-thinkers would hardly have favoured. There is "competition" and "competition," just as, in the words of Sganarelle, there is *fagot et fagot*.

its time, a great and necessary step forward in the development of *biological* science, which fully satisfied the strictest demands that this science could at the time make upon its workers. Can as much be claimed for the materialist conception of history? Can it be asserted that it was, in its time, a great and necessary step forward in the development of social science? And is it capable, at present, of meeting all the latter's demands? To this I can answer with complete assurance: "Yes, it can! Yes, it is capable of doing so!" And I hope I may to some degree show in these letters, that my assurance is not devoid of foundation.

But let us return to aesthetics. From Darwin's words, which I have quoted, it is evident that he regarded the development of *aesthetic taste* from exactly the same point of view as the development of *moral sense*. A sense of the beautiful is characteristic of man, as it is of many animals; i.e. he has the faculty of experiencing a special kind of ("aesthetic") pleasure under the influence of certain objects or phenomena. But exactly what objects and phenomena afford him such pleasure depends upon the conditions under which he is brought up, lives and acts. *Man's nature* makes it *possible* for him to have aesthetic tastes and concepts. *Environmental conditions* are the determining factor in the transition from this *possibility* to *reality*; it is these conditions that explain why social men (or rather, any particular society, people or class) possess their own distinct aesthetic tastes and concepts.

Such is the natural conclusion which ultimately emerges from what Darwin says on this matter. And this conclusion, of course, will not be disputed by a single supporter of the materialist conception of history. On the contrary, every such supporter will see in it a new confirmation of that conception. For none of them has ever dreamed of denying any of the well known characteristics of human nature, or embarking upon any arbitrary interpretation of them. All they have said is that if human nature is unchanging, it cannot explain the historical process, since this is nothing but a succession of constantly *changing* phenomena; while if it is *itself changed* in the course of historical development, then there is evidently some external reason for its changing. In either case the task of the historian and the sociologist must extend far beyond the limits of the consideration of the properties of human nature.

Supposing we take a feature such as the *tendency to imitation.* Tarde,[1] who wrote a very interesting study of the "laws of imitation," purports to see in this the soul, as it were, of society. According to his definition every social group is a totality of individuals who, in the first place, imitate each other at a given time, and in the second place have previously imitated one and the same model. There cannot be the slightest doubt that imitation has played a very great role in the history of all our ideas, tastes, fashions and customs. Even materialists of the last century were pointing to its tremendous significance: man consists entirely of imitation, said Helvetius. But that Tarde based his research into the laws of imitation on false foundations there can be equally little doubt.

When the restoration of the Stuarts temporarily re-established the rule of the old nobility in England, this nobility not only did not reveal the slightest aspiration to *imitate* the extreme representatives of the revolutionary petty-bourgeoisie, the *Puritans,* but showed the strongest inclination to habits and tastes which were the *direct opposite* of the Puritan rules of life. Puritan moral severity gave way to the most incredible dissoluteness. To admire and do all the things the Puritans had forbidden then became the fashion. The Puritans had been very religious; Restoration society made a display of its irreligion. The Puritans had persecuted the theatre and literature; their fall was the signal for a renewed enthusiasm for both. The Puritans had worn short hair and condemned elegance of dress; after the Restoration long wigs and luxurious attire came into fashion. The Puritans had forbidden card-playing; after the Restoration gaming became a passion, and so on and so forth.[2]

In short, it was *contradiction and not imitation* that was at work here, the former evidently also being rooted among the attributes of human nature. But why should contradiction, rooted among the attributes of human nature, become so evident in the relations

[1] *Gabriel Tarde* (1843–1904) French sociologist and psychologist who taught that imitation was at the basis of social psychology and that progress was made possible through the interaction of imitational trends. He did not accept the materialist basis of social phenomena, viewing collective psychology as based on the interaction of individual psychologies.—TRANS.

[2] Cf. Alexandre Beljame, *Le Public et les Hommes de Lettres en Angleterre du Dix-huitième Siècle,* Paris, 1881, pp. 1–10. Cf. also Taine, *Histoire de la Littérature Anglaise,* Vol. II, p. 443.

between the bourgeoisie and nobility in seventeenth century England? Because it was a century which saw a very marked sharpening of the struggle between the nobility and the bourgeoisie—or rather, the whole "third estate"—And so we can say that although man undoubtedly has a strong tendency to imitate, this tendency is manifested only where certain *social relations* exist—for instance, the relations which existed in France in the seventeenth century, when the bourgeoisie was fond of imitating the nobility, although it did not do so very successfully: you will recall Molière's *Le Bourgeois Gentilhomme*. But with other social relations the tendency to imitation disappears, yielding to its opposite, which I shall call for the time being the tendency to *contradiction*.

A moment though: I have stated the matter quite incorrectly. The English did not lose the striving to imitate in the seventeenth century: as we know, it manifested itself as strongly as ever in the mutual relations of persons *of one and the same class*. Speaking of the Englishmen of the highest society at that time, Beljame says: "These people were not in fact unbelievers; they denied religion *a priori*, so as not to be taken for Roundheads and to save themselves the trouble of thinking."[1] Without fear of error we may say of these people that they denied religion through *imitation*. But in imitating convinced *unbelievers* they thereby *contradicted the Puritans*. And so *imitation became a source of contradiction*. But we know that, though the weaker-minded members of the English aristocracy imitated the stronger in their scepticism, they did so because it was considered to be good form; and this came about solely by virtue of *contradiction*, solely as a reaction against Puritanism—a reaction which, in its turn, was the outcome of the *class struggle* to which we have already drawn attention. And so, *at the basis of these complex dialectics in mental phenomena lay facts of a social nature*. And hence it is clear in what degree and in what sense the conclusion which I drew above from certain theses of Darwin is correct: man's nature provides the possibility of his developing certain concepts (or tastes, or inclinations), but the transition from this *possibility to reality* depends on the conditions under which he lives; it is these conditions that cause the particular concepts (tastes, or inclinations) concerned to manifest themselves rather than others. If I am not mistaken this is just

[1] Alexandre Beljame, *op. cit.*, pp. 7–8.

what a certain Russian supporter of the materialist conception of history expressed some time before me:

> Once the stomach has been supplied with a certain quantity of food, it sets about its work in accordance with the general laws of stomachic digestion. But can one, with the help of these laws, reply to the question of why savoury and nourishing food descends every day into your stomach, while in mine it is a rare visitor? Do these laws explain why some eat too much, while others die of hunger? It would seem that the explanation must be sought in some other sphere, in the working of some other kind of laws. The same is the case with the mind of man. Once it has been placed in a definite situation, once its environment supplies it with certain impressions, it co-ordinates them according to certain general laws (moreover here, too, the results are varied in the extreme by the variety of impressions received). But what places it in that situation? What determines the influx and the character of new impressions? That is the question which cannot be answered by any laws of thought.
>
> Furthermore, imagine that a resilient ball falls from a high tower. Its movement takes place according to a universally known and very simple law of mechanics. But suddenly the ball strikes an inclined plane. Its movement is changed in accordance with another, also very simple and universally known mechanical law. As a result, we have a broken line of movement, of which one can and must say that it owes its origin to the joint action of both the laws which have been mentioned. But where did the inclined plane which the ball struck come from? This is not explained either by the first or the second law, or yet by their joint action. Exactly the same is the case with human thought. Whence came the circumstances thanks to which its movements were subjected to the combined action of such and such laws? This is not explained either by its individual laws or by their combined action.[1]

I am firmly convinced that the history of ideology can only be understood by those who have fully mastered this clear and simple truth.

Let us proceed further. In speaking of imitation I mentioned the exactly opposite tendency, which I called the tendency to contradiction.

This must be studied more carefully.

We know what an important role, according to Darwin, the "principle of antithesis" plays in the expression of emotions among men and animals.

> Certain states of the mind lead . . . to certain habitual movements which were primarily, or may still be, of service. . . . When a directly opposite state of mind

is induced, there is a strong and involuntary tendency to the performance of movements of a directly opposite nature, though these have never been of any service.[1]

Darwin quotes a number of examples which quite convincingly show that "the principle of antithesis" actually does explain a great deal concerning the expression of emotions. I ask whether it is not found at work in the origin and development of *customs*?

When a dog rolls over, belly upwards, in front of its master, its attitude, which amounts to the very reverse of anything that could be conceived as suggesting resistance, serves as the expression of absolute submission. Here the operation of the "principle of antithesis" strikes the eye immediately. It seems to me none the less striking, however, in the following instance related by the traveller, Burton. Negroes of the *Wanyamwezi* tribe, when they are passing not far from villages inhabited by hostile tribes, refrain from carrying weapons with them so as not to provoke the latter by their display. Whereas, at home, each one of them is always armed with at least a club.[2] If, as Darwin remarks, a dog, in rolling over on to its back, is, as it were, telling a man, or another dog: "Behold, I am your slave!", the Wanyamwezi negro in disarming himself at the very time when it would seem indispensable to carry arms, is, by this act, telling his enemy: "I have no thought of self-defence, but am relying fully on your magnanimity."

In either case both the purpose and its mode of expression are identical; that it to say, the purpose is expressed by an action the very opposite of that which must have been taken, had there been hostile intentions instead of a sense of submission.

The action of the "principle of antithesis" stands out with equally striking clarity in customs observed for the expression of grief. David and Charles Livingstone say that the negress never goes out without ornaments *except in those cases where she is in mourning.*[3]

When a negro of the *Niam-Niam* tribe loses one of his relatives, as a sign of his grief he immediately cuts off his hair, to the

[1] *The Expression of the Emotions in Man and Animals*, London, 1892. (The text available to Plekhanov was the Russian translation of 1872. There is no essential difference between the latter and the passage quoted above.—TRANS.)

[2] *The Lake Regions of Central Africa*, London, 1860, Vol. II, p. 301.

[3] *The Zambesi and its Tributaries*, London, 1865, p. 115.

coiffeur of which both he and his wives devote great care and attention.[1] In Africa, when a man who has held an important position in his tribe dies, according to du Chaillu, *many negro peoples put on soiled garments.*[2] On the island of Borneo some natives, to express their grief, take off the *cotton garments* which they nowadays normally wear and put on *garments made from tree bark*, which they used to wear in former times.[3] Certain Mongol tribes for the same purpose turn their clothing *inside out.*[4] In all these cases it is an *action contrary to the one which would be considered natural, necessary, useful or pleasant in the normal course of life, that serves to express the emotions.*

Thus, in the normal course of events, it is considered best to change from dirty clothing into clean; but in the case of grief, on the principle of antithesis, clean garments make way for dirty ones. The islanders of Borneo, mentioned above, liked exchanging their bark clothing for cotton; but the operation of the principle of antithesis has led to their wearing bark clothing in those instances where they wish to express their grief. It was natural for the Mongols, as for all other people, to wear their clothes with the right side of the material exposed and not inside-out, but for the very reason that this seems natural in the normal course of events they turn the material inside out when the normal tenor of their life is interrupted by some unhappy event. And here is a still more striking example. Schweinfurth tells us that many African Negroes *put a rope around their neck* to express their grief.[5] In this case grief is shown in the very opposite sense to any that might be suggested by the instinct of self-preservation. And it is possible to point to a great many instances of this sort.

I am therefore convinced that a quite considerable proportion of customs owe their origin to the operation of the principle of antithesis.

If my conviction is well-founded—and I think it is quite well founded—it may be supposed that the development of our *aesthetic tastes* also takes place under the same influence. Do the facts confirm such a supposition? I think that they do.

In Senegambia rich negresses wear shoes much too small for

[1] Schweinfurth, *Au Cœur de l'Afrique*, Vol. II, p. 33.

[2] *Voyage et Aventures à l'Afrique Equatoriale*, p. 268.

[3] Ratzel, *Voelkerkunde*, Vol. I, *Einleitung*, p. 65.

[4] Ratzel, *op. cit.*, Vol. II, p. 347.

[5] *Au Cœur de l'Afrique*, Vol. I, p. 151.

their feet, and for this reason these ladies have a noticeably awkward gait. But this gait of theirs is in fact considered extremely attractive.[1]

What is the explanation?

We must in the first place note that the poor negresses, who work, do not wear such shoes and walk normally. They cannot walk like the rich coquettes, because this would cause them to waste a great deal of time; but it is for this very reason that the rich women's awkward way of walking seems attractive; for them time is not precious, since they are absolved of the need to work. In itself, this manner of walking is quite pointless, and it acquires significance *only by contrast with the walk of women burdened with work (and hence poor)*. The action of the "*principle of antithesis*" is evident here. But note that it is called forth by *social conditions*: inequalities of wealth that exist among the negroes of Senegambia.

Remembering what has already been said about the English aristocracy at the time of the Stuart Restoration you will, I am sure, find no difficulty in agreeing that their tendency to contradiction represents in itself an example of the operation of Darwin's principle of antithesis in the field of social psychology. But here we must make the following remark.

Such virtues as industriousness, patience, sobriety, thriftiness, strict observance of domestic morality and so forth, were very useful for the English bourgeoisie as they strove to win for themselves a higher position in the social system. But the vices opposite to these bourgeois virtues were, at the very least, useless to the English nobility in its struggle for existence against the bourgeoisie. They did not provide it with new means of carrying on the struggle and were nothing more than its psychological result. What was useful for the English nobility was not this tendency to vice as opposed to the bourgeois virtues, but the emotion that evoked this tendency i.e. hatred of the class whose complete victory would have meant complete destruction of all the privileges of the aristocracy. The tendency to vice came only as a *correlated variation* (if I may here use a term that I have borrowed from Darwin). *Correlated variations* of this kind often occur in social psychology. It is essential to take them into account. But it is equally essential to remember when we do so that in the *final instance* they too are evoked by social conditions.

[1] L. J. B. Béranger-Féraud, *Les Peuplades de la Sénégambie*, Paris, 1879, p. 11.

We know from the history of English literature how strongly the psychological effect of the principle of antithesis, to which I have referred and which was evoked by the class struggle, was reflected in the aesthetic concepts of the upper class. The English aristocrats, who had been living in France during their exile, became acquainted there with French literature and the French theatre, which were in themselves models, unique of their kind, of what a refined aristocratic society could produce; and which therefore corresponded much more closely to their own aristocratic tendencies than did the English theatre and literature of the Elizabethan age. After the Restoration the reign of French taste began on the English stage and in English literature. Shakespeare began to be treated in the same way as the French, firmly holding to the classical traditions, treated him, when they made his acquaintance later on—that is to say, as *"a drunken savage." Romeo and Juliet* was considered a "poor play" at that time, and *A Midsummer Night's Dream* "foolish and ridiculous"; *Henry VIII*, was "naïve," and *Othello* "mediocre."[1] This attitude to Shakespeare had not entirely disappeared even in the succeeding century. Hume thought that Shakespeare's dramatic genius was commonly overrated for the very same reason that deformed and ill-proportioned bodies appear very large. He reproaches the great dramatist with "total ignorance of all theatrical art and conduct." Pope regretted that Shakespeare wrote "for the people" and managed without "the protection of his prince and the encouragement of the court." Even the famous Garrick, an enthusiastic admirer of Shakespeare, tried to add *gentility* to his "idol." In his performance of *Hamlet* he omitted the gravediggers scene as too coarse. For *King Lear* he provided a happy ending. On the other hand, however, the democratic section of the English public continued to cherish the keenest attachment to Shakespeare. Garrick was aware that in revising the plays he risked evoking the stormy protests of this section of the public. His French friends wrote and complimented him on his "courage" in facing this danger: and one of them added, "Car je connais la populace anglaise."[2]

[1] Beljame, *ibid.*, pp. 40–41. Cf. Taine, I, *op. cit.*, pp. 508–12.

[2] "For I know what the English mob is like." In this connection see J. J. Jusserand's interesting study, *Shakespeare en France sous l'ancien Régime*, Paris, 1898, pp. 247–8.

The dissoluteness of aristocratic morals during the second half of the seventeenth century was, as we know, reflected on the English stage, where it really did go to incredible lengths. As Eduard Engel says, almost all the comedies written in England during the period from 1660 to 1690 belong to the domain of pornography.[1] In view of this we can say *a priori*, on the principle of antithesis, that sooner or later a type of drama was bound to appear, which would have as its main aim the depiction and exaltation of the domestic virtues and the purity of lower middle class morality. And this type of drama was actually created later on by the intellectual representatives of the English bourgeoisie. But I shall come back to this later, when we have occasion to talk about the French "comédie larmoyante."

To the best of my knowledge Hippolyte Taine,[2] better than anyone else, has perceived and, with greater subtlety, revealed the significance of the principle of antithesis in the history of aesthetics.[3]

In his witty and interesting book, *Voyage aux Pyrénées*, he recounts a conversation with one of his "table companions," Monsieur Paul, who to all appearances expresses the views of the author himself: "You go to Versailles," says Monsieur Paul, "and you cry out against the taste of the seventeenth century. . . . But for a moment stop considering it from the point of view of your own needs and habits of today. . . . We have a right to admire wild scenery, just as they had a right to be bored by the same sort of scenery. In the seventeenth century nothing was more ugly than a real mountain.[4] It recalled a thousand memories of misfortune. People who had just emerged from civil war and semi-barbarity

[1] *Geschichte der englischen Literatur*, third edition, Leipzig, 1897, p. 264.

[2] *Hippolyte Taine* (1828–93) French psychologist, historian and man of letters. One of the founders of the historical method of studying literature and the arts. Believed in a scientific approach on the basis of racial, environmental and historical factors. Main works: *The History of English Literature* (1863) and *The Philosophy of the Arts* (1869). After the Paris Commune he forsook his liberal views for an extremely reactionary outlook.—TRANS.

[3] Tarde had the most excellent opportunity of studying the effect of this principle in his book: *L'Opposition Universelle, Essai d'une Théorie des Contraires*, which appeared in 1897. But for some reason he did not make use of it and limited himself to a very few remarks on the process referred to. He did, it is true, say (p. 245) that his book was not a sociological treatise. In a treatise specially devoted to sociology he would almost certainly not have been able to cope with his subject without abandoning his idealistic point of view.

[4] Remember that the conversation is taking place in the Pyrenees.

remembered the hunger, the long treks on horseback in rain and snow, the bad black bread, half made of chaff, the dirty wayside inns infested with vermin. They were weary of barbarity, just as we are weary of civilisation. . . . These old mountains . . . give us a rest from our pavements, offices and shops. This is the only reason why you like them. And if it wasn't for this they would be every bit as repugnant to you as they were to Madame de Maintenon."[1]

We take pleasure in a wild landscape, because it is in contrast to the city sights we are surfeited with. Eighteenth-century people delighted in city sights and close-clipped, formal gardens because of the contrast with wild and desolate places. Here, too, the operation of the "principle of antithesis" is not open to doubt. And precisely for this reason it is a graphic demonstration of the degree to which psychological laws may serve as a key to the explanation of the history of ideas in general, and of the history of art in particular.

The principle of antithesis played exactly the same role in the psychology of seventeenth-century people as it does in the psychology of our contemporaries. Why, then, are our aesthetic tastes opposed to those of the seventeenth century?

Because the situation we are in is a completely different one. And so we come to a conclusion with which we are already familiar: man's psychological nature makes it possible for him to have aesthetic notions and for the Darwinian *principle of antithesis* (Hegelian "contradiction") to play an extremely important role in the mechanism of these notions, a role which has as yet been insufficiently appreciated. But the reason why the social man in question has these specific tastes and not others; the reason why he likes certain objects and not others, depends on the conditions under which he lives.[2] The example quoted by Taine also demonstrates very well the character of these conditions: it shows that

[1] *Voyage aux Pyrénées*, Paris, 1910, pp. 190–3. The English here is translated direct from the original of Taine and differs slightly from the Russian translation by Plekhanov.—TRANS.

[2] Already in the early stages of culture the psychological principle of antithesis was brought into action by the division of labour between man and woman. According to V. I. Jochelson, "the antithesis between men and women as two separate groups is typical of the primitive social structure of the Yukagirs. This comes out in their games, where the men and women are ranged on opposite sides, in their language, where certain sounds are pronounced differently by

they are social conditions, the sum-total of which is defined—I am expressing myself for the time being in general terms—by the course of development of human culture.

Here I foresee an objection on your part. "Let us suppose" you will say, "that the example given by Taine suggests that *social* conditions explain the functioning of the basic laws of our psychology; let us suppose that the examples you have given yourself point to the same conclusion. But surely examples could be given to prove something quite different. Are there not examples to show that the laws of our psychology become effective under the influence of our *natural surroundings*?"

Of course there are, I shall answer; and in the example cited by Taine the question of our attitude to the impressions we receive from *nature* does in fact arise. But the point is that the influence such impressions have on us changes in accordance with the manner in which our own attitude to nature changes, and

women, in the fact that female descent is more important for women and male descent more important for men, as well as in a certain specialisation of occupations among the sexes which has, for each of them, brought about a special, independent sphere of activity" (*Ancient Yukagir Life and Writings on the Yasachnaya and Kirkidon Rivers*, St. Petersburg, 1898, p. 5).

Mr. Jochelson appears not to notice, here, that it was division of labour among the sexes that was the reason for the antithesis to which he refers, and not the other way round.

Many travellers bear witness to the fact that this antithesis is reflected in the ornaments of the different sexes. For example: "Here, as in other places, the stronger sex takes special care to distinguish itself from the other sex and the male dress is very markedly different from the female" (Schweinfurth, *Au Cœur de l'Afrique*, Vol. II, p. 281). ". . . and the men (in the Niam-Niam tribe) take far greater pains in doing their hair, whereas the women's coiffeur is quite simple and modest" (*ibid.*, Vol. II, p. 5). On the influence of the division of labour between men and women in dances, see von den Steinen: *Unter den Naturvoelkern Zentral-Brasiliens*, Berlin, 1894, p. 298. It can confidently be asserted that the tendency in men to contrast themselves to *women* arose earlier than the tendency to contrast themselves to *the lower animals*. Do not the fundamental features of man's psychological nature find somewhat paradoxical expression here?

V. I. Jochelson was born in 1855 in Vilna, Lithuania. In the early years of his life he was an active Narodnik revolutionary and took part in conspiratorial work in St. Petersburg. He emigrated in 1880 and ran the *Narodnaya Volya* printing press in Geneva, returning illegally to Russia in 1885. In 1888 he was arrested and exiled to Siberia for ten years. Here he took up the study of the peoples of the Yakutian region and became an outstanding ethnographer. Much of his work has been published in English.—TRANS.

this latter is determined by the course of development of our (social) culture.

In the example quoted by Taine, he talks about *landscape.* Notice, my dear sir, that landscape holds a far from permanent place in the history of painting. Michelangelo and his contemporaries despised it. It did not begin to flourish in Italy until the period of decline at the very end of the Renaissance.

Neither did the French artists of the seventeenth nor even of the eighteenth century attach any independent significance to it. In the nineteenth century the position changes markedly: landscape begins to be valued for its own sake, and young artists—Fleury, Cabat, Théodore Rousseau—sought such inspiration in the bosom of nature, in the environs of Paris, at Fontainebleau and at Melun, as artists of the time of Le Brun and Boucher had never even suspected to be possible. Why was this? Because French social relationships had changed and consequently the psychology of the French had also changed. Thus, man's impressions of nature differ in the various epochs of his social development, since in each he views it from a different standpoint.

Of course, the general laws of human psychology do not lose their validity in a single one of these periods. But since the material that comes to men's minds in different periods because of the difference in social relations, is by no means identical, it is not surprising that the results of its refashioning are by no means identical.

One more example. Certain writers have expressed the idea that everything in man's appearance which reminds us of the lower animals seems to us ugly. This is right in so far as it applies to civilised peoples, though even here there are not a few exceptions: none of us regards "a leonine head" as misshapen. However, despite such exceptions, it can be said that man, conscious that he is an incomparably higher being in comparison with all his relatives in the animal world, is afraid of likening himself to them and even tries to *accentuate* and to *exaggerate* his dissimilarity to them.[1]

[1] "In this idealisation of nature, sculpture followed the direction indicated by nature herself; it lent new emphasis mainly to those features which differentiated man from the animals. His upright posture led to greater slenderness and length of leg, the growing elevation of the forehead in the animal world to the portrayal of the Grecian profile, to the general principle already enounced

But to apply this to primitive peoples is definitely wrong. We know that some of them extract their upper incisors in order to make themselves more like the ruminant animals, while others file them, so as to look like beasts of prey, and still others plait their hair so as to make horns of it, and so on, almost *ad infinitum.*[1] These tendencies to imitate animals are often connected with religious beliefs among primitive peoples.[2]

But this does not in the least change the position.

After all, if primitive man had looked on the lower animals with our eyes, they would probably have found no place in his religious conceptions. He looks on them differently. Why is this so? Because *he stands at a different stage of culture.* In other words, if man in one instance seeks to liken himself to the lower animals and in another contrasts himself to them, this depends on the state of his culture, again, that is, on those same social conditions of which I have already spoken. Incidentally, here I may express myself with more exactness; I shall say that this depends on the degree of development of his productive forces, on his *mode of production.* And lest you should accuse me of exaggerating, or of being "narrow," I shall ask the learned German traveller, von den Steinen, from whom I have already quoted, to speak for me. "We shall not understand these people," he says of the Brazilian Indians, "until we study them as the products of a hunting mode of life.

by Winkelmann that Nature, when she interrupts surfaces does not round off the break, but acts decisively making the sharp edges of the eye-sockets and nasal bones stand out, as well as the lips, no less sharply delineated." *Lotze, Geschichte der Aesthetik in Deutschland,* Muenchen, 1868, p. 568.

[1] The missionary Heckewelder, relates how once, when calling on an Indian acquaintance, he found him preparing for a dance, which, as we know, has an important social significance among primitive peoples. The Indian was painting his face in the following subtle manner: "When I looked at his profile from one angle his nose took the form of a very well simulated eagle's beak. When I saw him from the other side the same nose looked like the snout of a pig. . . . The Indian was obviously very pleased with his work and as he had brought a mirror with him he looked at himself in it with satisfaction and some pride," *Histoire, moeurs et coutumes des nations indiennes, qui habitaient autrefois la Pennsylvanie et les etats voisins, par le révérand Jean Heckewelder, missionaire morave, trad. de l'anglais pa le chevalier Du Ponceau,* Paris, 1822, p. 324. I have given the title of this book in full since it contains a great deal of interesting information and I should like to recommend it to the reader. I shall have occasion to refer to it again more than once.

[2] Cf. J. G. Frazer, *Totemism,* Edinburgh, 1887, p. 26 ff. Schweinfurth, *Au Cœur de l'Afrique,* Vol. I, p. 381.

The greater part of their experience is bound up with the animal world, and it is on the basis of this experience that their philosophy of life has been built up. Similarly their artistic themes, too, are taken with depressing monotony from the animal world. It can be said that all their surprising wealth of art has its roots in a hunter's existence."[1]

In his thesis, *The Aesthetic Relationships of Art and Reality*, Chernyshevsky once wrote: "In plants we like the freshness of the bloom and the luxurious wealth of form that reveals fresh life, rich in strength. A drooping plant is not good; a plant in which there is little of the sap of life is a poor thing." Chernyshevsky's thesis is an extremely interesting example, unique of its kind, of the application of the general principles of Feuerbach's materialism to questions of aesthetics.

But history was always the weak point of Feuerbach's materialism, and this is well exemplified in the lines I have just quoted: "In plants we like . . ."

Who are "we"? People's tastes are, after all, exceedingly variable, as Chernyshevsky himself more than once pointed out in the same work. We know that primitive tribes—for instance, the Australian bushmen—never adorn themselves with flowers, although they live in lands where there is an abundance of them. It is said that the Tasmanians were an exception to this rule, but it is no longer possible to check the accuracy of this information: the Tasmanians are extinct. But in any case, we do know very well that plants are completely absent from the *ornamentation* of primitive—to be more accurate, of *hunting*—peoples, who take their themes from the animal world. Modern science explains this too by the state of their productive forces.

"The ornamental themes borrowed from nature by hunting tribes consist exclusively of animal and human forms," says Ernst Grosse. "Consequently they choose those particular phenomena which present the greatest measure of practical interest for them. The gathering of plants, which is, of course, also necessary for him, the primitive hunter allots to women as an occupation of a lower sort and does not himself take any interest in it. This explains why we do not meet even a trace of plant motives in his ornamentation—motives so richly developed in the decorative art of civilised peoples. In actual fact, the transition

[1] *Op. cit.*, p. 201.

from animal themes to plant themes is a symbol of the greatest progress in the history of culture—of the transition from a hunting to an agricultural economy."[1]

Primitive art provides such a clear reflection of the state of productive forces that in doubtful instances the state of those forces is now judged from the evidence of art. Thus, for example, the Bushmen are very fond of drawing people and animals, and they do so comparatively well. In the localities they inhabit, certain caverns assume the aspect of a regular picture gallery. But the Bushman does not draw any plants. In the only known exception to this general rule, the depiction of a hunter hiding behind a bush, the clumsy drawing of the *bush* shows, better than anything else could, how unaccustomed a subject this was for the primitive artist. On these grounds certain ethnologists conclude that if the Bushmen did, at one time, approach a somewhat higher level of culture than that at which they stood at present—which, generally speaking, would not be impossible—they certainly never practised *agriculture*.[2]

If all this is correct, we can now modify as follows the conclusion we previously drew from Darwin's statement: the psychological nature of the primitive hunter is the conditioning factor of his general capacity to develop aesthetic tastes and concepts, while the state of his productive forces, his hunting economy, leads to the formation of his particular aesthetic tastes and concepts, as distinct from others. This conclusion, which throws clear light upon the art of the hunting tribe, is at the same time an additional argument in favour of the materialist conception of history.

Among civilised people the technique of production far less often exercises any direct influence on art. This fact, which would appear to contradict the materialist conception of history, serves in actual fact as a magnificent confirmation of its truth. But we shall consider this elsewhere.

I am going to deal with another psychological law which also has played an important role in the history of art—a law, moreover, to which insufficient attention has been paid.

Burton says that certain African negroes known to him have a

[1] *Die Anfaenge der Kunst*, p. 149. Re-translated from Plekhanov's Russian.—TRANS.

[2] See the interesting introduction by Raoul Allier to Frédéric Christol's book, *Au sud de l'Afrique*, Paris, 1897.

poorly developed ear for music, but that they are, on the other hand, surprisingly sensitive to rhythm: "The rower sings in time to the movement of his oars, the porter sings as he walks, the housewife hums as she grinds grain."[1] Casalis says the same thing of caffres of the *Basuto* tribe, whom he studied closely. "The women of this tribe wear metal rings on their arms, they frequently gather together and accompany the measured movements of their hands with singing that strictly accords with the sound cadences made by their rings."[2] The men of the same tribe, when dressing leather, says Casalis, "at every movement utter a strange sound, the significance of which I could not account for."[3] This tribe especially takes pleasure in the rhythm of music, and the stronger it is in a given refrain, the more they like that refrain.[4] During their dances the Basutos beat time with their feet and hands, and to accentuate the sounds thus produced they hang rattles of a special kind around their bodies.[5] A sense of *rhythm* is also very strongly marked in the music of the Brazilian Indians, whereas they are very weak in their sense of *melody* and evidently have not the slightest conception of *harmony*.[6] The same must be said of the Australian aborigines.[7] In a word, rhythm has a truly tremendous significance for all primitive peoples. Response to rhythm, and musical ability in general, is evidently one of the basic attributes of man's psycho-physiological nature. And not only of man's. "The perception, if not the enjoyment, of musical cadences and of rhythm," says Darwin, "is probably common to all animals, and no doubt depends on the common physiological nature of their nervous system."[8] In view of this it might be supposed, perhaps, that the appearance of this capacity, which man holds in common with other animals, does not depend upon the conditions of his social life as a whole, nor upon the state of his productive forces in particular. But although such a supposition would seem at first glance extremely natural, it will not stand up to the criticism of facts. Science has shown that such a connection

[1] F. Christol, *Au sud de l'Afrique*, Vol. II, p. 291. A handmill is implied here.

[2] *Les Bassoutos*, by E. Casalis, a former missionary, Paris, 1863, p. 150.

[3] *Ibid.*, p. 141.

[4] *Ibid.*, p. 157.

[5] *Ibid.*, p. 158.

[6] Von den Steinen, *op. cit.*, p. 326.

[7] *Vide* E. J. Eyre, *Manners and Customs of the Aborigines of Australia*, in *Journal of the Expeditions of Discovery into Central Australia and Overland*, London, 1847, Vol. II. p. 229. See likewise Grosse, *Anfaenge der Kunst*, p. 271.

[8] *The Descent of Man*, London, 1872, Vol. II, p. 317.

exists. And take note, my dear sir, that science has done this in the person of one of the most outstanding *economists*, Karl Buecher.

The facts I have quoted above make it clear that because man has the capacity to recognise and take pleasure in rhythm, as a primitive producer he is ready to submit in the course of his labour to the beating of time and to accompanying his bodily movements by measured vocal sounds or the cadenced ring of various pendants. But what is it that determines this rhythm to which the primitive producer submits? Why is it that the movements of his body in the course of production observe one particular measure and not another? It depends *upon the technological character of the given productive process, upon the technique of the particular form of production*. With primitive tribes each form of labour has its song, whose refrain is always made to accord very exactly with the rhythm of the productive movements peculiar to this type of labour. With the development of productive forces the significance of rhythmic activity in the productive process diminishes, but even amongst civilised peoples, for instance, in German villages, each season of the year, as Buecher puts it, has its own characteristic sounds of work, and each form of work its own music.[1]

But it should also be noted that solos or entire choruses arise according to the manner in which the work is done, either by one producer or by a whole group, the latter also subdividing into several sections. And in all these instances the rhythm of the song is invariably determined by the rhythm of the productive process. But this is not all. The technical character of this process has also a decisive influence on the *content* of the songs accompanying the work. A study of the interconnection of work, music and poetry has brought Buecher to the conclusion "that in the first stage of their development, work, music and poetry were most intimately connected with one another, but that the basic element of this trinity was work, while the other two elements had only a subordinate significance."[2]

Since the sounds accompanying many productive processes have in themselves a musical effect; since, moreover, the main thing in music for primitive peoples is *rhythm*, it is not hard to understand

[1] K. Buecher, *Arbeit und Rhythmus*, Leipzig, 1896, pp. 21, 22, 23, 35, 50, 53, 54; Burton, *op. cit.*, Vol. I, p. 641.

[2] Buecher, *ibid.*, p. 78.

how their unassuming works of music grew out of the sounds evoked by the contact of tools with the *materials* being worked. This was brought about by accentuating these sounds, by introducing a certain diversity in their rhythm and, in general, by adapting them to the expression of human emotions.[1] But for this purpose it was necessary to alter the primitive *instruments of labour*, which were thus transformed into *musical instruments.*

Those instruments which the producer used simply to *beat* the object of his labour must have undergone such a transformation earlier than the others. We know that the *drum* is extremely widespread among primitive peoples and that for some of them it has remained to this day their sole musical instrument. String instruments belong primarily to the same category, since primitive musicians, when they play, *beat the strings.* Among these peoples, however, wind instruments are entirely relegated to the background: the flute is more often met with than others and not infrequently accompanies certain combined forms of labour to impart the correct rhythm to them.[2] I cannot speak here in detail of Buecher's views on the origin of poetry; it will be more convenient to do so in one of the letters that are to follow. I shall say briefly that Buecher is convinced that energetic rhythmical movements of the body, especially those movements which we term work, led to its inception, and that this is true not only in regard to poetic *form*, but also in regard to *content.*[3]

If Buecher's remarkable conclusions are correct we have a right to say that human nature (the physiological nature of man's nervous system) has provided him with the faculty of recognising the musical nature of rhythm and of enjoying it, whilst the technique of his production has been the determining factor in the further development of this faculty.

Research workers have long been aware of the intimate connection between the state of the productive forces of so-called primitive peoples and their art. But as these research workers in the great majority of instances have held idealist views, they recognised the existence of this connection against their will, as it were, and explained it incorrectly. Thus Wilhelm Luebke, the well-known art historian, says that works of art among primitive peoples bear the imprint of *natural necessity*, whereas with

[1] K. Buecher, *Arbeit und Rhythmus*, p. 91. [2] *Ibid.*, pp. 91–2.
[3] *Ibid.*, p. 80.

civilised nations they are imbued with *spiritual consciousness*. Such a contrast is entirely based on idealist prejudice. In actual fact artistic creation among civilised no less than among primitive peoples, is subject to necessity. The difference consists only in the fact that the *direct* dependence of art on technique and the modes of production disappears with civilised peoples. Of course, I know that this is a very big difference. But I know also that it is due solely to the development of those very social forces of production, which lead to the division of social labour between different classes. It does not refute the materialist conception of history, but, on the contrary, provides new and convincing evidence in its favour.

Let me point as well to the "law of symmetry." Its significance is great and undoubted. From what does it stem? Probably as much from the structure of the human body itself as from that of animals: only cripples and monstrosities have bodies that are not symmetrical, and these were always bound to make an unpleasant impression in the physically normal man. Thus ability to appreciate symmetry is also given us by nature. But it is not known how far this faculty would have developed had it not been reinforced and cultivated by the actual mode of life of primitive peoples. We know that primitive man is predominantly a hunter. This mode of life leads, as we are already aware, to a predominance in his ornamentation of themes taken from the animal world. And this compels primitive man—from a very early age—to take the law of symmetry carefully into account.[1]

The fact that savages (and not only savages, either) are more fond in their ornamentation of *horizontal* than of *vertical* symmetry clearly shows that the sense of symmetry as a human attribute is cultivated precisely by these models: look at the first figure of a man or animal you come across (not a deformed one, of course)

[1] I say "from a very early age" because, with primitive man, children's games at the same time serve as a school for developing their artistic talents. Thus, according to the missionary Christol (*Au Sud de L'Afrique*, p. 95 ff.), the children of the Basuto tribe make their own toy bulls, horses and so forth, out of clay. Of course, this sculpture by children leaves a great deal to be desired; nevertheless civilised children could not compare in this respect with the little African "savages." In primitive society children's amusements are most intimately connected with the productive activities of adults. This circumstance throws a clear light on the question of the relationship of "play" to social life, as I shall show in one of my later letters.

and you will see that its symmetry is horizontal and not vertical. Besides this it must be borne in mind that tools and utensils often required symmetrical form by virtue of their very character and purpose. Finally, if the Australian aborigine when decorating his shield, as Grosse quite rightly remarks, accepts the significance of symmetry every bit as much as did the highly civilised builders of the Parthenon,[1] then it is clear that a sense of symmetry in itself still throws no light whatever on the history of art, and that in this, as in all other cases, we have to say: nature provides man with the faculty, while the exercise and practical application of this faculty is determined by the course of development of his culture.

Here again I am purposely using an indeterminate expression: *culture*. On reading it you will angrily exclaim: "Why, who on earth has denied it and when? We are only saying that the development of culture is not solely conditioned either by the development of productive forces or by economics."

Alas! I am too well acquainted with such objections. And I admit, I could never understand why even clever people fail to notice the terrible logical blunder upon which these objections are founded.

Indeed, sir, you want the course of culture to be determined by other "factors" as well. I will put the question to you: is art one of them? You will, of course, answer that it is. Then this is the position we are left in: the course of development of human culture is determined, among other things, by the development of art, and the development of art is determined by the course of development of human culture. And you will have to say the same thing about all the other "factors": economics, civil law, political institutions, morality and so forth. What is the result? The result is as follows: the development of human culture is determined by the effect of all the factors referred to, and the development of all the factors referred to is determined by the development of culture. Why, this is the old logical mistake, in which our forefathers involved themselves: "What supports the earth?"—"Whales."—"And the whales?"—"Water."—"And the water?"—"The earth."—"And the earth?"—"Whales" . . . and so on, in the same amazing order.

You will agree that in conducting research on serious questions

[1] See the drawings of Australian shields in Grosse, *Anfaenge der Kunst*, p. 145.

of social development we can and must, after all, try to reason more seriously.

I am deeply convinced that criticism (to be more exact: the scientific theory of aesthetics) will from now on only be able to advance on the basis of the materialist conception of history. I also believe that criticism in its past development as well acquired more solid foundations in so far as its representatives approached the historical view I am defending. I will refer you to *the evolution of criticism* in France as an example.

This evolution is intimately connected with the development of general historical ideas. The philosophers of the Enlightenment in the eighteenth century, as I have already said, looked on history from the idealist point of view. They saw the accumulation and dissemination of knowledge as the chief motive force, more profound than all others, behind mankind's historical development. But if the successes of science and the development of human thought in general do indeed amount to the most important and profound reason for historical development the question naturally arises: what conditions the development of thought itself? From the point of view of the eighteenth century there was *only one possible answer* to this: man's nature, the immanent laws of development of his thought. But if man's nature is the conditioning factor for the development of his thought, it is clear that the *development of literature and art*, too, is conditioned by it. And so human nature—and that alone—can and must give us the key to an understanding of the development of literature and art in the civilised world.

The attributes of human nature lead to man's passing through different ages: childhood, youth, maturity and so on. Literature and art also pass through these ages in their development.

"What people has not been first a poet, and afterwards a thinker?" asks Grimm in his *Correspondance Littéraire*,[1] meaning

[1] *Friedrich Melchior (Baron von) Grimm* (1723–1807), not to be confused with the brothers Jacob and Wilhelm Grimm, well known for their work on linguistics and folklore. Friedrich Grimm studied at Leipzig under Gottsched, the German proponent of the classical school of literature. He went to Paris in 1748 and remained in France for a large part of his life. He became a friend of Rousseau and of the French Encyclopaedists, by whom he was greatly influenced. He wrote in French, and his *Correspondance Littéraire*, posthumously published, was conducted with a number of European monarchs, including Catherine II of Russia, whose friend and confidant he became.—TRANS.

thereby that the flowering of poetry corresponds with the childhood and youth of peoples and the advance of philosophy with their maturity. This 18th century viewpoint was inherited by the 19th century. We meet it even in Mme. de Staël's famous book, *De la Littérature considérée dans ses rapports avec les institutions Sociales*,[1] where there are at the same time extremely significant rudiments of a completely different outlook. "In studying the three different epochs of Greek literature," says Mme. de Staël, "the natural course of the human mind can be very distinctly perceived. . . . It is Homer who characterises the first period of Greek literature; in the age of Pericles dramatic art, eloquence and ethics make rapid progress, whilst philosophy makes its first steps; in the period of Alexander a deeper study of the philosophical sciences becomes the main occupation of persons outstanding in the literary field. Of course, a certain level of development of the human mind is necessary in order to achieve the heights of poetry: but this aspect of literature must nevertheless lose some of its effect at a period when, thanks to progress, civilisation and philosophy, certain errors of the imagination are being corrected."[2]

This means that once a given people has emerged from the epoch of its youth, its poetry is bound to fall into a certain decline.

Mme. de Staël knew that modern nations, despite all the achievements of their intellect, had not produced a single poetic work that could possibly be placed higher than the *Iliad* or the *Odyssey*. This circumstance threatened to undermine her confidence in the permanent and unfaltering improvement of mankind, and therefore she did not wish to give up the theory of different ages which she had inherited from the eighteenth century, and which enabled her to cope satisfactorily with the difficulty above mentioned.

Indeed, from the standpoint of this theory, we can see that the decline of poetry was a sign of the intellectual maturity of the civilised peoples of the modern world. But when Mme. de Staël leaves this comparison and transfers her attention to the literature of modern nations, she can look upon the problem from a com-

[1] *Mme. de Staël, née* Germaine Neckar (1766–1817), noted French novelist and writer on literary and philosophical subjects. Her three most important works were the novel *Corinne* (1807) and two studies *De la Littérature considérée dans ses rapports avec les institutions Sociales* and *De l'Allemagne*.—TRANS.

[2] *De la Littérature*, etc., *Oeuvres Complètes*, Paris, 1836, Vol. I, pp. 209–10.

pletely different point of view. In this sense those chapters of her book which deal with French literature are particularly interesting. "French vivacity and French taste had become proverbial in all European countries," she remarks in one of these chapters, "and this taste and this vivacity were generally attributed to the national character; but what is national character if not the result of the institutions and conditions which have influenced the welfare of a people, its interests and its habits? In the course of the last ten years, even at moments when there has been the most marked lull in the Revolution, the most piquant contrasts have not afforded a pretext for a single epigram, nor for a single witty joke. Several of those who have had the greatest influence on the fate of France were completely lacking in elegance of expression and brilliance of mind; it is perfectly possible, in fact, that a part of their influence was due originally to their dourness, taciturnity and cold heartlessness . . ."[1] It is not important for us to know here at whom these words were directed or in what degree the suggestion they contain corresponds with reality. We have to note only that, in Mme. de Staël's opinion, *national character is created by historical conditions.* But what is national character if not human nature as manifested in the spiritual attributes of a *given nation*?

And if the nature of a nation is created by that nation's historical development it obviously cannot itself be the primary cause of this development. And hence it follows that *literature*, the reflection of a nation's spiritual nature, is the product of those same historical conditions that created that nature. In other words, it is not human nature, not the character of a given people, but its history and its social structure that explain its literature to us. It is from this very point of view that Mme. de Staël looks at literature. The chapter devoted to French literature of the seventeenth century represents an extremely interesting attempt to explain the predominant character of this literature by the social and political relations obtaining in France at that time, and by the psychology of the French nobility examined in its relations with the monarchical power.

Many exceedingly acute observations may be found in the book, touching the psychology of the ruling class of the time, and some very apt reflections on the future of French literature.

[1] *De la Littérature*, etc., *Oeuvres Complètes*, Paris, 1836, Vol. I, p. 278.

"Under a government of a different character, however it may be constituted, we shall not see anything similar again in France" (to the literature of the seventeenth century—G.V.P.), says Mme. de Staël, "and this will offer good proof of the fact that so-called French wit and French elegance were nothing but the direct and necessary product of monarchical institutions and customs, as they existed in France over a number of centuries."[1] This new view, according to which literature is the product of the social structure, little by little achieved a dominant place in the criticism of the nineteenth century.

In France, Guizot[2] repeats it in his literary essays.[3] Sainte-Beuve repeats it as well, though it is true that he does not accept it without reservations; finally, it finds full and brilliant expression in the works of Taine.

[1] *De la Littérature, Oeuvres Complètes*, Paris, 1836, Vol. I, p. 281.

[2] *François Guizot* (1787–1874). French politician and historian. Foreign Minister under Louis Philippe from 1840–7. In 1847 he became Premier. The Revolution of 1848 led him to seek refuge in England and retire from politics. His *History of the English Revolution* (1828) is interesting as one of the first attempts to interpret history in the light of class struggles.—TRANS.

[3] Guizot's views on literature throw such clear light on the development of historical ideas in France that it is worth while dwelling on them, if only in passing. In his book, *Vies des Poètes Français du Siècle Louis XIV*, Paris, 1813, Guizot says that Greek literature reflects historically the natural course of development of the human mind, whereas among modern nations the matter is far more complicated: here it is necessary to take into account a "whole multitude of secondary factors." When he goes on to deal with the history of literature in France and begins to explore these "secondary" factors, it turns out that they all have their *roots in the social relations* obtaining in France, under the influence of which the tastes and habits of her different social classes and strata were formed. In his *Essai sur Shakespeare* Guizot examines French tragedy as a reflection of class psychology. The fate of drama, in his opinion, is generally speaking intimately connected with the development of social relations. But even at the time of publication of his *Essai sur Shakespeare* Guizot does not abandon his views on Greek literature as the product of the "natural" development of the human mind. On the contrary, this view finds its parallel in his *natural-historical* outlook as well. In his *Essais sur l'Histoire de France*, published in 1821, Guizot expresses the idea that the political structure of a given country is determined by its "civil condition"—at all events among the nations of the modern world—while civil condition is connected with land-ownership, as cause to effect. This "at all events" is extremely noteworthy. It shows that the civil condition of the peoples of antiquity, in contrast to the same condition among modern nations, is seen by Guizot as the product *"of the natural development of the human mind,"* and not as the result of the history of land-ownership and of economic

Taine held firmly to the conviction that "every change in man's condition leads to a change in his psychology."

But the literature and art of any society are to be explained precisely by its psychology, because "the works of the human spirit, like the works of nature, are to be explained only by their environment." And so, in order to understand the history of the art and literature of any country, the history of those changes which have taken place in the condition of its inhabitants has to be studied. This is undoubtedly true. We need only read Taine's *Philosophie de l'Art*, *Histoire de la Littérature Anglaise* or *Voyage en Italie* to find a number of the most striking and well-chosen illustrations of this. But, like Mme. de Staël and his other predecessors, Taine nevertheless held to the idealist view of history, and this hindered him from making the fullest use which an historian of literature and art might have made of the undoubted truth which he illustrated so strikingly and with such talent.

Since an idealist looks on the progress of the human mind as the ultimate cause of historical development, in Taine's case the *psychology* of man is determined *by his condition* and his *condition by his psychology*. Hence a series of contradictions and difficulties, from which Taine, like the philosophers of the eighteenth century, escaped through recourse to *human nature*, which with him assumes the form of *race*. What kind of door this key opened for him is quite evident from the following example. We know that the Renaissance began in Italy earlier than anywhere else and that Italy, generally speaking, had finished with the mediaeval way of life before other countries. What was it that gave rise to this *change in the way of life* of the Italians? The qualities of the Italian

relations in general. Here we have a complete analogy with his view on the historical development of Greek literature. If we add to this the fact that, in his journalistic writings at the time when his *Essais sur l'Histoire de France* was published, Guizot expressed with great conviction and vigour the idea that France "was created by the class struggle," there can be not the slightest doubt left that modern historians came to perceive the class struggle in the womb of modern society sooner than they did the same struggle within the ancient states. It is interesting that ancient historians like Thucydides and Polybius looked on the struggle between the classes of their own contemporary society as something perfectly natural and taken for granted, in approximately the same way as the members of our Russian peasant communes look upon the struggle between those of its members with more land and those with less.

race, answers Taine.[1] I leave it to you to judge how far such an explanation is satisfactory, and will go on to another example. In the Palazzo Sciarra at Rome, Taine saw a landscape by Poussin which prompted him to remark that, by virtue of the special qualities of their race, the Italians understood landscape in a special way, that for them a landscape was much like a villa, only a villa of exaggerated proportions, whereas the German race loved nature for its own sake.[2] But elsewhere Taine, referring to the landscapes of the same Poussin, says: "To be able to take pleasure in them one must love (classical) tragedy, classical verse, the pomposity of etiquette and of aristocratic or monarchical magnificence. Such feelings are infinitely removed from those of our contemporaries."[3] Why, then, are the feelings of our contemporaries so unlike those of the people who loved pompous etiquette, classical tragedy and Alexandrine verse? Can it be because Frenchmen of the time of "le Roi Soleil," for example, were people of a *different race* from the Frenchmen of the nineteenth century? What an odd question to ask! Why, Taine himself repeats insistently and with conviction that the change in the mentality of men is consequent upon the changes in their condition. We have not forgotten this, and will repeat what he says: the condition of our contemporaries is extremely far removed from that of the men of the seventeenth century, and for this reason their feelings are very dissimilar to those of Boileau's and Racine's contemporaries. It remains to discover why that condition changed, i.e. why the *ancien régime* gave way to the present bourgeois order, and why the Stock Exchange now rules in a country where Louis XIV could once say, almost without exaggeration: "L'Etat, c'est moi."[4] And to this a quite satisfactory answer is given by the economic history of the country.

You are aware, Sir, that writers holding the most varied opinions objected to Taine's views. I do not know what you think of their objections, but I will say that none of Taine's critics succeeded in even shaking the principle which sums up nearly all that is true in his aesthetic theory, and which proclaims art to be the creation of man's mind, while man's mind changes in

[1] "As the Italians are a precocious race and were only partially covered by a Germanic veneer, the modern age developed earlier in their country than elsewhere . . ." *Voyage en Italie*, Paris, 1872, Vol I, p. 273.

[2] *Ibid.*, Vol. I, p. 330. [3] *Ibid.*, Vol. I, p. 331. [4] "I am the State."

accordance with man's condition. And in just the same way not one of them discerned the fundamental contradiction which made impossible the further fruitful development of Taine's views; not one of them noticed that, according to his view of history, man's mental make-up, determined by his condition, itself turns out to be the ultimate determinant of that condition. Why was it none of them noticed this? Because their own historical views were penetrated, through and through, by the same contradiction. But what is this contradiction? Of what factors does it consist? It consists of two, one of which is termed the *idealist* view of history and the other the *materialist* view of history. When Taine said that men's minds changed according to the changes in their condition he was a materialist, while when the same Taine said that men's condition was determined by their psychology, he was repeating the idealistic view of the eighteenth century. It need scarcely be added that it was not the latter view which prompted his most penetrating reflections on the history of literature and art.

What conclusion may be drawn from this? The answer is that anyone who wishes to rid himself of the contradiction in question, which hindered the development of the acute and profound views of the French art critics, can only do so by telling himself that the art of any people is determined by their psychology; that their psychology is the outcome of their condition and that this is itself determined in the last analysis by the state of their productive forces and their relations of production. But whoever said this would thereby be expressing the materialist view of history . . .

However, I can see that it is high time for me to stop. Till the next letter, then! Forgive me, if the "narrowness" of my outlook has irritated you. Next time I shall be dealing with art among primitive peoples, and in doing so I shall hope to show that my outlook is by no means so narrow as it may have appeared, and probably still does appear to you.

SECOND LETTER

PRIMITIVE SOCIETY

Dear Sir,—The art of any people has always, in my opinion, an intimate causal connection with their economy. In approaching the study of art among primitive peoples, therefore, I must first of all indicate the most important distinctive features of primitive economy.

It is on the whole natural, as one writer has graphically put it, for the "economic" materialist to start playing his tune on the "economic string." But in this instance I have also been prompted by a special and very important circumstance to take this "string" as the point of departure for my research.

Until very recently there was a widespread and firm conviction among sociologists and economists acquainted with ethnology that the economy of primitive society was a *communist* economy *par excellence*. "Nowadays the historical ethnographer, in approaching the study of primitive culture," wrote M. M. Kovalevsky[1] in 1879, "knows that the objects of his research are not isolated individuals, supposedly entering into an agreement with each other to live in comm. . under the leadership of authorities established by themselves, nor individual families that existed from time immemorial and grad. ally grew into tribal unions, but gregarious groups of individuals of different sex—groups within which a slow and spontaneous process of differentiation takes place, resulting in the emergence of the family as a unit and of individual property, which in the earliest times was movable property only."[2]

Originally even food, that "most important and essential form of movable property," was the common property of the members

[1] *M. M. Kovalevsky* (1851–1916). Russian historian and sociologist. Though an acquaintance of Karl Marx he was an eclectic in philosophy. He did not accept the theory of historical materialism, though he attached great importance to the role of economics in history. In 1901 he organised a School of Social Science in Paris, where for a time Lenin and Plekhanov taught.—Trans.

[2] *Communal Landownership; the Causes, Course and Consequences of its Disintegration*, pp. 26–7. (*Obshchinnoe zemlevladenie, prichiny, khod i posledstviya evo razlozheniya.*)

of the gregarious group, while the division of provender among separate families occurred only in tribes at a comparatively higher level of development.[1]

The late N. I. Sieber,[2] whose well-known book, *Essays on Primitive Economic Culture*, was devoted to a critical examination of "the thesis that the communal aspects of economy in their various phases are universal forms of economic activity in the early stages of development," took a similar view of primitive economic structure. On the basis of far-reaching factual material, the organisation of which, it is true, cannot be regarded as strictly systematic, Sieber came to the conclusion that "simple collaboration in catching fish, hunting, attack and defence, tending cattle, clearance of forest lots for cultivation, irrigation, cultivation of the land, construction of houses and heavy equipment, such as nets, boats and so on, was the factor that naturally determined the joint use of all that was produced and hence, also, the common ownership of immovable and even of movable property, in so far as it could be preserved from infringement by neighbouring groups."[3]

I could quote from many other authorities of no less standing. But, of course, you know of them yourself. I will not, therefore, multiply the quotations, but will go straight to the point that the theory of "*primitive communism*" is, at the present time under dispute. Thus Karl Buecher,[4] to whom I have already referred in

[1] *Ibid.*, p. 29.

[2] *N. I. Sieber* (1844–88). One of the first popularisers of Marxist theory in Russia. His main work, published in 1881 was *The Social and Economic Researches of Ricardo and Marx*, in which he showed that Marx's teaching was a development and deepening of Ricardo's labour theory of value. Sieber also conducted research into the history of primitive economy, where he was one of the first to apply Marxist method to the study of the history of culture.—TRANS.

[3] *Ocherki Pervobytnoi Ekonomicheskoi Kultury*, pp. 5–6, 1st Edn. (K. T. Soldatenkova, Moscow, 1883).

[4] *Karl Buecher* German economist of the historical school, well-known for his studies on stages of economic development. His classification of stages depended on the degree of removal of the product from the producer on its reaching the consumer: on this basis he distinguished a stage (1) of closed domestic production for use, (2) of city economy with direct exchange between producer and consumer, (3) of national economy in which the product passes from producer to consumer via a number of intermediaries. His theory ignored the differences in the class structure of economy, e.g. slave and feudal society are united under his first classification.—TRANS.

my first letter, considers that the theory does not accord with the facts. In his opinion, those peoples who actually can be termed primitive, are as far removed *from communism* as they possibly could be. It would be more correct to call their economy *individualist*; but even this term would be incorrect, since the very features essential to an "economy" are generally alien to their way of life.

"By economy we always understand collaboration by men for the purpose of acquiring goods," writes Buecher in his essay, *Primitive Economic Structure.* "Economy presupposes care, not merely for the present moment, but also for the future, a thrifty use of time and its expedient allocation; economy signifies labour, appreciation of the value of articles, the regulation of their use, the transmission of cultural attainments from generation to generation."[1] But only the barest rudiments of such features are to be met with in the lower tribes. "If we set aside the use of fire and the bow and arrow by the Bushmen and Veddas their whole life amounts to an individual search for food. Each individual Bushman has to feed himself quite independently. Naked and unarmed, he wanders, like the wild game, with his comrades within the narrow limits of a definite area. . . . Each one of them, man and woman alike, eats raw whatever he can manage to clutch with his hands or scrape from the ground with his nails—lower organisms, roots, fruit. At times they gather together in tiny groups or in large herds, at times they wander apart again, according to the extent to which the locality abounds in vegetable foods or game; but such groups do not turn into real communities. They do not make it any easier for the individual to exist. This picture is not perhaps a very pleasing one to the modern cultured person; however, empirically established facts simply compel us to present it in no other way. Nothing whatsoever has been invented. We have eliminated from the life of the lower hunters only those factors which, according to the commonly accepted view, are acknowledged to be already a mark of culture: the use of weapons and fire."[2]

It must be admitted that this picture is not at all like the one of primitive communist economy which rises in our minds under

[1] *Four Essays on the Subject of National Economy.* Articles from the book *The Origin of National Economy.* St. Petersburg, 1898, p. 91.

[2] *Ibid.*, p. 91.

the influence of the work of M. M. Kovalevsky and N. I. Sieber.

I do not know which of the two pictures you "like," my dear sir. But that matters little. It is not a question of what you, I or some third person may *like*, but as to whether the picture drawn for us by Buecher is true, whether it accords with reality, whether it corresponds with empirical material established by science. These questions are not only important in economic history, they are of tremendous significance for everyone conducting research into one or another aspect of primitive culture. Indeed it is not in vain that art has been termed the reflection of life. If the "savage" turns out to be an individualist of the kind depicted by Buecher, his art must certainly reproduce the features characteristic of his individualism. Moreover, art is predominantly a reflection of social life, and if you look on the savage with Buecher's eyes you will be quite consistent in pointing out to me that there can be no question of art where *the individual search for food* prevails and where men, practically speaking, do not collaborate at all.

To all this the following must be added: Buecher undoubtedly belongs to the ranks of those *thinking* savants, whose number, unfortunately, is by no means so great as might be desired, and therefore his views merit serious attention even if he is in error.

Let us examine more closely the picture of savage life which he has drawn for us.

Buecher based his description on data relating to the life of the so-called lower hunting tribes, setting aside from these data only the marks of culture: the use of weapons and fire. In doing so he has himself shown us the direction we must follow in analysing his picture. To be precise, we have first of all to check the empirical material used by him; that is, we must see how the lower hunting tribes *do live* in actual fact, and then we must choose the most probable thesis as to how they *used to live* in the far-off times when the use of fire and weapons was unknown to them. The facts first, the hypothesis after.

Buecher draws his evidence from the Bushmen and the Veddas of Ceylon. The question arises whether the life of these tribes, which undoubtedly belong to the lowest hunting tribes, may be described as devoid of all marks of any economy and whether the individual, in their case, is left completely to his own devices. I assert that this is not so.

Let us take the Bushmen first. We know they not infrequently gather together in parties of two to three hundred for collective hunting. Such hunting, which beyond all doubt represents co-operation between men for productive purposes, at the same time "presupposes" both labour and the expedient allocation of time, since, in these instances, the Bushmen have to build enclosures, sometimes stretching for several miles, dig deep ditches, set sharpened stakes at the bottom of them and so on.[1] It goes without saying that all this is not done merely for the satisfaction of immediate requirements, but with a view to future needs as well.

"Some people deny that they are possessed of any economic sense," says Theophil Hahn, "and in the volumes that discourse upon them, one author copies down the mistakes of the last. Of course, Bushmen do not understand political economy and State economy, but that does not prevent them from taking thought for a rainy day."[2]

And this is true: from the meat of the animals they have killed they organise stocks and hide them in caves, or leave them in well-covered ravines under the supervision of old men who are no longer capable of taking direct part in the hunt.[3] The bulbs of certain plants are also prepared for storing. These bulbs, gathered in vast quantities, are preserved by the Bushmen in birds' nests. Finally we know of the stocks of *locusts* made by the Bushmen, who also dig deep, long trenches in order to catch them.[4]

This shows how greatly mistaken Buecher is in affirming, with Lippert, that no one among the lower hunting tribes thinks of laying in stocks.[5]

True, on the conclusion of collective hunts the great hunting parties of Bushmen break up into small groups. But, in the first place, it is one matter to be a member of a small group and another matter to be left to one's own devices. In the second place, even when they disperse to different parts, the Bushmen do not break off mutual contact. The Bechuanas told Lichtenstein that the Bushmen keep on giving each other signals by means of fires and

[1] Cf. *Die Buschmaenner, "Ein Beitrag zur suedafrikanischen Voelkerkunde von Theophil Hahn." Globus*, 1870, No. 7, p. 105.

[2] *Ibid.*, No. 8, p. 120.

[3] Cf. *ibid.*, No. 8, pp. 120 and 130.

[4] G. Lichtenstein, *Reise im Suedlichen Afrika in den Jahren, 1803, 1804, 1805 und 1806; Zweiter Teil*, p. 74.

[5] *Four Essays*, p. 75, footnote.

thanks to these know all that is going on over a very wide area a great deal better than do all the other neighbouring tribes which, culturally, are at a much higher level than they are.[1] I do not think that such customs as these could arise among the Bushmen if individuals were left *to their own devices* and if the "*individual search for food*" prevailed among them.

I will now pass on to the Veddas. These hunters (I am speaking of the completely savage "Rock Veddas," as the English call them) live, similarly to the Bushmen, in small kinship groups, pooling forces to carry on their search for food. True, the German investigators, Paul and Fritz Sarasin, authors of the latest and in many respects the most complete work on the Veddas,[2] make them out to be substantially individualists. They say that all the hunting territory of the Veddas, when their primitive social relations had not yet been destroyed under the influence of neighbouring peoples at a higher level of cultural development, was divided between separate families.

But this view is completely mistaken. The evidence on which the Sarasins make their surmise about the primitive social structure of the Veddas by no means bears out the conclusions these research workers draw from it. Thus the Sarasins quote the evidence of a certain Van Goens, who was a governor of Ceylon in the seventeenth century. But all that emerges from Van Goens' account is that the territory inhabited by the Veddas was divided into separate areas, and certainly not that these areas belonged to *separate families*. Another seventeenth century writer, Knox, says that the forest Veddas "have boundaries, dividing them off from each other," and that "the parties must not infringe these boundaries during a hunt and the gathering of fruits."

Here it is a question of *parties* and not of *separate* families, and for this reason we must suppose that Knox had in mind the boundaries of areas belonging to more or less sizeable clans, and not to separate families. Furthermore the Sarasins refer to the Englishman, Tennant. But what precisely is it that Tennant says?

[1] *Op. cit.*, Vol. II, p. 472. The Fuegians are also known to communicate with each other by means of fire. See Darwin, *Journal of Researches*, etc., London, 1834, p. 238.

[2] Sarasin, *Die Weddahs von Ceylon und die sie umgebenden Voelkerschaften*, Wiesbaden, 1892–3.

He tells us that the territory of the Veddas is divided *between clans* ("clans of families associated by relationship").[1]

A clan and a separate family are not one and the same thing. Of course, the Vedda clans are not large: Tennant specifically states that they are "small clans." But this, after all, is comprehensible. Clans cannot be large where the stage reached by the productive forces is as low as among the Veddas. But this is not the point. What is important for us here is to know, not the size of the Vedda clan, but the role which it plays in the existence of the separate individuals of the tribe. Can it be said that this role is insignificant, or that the individual's existence is not made easier for him by the clan? Of course it cannot! We know that the Vedda clans roam about under the leadership of their chiefs. We also know that children and adolescents when passing the night sleep near the leader, while the adult members of the clan range themselves around them, thus forming a living chain ready to defend them against hostile attacks.[2] This custom undoubtedly makes existence easier alike for the individual and for the whole tribe. It is also eased in no less a degree by certain other manifestations of solidarity. Thus, for example, widows in these tribes continue to receive their portion of all that falls into the hands of the clan.[3]

If there were no social union among them and if the "individual search for food" prevailed, women deprived of their husbands' support would, of course, meet a completely different fate.

By way of concluding with the Veddas I will add, further, that they, like the Bushmen, *organise stocks of meat and other hunting products*, not only to consume themselves but to barter with neighbouring tribes.[4] Captain Ribeiro even asserts that the Veddas do not eat fresh meat at all, but cut it up into pieces and preserve it in the hollows of trees, drawing on their supplies only on the expiry of a year.[5] This is probably an exaggeration; but in any case I ask you, sir, to note that the Veddas, like the Bushmen,

[1] *Ceylon: An Account of the Island*, etc., London, 1880, Vol. II, p. 440.

[2] Tennant, *op. cit.*, Vol. II, p. 441.

[3] *Ibid.*, Vol. II, p. 445. Monogamy is known to prevail among the Veddas.

[4] *Ibid.*, Vol. II, p. 440.

[5] *Histoire de l'isle de Ceylon, écrite par le capitaine J. Ribeiro et présenté au roi de Portugal en 1685*, trad. par m-r L'abbé Legrand, Amsterdam, MDCCXIX, p. 179.

provide evidence to refute once and for all Buecher's theory that savages do not lay in stores. And the preparation of stocks after all, according to Buecher, is in itself one of the undoubted marks of an economy.

The inhabitants of the Andaman Islands, the Mincopies,[1] are little above the level of the Veddas in their cultural development, but they, as well, live in clans and often hold socially organised hunts. Everything that the celibate youth succeed in obtaining becomes *common property* and is distributed according to the instructions of the chief of the clan. Those who have not taken part in the hunt nevertheless receive their portion of the booty, since it is assumed that they have been prevented from doing so by some sort of work that is of benefit to the whole commune. On returning to their camp the hunters seat themselves round a fire and then the feasting, songs and dances are begun. Not only do the unsuccessful, who rarely make a kill when hunting, take part in the feast, but even the plainly lazy ones, who prefer to spend their time in idleness.[2] Does all this bear any resemblance to an "individual search for food," and can it be said, under the circumstances, that the Mincopies clans fail to make existence easier for their individual members? No. On the contrary, it must be stated that empirical evidence on the life of the Mincopies bears no resemblance whatever to the "picture" Buecher has given us.

In characterising the life of the lower hunting tribes Buecher borrows a description of Negrito life in the Philippines from Schadenberg. Anyone reading Schadenberg's article[3] attentively, can satisfy himself that the Negritos carry on their struggle for existence, *not as isolated individuals, but through the united forces of the clan*. One Spanish priest, whose evidence Schadenberg quotes, says that among the Negritos "father, mother and children, each armed with their arrows, go hunting together." On this basis it might be thought that they live, if not as isolated individuals, then as small families. But this is not true. The Negrito "family"

[1] A note once appeared in the London journal, *Nature*, in which it was asserted that the term "Mincopies," sometimes given to the Andaman Islanders, had no foundation and was not used either by the natives or by their neighbours.

[2] C. H. Man, *On the Aboriginal Inhabitants of the Andaman Islands*, "Journal of the Anthropological Institute of Great Britain and Ireland," Vol. XII, p. 363.

[3] *Ueber die Negritos der Philippinen*, in "Zeitschrift fuer Ethnologie," Vol. XII.

is a clan embracing from twenty to eighty persons.[1] The members of such a union roam together under the leadership of a chief who chooses spots for bivouacs, appoints the time for setting out on campaigns, and so forth. By day the old men, invalids and children sit around a large camp fire while the healthy, adult members of the clan hunt in the forest. By night they all sleep huddled together around the same fire.[2]

However, not infrequently the children go off hunting too, as do the women, a fact which deserves special attention. In such cases they all go together, "like a herd of orang-outangs setting off on a plundering raid."[3] Here again I can see no sign at all of any "individual search for food."

The Pigmies of Central Africa, who only comparatively recently have become the object of reliable observation, are at the same level of development. All the "empirical material" on them collected by the most recent explorers decisively refutes the theory of the "individual search for food." They hunt wild animals jointly, and jointly raid the fields of neighbouring agricultural tribes. "While the men form a vanguard and, in case of need, join battle with the owners of the fields which are being ravaged, the women seize their booty, make bundles and sheaves of it, and carry it off."[4] This is not a case of *individualism, but of co-operation* and even *division of labour*.

I shall not dilate on the Brazilian Botocudos nor on the Australian aborigines,[5] since I should be compelled in dealing with them to repeat what has already been said of a number of other lower hunting peoples. It will be more useful to cast a glance at the life of those primitive peoples whose productive forces have

[1] According to Schadenberg—from twenty to thirty, according to *de la Gironière*—from sixty to eighty. (*Vide* George Windsor Earle, *The Native Races of the Indian Archipelago*, London, 1853, p. 133.)

[2] Earle, *op. cit.*, p. 131.

[3] Earle, *ibid.*, p. 134.

[4] Gaetano Casati, *Dix Années en Equatoria*, Paris, 1892, p. 116.

[5] Of the Australians I will only say this: whereas from Buecher's point of view their social relations scarcely merit being called a social union, unprejudiced explorers tell us something quite different. For instance: "An Australian tribe is an organised society, governed by strict customary laws, which are administered by the headmen or rulers of the various sections of the community, who exercise their authority after consultation among themselves," etc. *The Kamilaroi class system of the Australian Aborigines*, by R. H. Matthews, in *Proceedings and Transactions of the Queensland Branch of the Royal Geographical Society of Australasia*, Vol. X, Brisbane, 1895.

already attained a higher level of development. There are many such peoples in America.

The Redskins of North America live in clans, and with them exclusion from the clan is a terrible punishment imposed only for the worst of crimes.[1] This alone is enough to show how far individualism is alien to them, although, in Buecher's opinion, it is the distinguishing feature of primitive tribes. For the Redskins the clan is both landowner and lawgiver, avenger of the violated rights of the individual, and, in many cases, his heir. The whole strength, the whole survival of the clan depends upon the number of its members and, therefore, the death of each separate member is a heavy loss to all the rest. The clan strives to make good such losses by accepting new members into its midst. *Adoption* is very widespread among the Redskins of North America.[2] This serves to show what great significance they attach to the struggle for existence by the group as a collective; whereas Buecher, led astray by preconceived ideas, only sees in it proof of a poorly developed sense of kinship among primitive peoples.[3]

How important this collective struggle for existence is to them is proved also by the great prevalence among these tribes of communal hunting and fishing.[4] But apparently such communal hunting and fishing is still more widespread among the Indians of South America. As an example I shall take the Brazilian Bororos, who, according to Von den Steinen, have maintained their existence

[1] See Powell, on exclusion from the clan: *Wyandot Government* in the First Annual Report of the Bureau of Ethnology to the Smithsonian Institution, p. 67–8.

[2] Cf. *Lafitau, Les Moeurs des Sauvages Américains*, Vol. 2, p. 163; *vide* also Powell, *op. cit.*, Vol. I, p. 68. On adoption among the Eskimos, see Franz Boas, *The Central Eskimo* in the Sixth Report of the Bureau of Ethnology, p. 580.

[3] M. M. Kovalevsky points out that the custom of adoption is poorly developed among the Svanetians and remarks that this is to be explained by the strength of their clan structure (*Law and Custom in the Caucasus—Zakon i Obychai na Kavkaze*—Vol. II, pp. 4–5). But among the Redskins of North America and the Eskimos the undoubted strength of their tribal unions does not hinder the marked development of adoption. (On the Eskimos see John Murdoch, *Ethnological results of the Point Barrow Expedition* in the Ninth Annual Report of the Bureau of Ethnology, p. 417. Hence it follows that if the Svanetians seldom practise adoption the explanation for this must be sought in something else and definitely not in the strength of the clan.

[4] Cf. the description of the communal hunting of bison in G. Catlin's *Letters and Notes on the Manners, Customs and Condition of the North American Indians*, London, 1842, Vol. I, pp. 199 ff.

solely by means of constant co-operation on the part of the male half of the tribe, which often undertook extremely prolonged collective hunting expeditions.[1]

And were anyone to say that collective hunting expeditions did not become a factor of such tremendous import in the life of the American Indians until after they had emerged from the lower level of hunting life, he would be very much mistaken. It must, of course, be admitted that one of the most important cultural acquisitions of the natives of the New World is *agriculture*, which a great many of their tribes pursue, some with more, some with less diligence and persistence. . . . But agriculture could only *weaken* the general significance of hunting for them, and consequently, the particular significance of collective hunting by a large number of the tribe. Therefore the collective hunting expeditions of the Indians must be seen as a natural and most characteristic creation of that lower level of hunting life.

Nor, for that matter, has agriculture narrowed the role of co-operation in the life of the primitive tribes of America. Far from it. Whilst collective hunting expeditions to some extent lost their importance with the growth of agriculture, cultivation of the land created a new and very wide sphere of co-operation: among American Indians the land is cultivated (or, at least, was cultivated) *collectively* by the women, whose lot was to work in the fields. Indications to this effect are already to be found in Lafitau.[2] But modern American ethnology leaves not the slightest doubt on this score: I need only refer to the work by Powell, previously cited:—*Wyandot Government*. "Cultivation," says Powell, "is communal; that is, all of the able-bodied women of the gens take part in the cultivation of each household tract. . . ."[3] I could cite a number of examples showing the great importance of collective work in the life of primitive tribes in other parts of the world, but

[1] *Unter den Naturvoelkern Zentral-Brasiliens*, Berlin, 1894, p. 481: "Existence could only be maintained through the closed collective of the majority of the men, who had often to spend a long time together away hunting, which would not have been feasible for the individual tribesman."

[2] *Les Mœurs des Sauvages* . . . Vol. II, 77. Cf. Heckewelder, *Histoire des Indiens*, etc., p. 238.

[3] It is almost superfluous to add that the lots are not the property of the separate families, but only for their use and are allotted to them by the tribal council which, I will note in passing, is composed *of women*. Powell, *ibid.*, p. 65.

lack of space compels me to limit myself to a reference to collective fishing among the *New Zealanders.*

The combined forces of a whole clan among the New Zealanders, would prepare nets *several thousand feet in length* which they would use for the benefit of all the members of the clan. "This system of universal help," says Polack, "appears to have been the original plan of the earliest society, from the creation to the present period, inclusive."[1] Enough has been said, I think, for a critical assessment of the picture of savage life drawn by Buecher. The facts are sufficiently convincing to show that it is not the individual search for food of which Buecher speaks, that prevails among savages, but a struggle for existence by the combined forces of the whole—more or less extensive—kinship union,—the struggle of which the writers who took the point of view of N. I. Sieber and M. M. Kovalevsky spoke. This conclusion is very useful to us in our research into art. We must hold it firmly fixed in our memory.

And now let us continue. The manner in which people live naturally and inevitably determines the whole make-up of their character. If the "individual search for food" prevailed among savages, they would, of course, be bound to become complete individualists and egoists, amounting, as it were, to an embodiment of Max Stirner's well-known ideal. Such, in fact, Buecher considers them. "The instinct to maintain existence which dominates the animal," he says, "is also the dominant, instinctive striving of the savage. The operation of this instinct is limited in extent to the individual and, in time, to the moment at which the requirement is felt. In other words, the savage thinks *only of himself, and he thinks only of the present.*"[2]

Here, again, I am not going to ask you whether you like this picture or not; I shall ask, however, whether the facts do not contradict it. In my opinion they do completely.

In the first instance we are already aware that the organisation of stocks is something known even to the very lowest hunting tribes. This proves that even they are not completely ignorant of thought for the future. But even if they did not organise stocks it would still not follow from this that they thought only of the present. Why does the savage keep his weapon even after he has

[1] J. F. Polack, *Manners and Customs of the New Zealanders*, Vol. II, p. 107, London, 1840.

[2] *Four Essays*, p. 79.

had a successful hunt? Because he is thinking of future hunts and of future clashes with an enemy. And the sacks which the women of savage tribes carry on their backs during their ceaseless moves from place to place! It is enough to acquaint oneself, even in the most superficial manner, with the content of these sacks in order to form a fairly high opinion of the savage's husbandry. What do they not contain! You will find flat stones there for grinding edible roots, pieces of quartz for cutting, tips for spears, spare stone axe-heads, strings made from kangaroo tendons, the fur of the opossum, clay of different colours, the bark of trees, pieces of fat, fruits and roots gathered by the way.[1] It is a complete economy! If the savage were not thinking of the morrow, why should he compel his wife to carry all these things? Of course, to the European, the household goods of the Australian woman appear quite pitiable. But all things are relative, both in history as a whole and in economic history in particular.

But what interests me more here is the psychological side of the question.

Since the individual search for food is far from dominant in primitive society, it is not surprising that the savage is by no means such an individualist and egoist as he appears to Buecher. This is excellently brought out by quite unmistakable evidence provided by most reliable observers. Here are a few vivid examples.

"As far as food is concerned," writes Ehrenreich of the Botocudos, "the strictest communism prevails among them. Booty is divided amongst all the members of the horde, as well as the gifts they receive, even if this means that each separate member has to have the tiniest of portions."[2] We see the same occur among the Eskimos, whose stores of food and other movable property, according to Klutschak, appear to constitute common property. "So long as a single piece of meat is to be found in the camp it belongs to all, and when it is divided up everyone is taken into consideration, especially the sick and the childless widows."[3] This evidence of Klutschak's fully accords with earlier evidence

[1] Cf. Ratzel, *Voelkerkunde*, Vol. I, pp. 320–1.

[2] *Ueber die Botocudos der brasilischen Provinzen Espiritu Santo und Monos Geraes*, Zeitschrift fuer Ethnologie, Vol. XIX, p. 31.

[3] *Als Eskimo unter den Eskimos*, von H. Klutschak, Wien, Pest, Leipzig, 1881, p. 233.

from another expert on the Eskimos, Kranz, who also characterises Eskimo life as very near to communism. The hunter, who returns home with plenty of game will be certain to share it with the others, and in the first place with widows who have nothing.[1] Usually each Eskimo knows his genealogy well, and this knowledge is of great advantage to the poor "because no one is ashamed of his poor relations, and it is enough for anyone to prove even very distant relationship with some rich man in order not to want for food."[2]

The most recent American ethnologists, among them Boas, point out this very same trait in the Eskimo character.[3]

The Australians, whom earlier explorers depicted as great individualists, on closer acquaintance appear in a completely different light. Letourneau says that, within the limits of the clan—*everything they have belongs to all.*[4] This statement may, of course, be taken *cum grano salis,*[5] because certain undoubted rudiments of private property do exist among the Australians. But from the rudiments of private property it is still a long way to the individualism of which Buecher speaks.

The same Letourneau describes in detail, after Fison and Howitt, the rules that are observed in the division of booty by certain Australian tribes.[6]

These rules, which are most intimately connected with the system of relationship, convincingly prove by their very existence that the provender acquired by individual members of the Australian clan does not become their personal property. And provender would certainly have become the unrestricted private property of the individual members if the Australians were individualists exclusively engaged in the "individual search for food."

The social instincts of the lower hunters sometimes lead to rather unexpected consequences from the European viewpoint. Thus, when the Bushman succeeds in stealing one or several head of cattle from some farmer or stock-breeder, all the other Bushmen

[1] Kranz, *Historie von Groenland,* 1770, Vol. I, p. 222.

[2] *Ibid.,* p. 291.

[3] Franz Boas, *The Central Eskimo,* Sixth Annual Report of the Bureau of Ethnology, pp. 564 and 582.

[4] *L'évolution de la proprieté,* Paris, 1889, pp. 36 and 49.

[5] With a grain of salt.

[6] *Ibid.,* pp. 41–6.

consider it their right to take part in the feasting which, with this tribe, usually accompanies their daring exploits.[1]

Primitive communist instincts are also preserved quite late in the higher stages of cultural development. Modern American ethnologists depict the Redskins as real communists. Powell, the director of the North American Ethnological Bureau whom I have already quoted, says categorically that *all property* among the Redskins belonged to the gens or clan, and that its most important aspect, *food*, by no means came within the exclusive control of separate persons or families. The meat of animals killed in the hunt was allotted on the basis of different rules according to each tribe, but in practice all these different rules uniformly led to an equal division of provender.

"The hungry Indian had but to ask to receive, and this no matter how small the supply or how dark the future prospect."[2] And note, dear sir, that this right of the asker to receive what he asks for is not restricted in this case to the limits of the clan alone, nor only of the tribe. "What was originally a right based on kinship afterwards assumed broader dimensions and was transformed into completely unlimited hospitality."[3] We learn from Dorsey that when the Omaha Indians had plenty of grain while the Ponka tribe or the Pawnee felt a shortage, the former divided their stocks with the latter, and the Pawnee and the Ponka, when the Omaha were short of grain, did the same.[4] Late in years, Lafitau still referred to this praiseworthy custom with the just remark that "Europeans do not behave like this."[5]

As regards the Indians of South America, it will suffice to refer to Marzius and Von den Steinen. According to the former, where a number of the members of Brazilian Indian communes combined their labour, the objects they produced remained the

[1] Lichtenstein, *Reisen*, Vol. II, p. 338.

[2] *Indian Linguistic Families*, Seventh Annual Report of the Bureau of Ethnology, p. 34. I will add here that according to Matilda Stevenson, among the American Indians the strong have no advantages over the weak when it comes to the division of provender. (*The Siou*, by Matilda Coxe Stevenson, Seventh Annual Report, p. 12.

[3] Powell, *op. cit.*, p. 34.

[4] *Omaha Sociology*, by Owen Dorsey, Third Annual Report of the Bureau of Ethnology, p. 274.

[5] Lafitau, *Les Mœurs des Sauvages* . . . Vol. II, p. 91.

common property of those members. The latter states that the Brazilian Bakairi, whom he studied closely, lived as one family, constantly dividing among themselves the provender acquired in hunting or fishing.[1] Among the Bororos a hunter, when he kills a jaguar, invites the other hunters and consumes with them the meat of the slain beast, *while its skin and teeth are given to the man or woman most closely related to the last member of the commune to die.*[2]

The South African Caffre hunter has not the right to dispose of his booty as he himself deems best, but is bound to share it with others.[3] When one of them kills a bull all his neighbours come to him as guests and stay until such time as all the meat has been eaten up. Even a "king" submits to this custom and patiently regales his subjects.[4] Again, in Lafitau's words—Europeans do not behave like this!

We have already learnt from Ehrenreich that when one of the Botocudos receives a gift he shares it among all the members of his clan. Darwin tells us the same of the Fuegians[5] as does Lichtenstein of the primitive peoples of South Africa. According to the latter, a man who does not divide the gift he has received among his fellows is subjected, as a result, to the most insulting ridicule.[6] When the Sarasins gave any Vedda a silver coin the latter would make as though to chop it in pieces and after this expressive gesture, ask to be given more coins so as to be able to share them with the others.[7] Miligavang, the King of the Bechuanas, asked one of Lichtenstein's fellow travellers to give him a present *in secret*, since otherwise his dark-skinned majesty would be compelled to share it among his subjects.[8] Nordenskiöld relates that, during his visit to the Chukchi, one of the adolescent members of this tribe was given a piece of sugar. This dainty immediately began to go the rounds, from mouth to mouth.[9]

Enough. Buecher is making a great mistake in saying that the

[1] Von den Steinen, *Unter den Naturvoelkern Zentral-Brasliens*, pp. 67–8. Marzius, *Von dem Rechtzustande unter den Ureinwohnern Brasiliens*, p. 35.

[2] Von den Steinen, *ibid.*, p. 491.

[3] H. Lichtenstein, *Reisen*, I, p. 444.

[4] *Ibid.*, p. 450.

[5] *Journal of Researches*, etc., p. 242.

[6] *Reisen*, I, p. 450.

[7] *Die Weddahs von Ceylon*, p. 560.

[8] Lichtenstein, *ibid.*, Vol. II, pp. 479–80.

[9] *Die Umsegelung Asiens und Europas auf der "Vega,"* Leipzig, 1882, Vol. II, p. 139.

savage thinks only of himself. The contemporary ethnological data at our disposal leave not the slightest doubt on this score. We can now, therefore, pass from the facts to the hypothesis, and ask ourselves how we are to picture the relationships of our savage forefathers in the extremely far-off times when the use of fire and weapons was still unknown to them. Have we any grounds whatever for believing that age to have been dominated by individualism and that the life of the individual in those times was not made at all easier by social solidarity?

To me it seems that we have not the slightest foundation for thinking so. All that I know of the apes of the Old World compels me to believe that our forefathers were already social animals while they were still only "similar" to man. Espinas tells us: "A herd of apes differs from a herd of any other animals, firstly by the mutual help its members give each other, in other words the *solidarity* of its members—by the subordination or the *obedience* of all, even of the males, to a leader who takes care for the common welfare."[1] As you see, this is already a social union in the full sense of the word.

True, the great anthropoid apes are apparently not very inclined to social life. But they cannot be termed complete individualists either. Numbers of them often gather together and chant in chorus, striking on the hollow trunks of trees. Du Chaillu met with gorillas in groups of eight to ten individuals; gibbons have been seen in herds of up to a hundred and even a hundred and fifty head. While orang-outangs live in small, separate families, we are bound to take into account the exceptional conditions under which these animals live. The anthropoid apes are no longer in a position to continue the struggle for existence. They are degenerating and becoming very rare, and for this reason—as Topinard has very rightly remarked—the way they live at present cannot give us the least conception of their former mode of existence.[2]

In any case, Darwin was convinced that our anthropoid forbears[3] lived in communities, and I know of no argument to make us regard him as mistaken. But if our anthropoid forbears lived in communities the question arises as to *when in fact*, at what point

[1] *Des sociétés animales*, deuxième édition, Paris, 1878, p. 502.

[2] *L'Anthropologie et la science Sociale*, Paris. 1900, pp. 122–3.

[3] *The Descent of Man*, 1883, p. 502.

in their further zoological development, and *for what reason* their social instincts had to give way to the individualism supposed to be inherent in primitive man? I do not know. Nor does Buecher. At any rate he tells us precisely nothing on the subject.

And so we find his views no more supported by *hypothetical* considerations than they are by the evidence of facts.

LABOUR, PLAY AND ART

How did human economy develop from the individual search for food? In Buecher's opinion, we can at present form practically no conception of this; I think, however, that we shall arrive at one if we accept the fact that *the search for food was originally social, and not individual.* Men originally "sought" food just as the social animals seek it: groups of varying size combined forces in order to acquire the *ready gifts* of nature. Earle, from whom I have already quoted in my previous letter, is right in remarking, after De la Gironière, that when the Negritos go hunting in whole clans they remind one of a herd of orang-outangs setting off on a predatory raid. The ravaging of fields carried on by the united forces of the Akka pigmy tribe also call such raids to mind. If, by economy, we have to understand the combined activity of men for the purpose of acquiring goods, then such raids must be recognised as one of the very earliest aspects of economic activity.

The original form of acquiring goods was *collection of the ready gifts of nature.*[1] This collection itself can, of course, be sub-divided into several categories, among which were fishing and hunting. After *collection* follows *production*—as seen, for example, in the history of primitive agriculture—sometimes linked with it by a series of scarcely perceptible transitions. Agriculture, of course —even the most primitive—already shows all the marks of economic activity.[2]

[1] "Accordingly it was the collecting people and not the hunting people who must have stood at the foot of the ladder of human economic development," as Pankow correctly remarks in *Zeitschrift der Gesellschaft fuer Erdkunde zu Berlin*, Vol. XXX, No. 3, p. 162. This is also the view of the Sarasins, in whose opinion hunting only becomes an important "means of obtaining food at a comparatively higher level of development." *Die Weddahs*, p. 401.

[2] Certain customs of the Australian aborigines show them as disposed to economic activity and again provide evidence that they, too, think of the future. Among these people it is forbidden to root up the plants whose fruit they use for food, as well as to destroy the nests of birds whose eggs they eat, etc. Ratzel, *Anthropo-Geographie*, Vol. I, p. 348.

And since primitive cultivation is very often carried on by the united forces of the clan, a graphic instance is provided of the way in which the social instincts, inherited by primitive man from his anthropoid forbears could be widely applied in his economic activity. The further fate of these instincts was determined by those (constantly changing) mutual relations into which people entered through this activity, or, as Marx expressed it, "in the social production of their means of existence."[1] All this is as natural as could be and *I do not understand what perplexities there can be about this natural course of development.*

Just a moment, though.

According to Buecher the difficulty is as follows. "It would be fairly natural to suppose," he says, "that this upheaval (the transition to an economy from the individual search for food) begins when, in place of the simple appropriation of the gifts of nature for immediate consumption, production for some more remote purpose arises, and labour, as an application of physical force with a conscious aim, replaces the instinctive activity of the organs. But in establishing a purely theoretical postulation of this kind we shall have gained but little. *Labour*, as known among the primitive peoples, is in itself a somewhat vague phenomenon. The closer we approach the point where its development commences the nearer it approaches, both in form and content, to *play*."[2]

And so the obstacle to understanding the transition from the simple search for food to economic activity lies in the difficulty of drawing a line between labour and play.

The solution of this problem, the relationship of labour to play—or, if you prefer it, of play to labour—is in the highest degree important for the clarification of the *genesis of art*. Therefore I invite you, Sir, to give your patient attention and *weigh up painstakingly* all that Buecher has to say about this. Let him expound his views himself.

"In leaving the restricted limits of the simple search for food man was probably prompted by instincts similar to those observable among higher animals, especially by the instinct of imitation and by an instinctive inclination towards all kinds of experiment. The taming of domestic animals begins, for example, not with useful animals, but with those which man maintains solely for

[1] Preface to the *Contribution to the Critique of Political Economy*.—TRANS.

[2] *Four Essays*, pp. 92, 93.

his own pleasure. The development of manufacture apparently always begins with the painting of the body, the tattooing, piercing or distortion of various parts of the body, after which, little by little the preparation of ornaments, masks, drawings on bark, hieroglyphs and similar occupations develop. . . . Thus, technical skills are elaborated in play and only gradually acquire useful application. And therefore the previously accepted sequence of stages in development must be replaced by their direct opposite: play is older than labour, and art is older than the production of useful objects."[1]

You hear what he says: *play is older than labour, and art is older than the production of useful objects.*

Now you can understand why I asked you to pay particular attention to Buecher's words: they have the closest relationship to the historical theory which I am defending. If play is indeed older than labour and if art is indeed older than the production of useful objects, then the materialist explanation of history, at any rate as expounded by the author of *Capital, will not stand up to the criticism of the facts* and all my reasoning must be turned upside down: I shall have to argue about the dependence of economics on art and not about the dependence of art on economics. But is Buecher right?

Let us first test what he has said about play. We shall deal with art later on.

According to Spencer the chief distinctive feature of play lies in the fact that it does not directly assist the processes essential for the support of life. The activity of the individual at play is not undertaken for any specific, utilitarian purpose. True, the exercise of the organs brought into action by the game is useful for the individual who is playing and so, in the final count, for the whole of his kind. But exercise is not precluded by activity for utilitarian purposes either. It is not a question of exercise, but of the fact that utilitarian activity, besides the exercise and the pleasure it affords, leads to the achievement as well of some practical aim—for instance, that of obtaining food—whereas in play any purpose of this sort is absent. When a cat catches a mouse, besides the pleasure afforded her by the exercise of her limbs she has a welcome morsel of food, while the same cat, when she runs after a ball of thread rolled across the floor, gets nothing

[1] *Four Essays,* pp. 93–4.

but the pleasure afforded by the game. But if this is so, how can such aimless activity arise?

We know how Spencer answers this. Among lower animals the whole strength of the organism is expended on the fulfilment of functions essential to the support of life. Only utilitarian activity is known to the lower animals. But on higher rungs of the animal ladder it is quite a different matter. Not all their powers, here, are absorbed by utilitarian activity. Thanks to better nourishment the organism accumulates a certain surplus of strength which demands an outlet and, when the animal plays, it is this demand that it is obeying. Play is the artificial exercise of strength.[1]

Such is the *origin* of play. And what is its *content*? In other words: if, in playing, the animal exercises its strength, why does one animal exercise it in one way and another differently; why are various kinds of play peculiar to different varieties of animal?

According to Spencer, beasts of prey clearly show us that their play consists of sham hunting and sham fighting. All this is "a dramatising of the pursuit of prey—an ideal satisfaction for the destructive instincts in the absence of real satisfaction for them."[2] What does this mean? It means that in animals the content of play is determined by such activity as assists in the support of their existence. Which comes first then—play before utilitarian activity, or utilitarian activity before play? It is clear that utilitarian activity *precedes play, that the former is "older" than the latter*. And what do we find amongst men? Children's "plays," nursing dolls, giving tea-parties and so on are dramatisings of adult activities.[3] But what aims do adults pursue in their activities? In the overwhelming majority of cases they pursue *utilitarian aims*. In other words *activity among human beings in pursuit of utilitarian ends*, that is, activity essential to support the existence of individuals and the whole of society, *also precedes play and is the factor which determines its content*. Such is the conclusion that follows logically from what Spencer says about play.

This logical conclusion completely coincides with the views of Wilhelm Wundt on the same subject.

"Play is the child of labour," says the famous psychophysiologist. "There is not a single form of play which has not its model in

[1] Cf. Herbert Spencer, *Principles of Psychology*, London, 1872, Vol. II, p. 630.
[2] *Ibid.*, p. 631.
[3] *Ibid.*, p. 631.

one or another kind of serious occupation which, it goes without saying, precedes it in time. For the needs of life compel man to work, and in labour he learns little by little to look upon the use of his strength in the work he is doing as a pleasure."[1]

Play is born of the urge to experience anew the pleasure afforded by the purposive use of strength. And the greater the reserve of strength, the greater the urge to play—other conditions being equal, of course. Nothing is easier than to convince oneself of this fully.

Here, as in all other instances, I shall prove and clarify my argument by examples.

We know that savages in their dances often reproduce the movements of different animals.[2] What is the explanation of this? It is nothing but the urge to experience anew the pleasure afforded by the use of their strength in hunting. Observe how the Eskimo hunts the seal: he crawls up to him on his belly; he tries to hold his head in the same way as the seal does; he imitates all its movements, and only when he has crept up to within a short distance of it does he at last decide to shoot it.[3] The imitation of the animal's movements thus forms a most essential part of the hunt. It is not surprising, therefore, that when the hunter desires to experience the pleasure afforded by the use of his strength in hunting he again starts to imitate the movements of the animals and creates his own original hunting dance. But what is it which, in this case, determines the character of the dance, that is, of his *play*? The character of the serious occupation does, in other words, the hunt. Play is the child of labour, which necessarily precedes it in time.

Another example. Among one of the Brazilian tribes Von den Steinen saw a dance which, with staggering dramatic power, depicted the death of a wounded warrior.[4] What is your opinion as to which came first in this instance? The war before the dance, or the dance before the war? I believe that war occurred first and that the dances, depicting different war scenes, arose afterwards; first

[1] *Ethik*, Stuttgart, 1886, p. 145.

[2] "So they (the savages) talked of a monkey dance, a sloth dance, a bird dance and so on." Schomburg, *Reisen in Britischer Guiana*, Leipzig, 1847, Erster Teil, p. 154.

[3] Cf. Kranz, *Historie von Groenland*, Vol. I, p. 207.

[4] *Unter den Naturvoelkern Brasiliens*, p. 324.

came the impression produced on the savage by the death of his comrade wounded in battle, and then came the urge to reproduce this impression by means of a dance. If I am right, and I am convinced that I am, then in this instance, too, I have every ground for saying that activity in pursuit of utilitarian aims is older than play and that play is its offspring.

Buecher would say, perhaps, that for primitive man both war and hunting constitute not so much labour as amusement, in other words, play again. But to talk like this is to equivocate. At the stage of development of the lower hunting tribes, hunting and war are essential activities for the maintenance of the hunter's existence and for his self-defence. Both the one and the other pursue perfectly definite utilitarian aims, and to identify them with play, which is characterised precisely by the lack of such aims, is only possible by the crass and almost deliberate misuse of terms. Moreover, experts on the life of the savage say that he never hunts for the sake of pleasure alone.[1]

However, let us take a third example which can leave not the slightest doubt as to the correctness of the view I am defending.

Earlier I pointed to the great importance of social labour in the life of those primitive peoples who, together with hunting, also engage in agriculture. Now I want to draw your attention to the manner in which the Bagobos—one of the native tribes of Southern Mindanao—cultivate the land socially. In this tribe both sexes take part in agricultural work. On the day for rice sowing men and women gather together very early in the morning and set to work. The men go ahead and, *dancing*, poke iron picks into the ground. After them follow the women, who throw the rice grains into the holes made by the men and cover them with earth. All this is performed with solemnity and dignity.[2]

Here we see a unification of *play* (dancing) and *labour*. But this unification does not obscure the true connection of the phenomena. Unless you believe that the Bagobos originally poked their picks

[1] "The Indian never hunted game for sport." Dorsey, *Omaha Sociology*, Third Annual Report, p. 267.

Cf. Hellwald: "Hunting, however, is in itself at the same time work, an exertion of physical force, and that it is understood as such by the actual hunting tribes, and not as a kind of amusement, we have just now been convinced." *Kulturgeschichte*, Augsburg, 1876, Vol. I, p. 109.

[2] *Die Bewohner von Sued-Mindanao und der Insel Samal*, von Al. Schadenberg; *Zeitschrift fuer Ethnologie*, Vol. XVII, p. 19.

into the ground and sowed rice for amusement and only afterwards began to cultivate the land to support themselves, you must admit that labour in this case is older than play and that play *arose* from the special condition under which sowing took place among the Bagobos. Play is the child of labour, which precedes it in time.

Note that the dances themselves are in such cases *simple reproductions of the movements of the worker.* In confirmation of this I will refer to Buecher himself, who, in his book *Arbeit und Rhythmus*[1] also says that "many dances of primitive peoples amount to no more nor less than a conscious imitation of certain productive activities. Thus, in the case of this mimetic depiction, labour is bound to precede the dance."[2] I simply cannot understand how, after this, Buecher can assert that play is older than labour.

It can in general be said without any exaggeration that the book, *Arbeit und Rhythmus,* is a complete and brilliant refutation in its whole content of Buecher's views on the relationship of play and art to labour, which I am at present examining. It is surprising in the extreme that Buecher himself fails to notice such a crying contradiction as this which must immediately strike the eye.

Evidently he has been led astray by the theory of play recently offered to scientists by Karl Groos, Professor at Giessen.[3] It will therefore, not be without point to acquaint ourselves with Groos' theory.

In Groos' opinion, the view that play is a manifestation of surplus strength is not fully confirmed by the facts. Puppies play with each other until quite exhausted and renew the game after the shortest of rests, which provides them, not with a surplus of strength, but with only so much as is barely sufficient to renew their sport. In the same way children, too, although they may be weary after a long walk, for example, immediately forget their tiredness the moment they begin to play. They do not stand in need of prolonged rest and accumulation of surplus energy: "instinct prompts them to activity not only when, to use a figurative expression, the cup is overflowing, but even when it contains no more than a single drop."[4] A surplus of strength is not the *conditio sine qua non* for play, but only a favourable condition for it.

1 (Work and Rhythm), p. 79, 1896, Leipzig.

2 *Ibid.*

3 In the book *Die Spiele der Tiere,* Jena, 1896.

4 *Ibid.*, p. 18.

But even if this were not so, all the same Spencer's theory (Groos calls it the Schiller-Spencer theory) would be inadequate. It seeks to clarify the *physiological* significance of play but does not clarify its *biological* significance. And this significance is very great. Play, especially the play of young animals, has a quite definite biological purpose. As with men, so with animals, the play of the young amounts to an exercise of attributes useful to the individual separately or to the whole kind.[1] Play prepares the young animal for his future activity in life. But for the very reason that it *prepares* the young animal for its future activity, it *precedes* it, and therefore Groos refuses to admit that play is the child of labour. He says, on the contrary, that *labour is the child of play.*[2]

This, as you see, is the very same view that we met with in Buecher. All that I said, therefore, about the true relationship of labour and play is fully applicable to him. But Groos approaches the question from a different angle: he has in mind, above all, the play of the young, and not of adults. How will the matter appear to us if, like Groos, we look at it from this point of view?

Let us take an example again. Eyre tells us[3] that the children of the Australian aborigines often play at war, and that this game is very much encouraged by adults, since it develops their skill as future warriors. We see the same thing, too, among the Redskins of North America, where many hundreds of children sometimes take part in such games under the guidance of experienced warriors. According to Catlin this kind of play constitutes a substantial branch of the Redskins' system of education.[4] Here, we have a clear case of the preparation of young persons for their future activity in life, such as Groos speaks of. But does this case confirm his theory? It does—and it does not! The "system of education" in existence among the primitive peoples I have named causes *playing* at war to precede actual participation in war *in the life of the individual.*[5] And so Groos turns out to be right: from the point of view of the individual as such play is actually older than utilitarian activity. But why is it that a system of

[1] *Die Spiele der Tiere*, pp. 19–20 [2] *Ibid.*, p. 125.

[3] *Manners and Customs of the Aborigines of Australia*, p. 228.

[4] Catlin, *Letters and Notes on the Manners, Customs and Condition of the North American Indians*, Vol. I, p. 131.

[5] Letourneau, *L'Evolution Littéraire dans les Diverses Races Humaines*, Paris, 1894, p. 34.

education has become established among the Redskins, in which war games play such an important role? The reason is clear: it is because it is so important for them to have well-trained warriors, accustomed from childhood to various military exercises: in other words, from the point of view of society (of the kind), the matter appears in quite a different light: first comes real war and the demand created by it for good warriors, and only then come war games in order to satisfy this demand. In other words, from the point of view of society, utilitarian activity is older than play.

Another example. An Australian woman in her dancing depicts, amongst other things, how she pulls edible roots up from the ground.[1] Her daughter sees this dance and, following the tendency of children to imitate, she reproduces the movements made by her mother.[2] She does this at an age when she does not yet have seriously to take part in the gathering of food. And so, in her life, playing (dancing) at pulling up roots precedes their actual extraction; for her, play is older than labour. But in the life of society, of course, the actual extraction of roots comes before the reproduction of this process in adult dances and children's games. *In the life of society, therefore, labour is older than play.*[3] This seems perfectly clear. And if it is clear it only remains for us to ask ourselves from what point of view the economist or any person interested in social science ought to look at this problem of labour's relation to play? I believe the answer is clear in this case, too: nobody interested in social science can look at this question—or for that matter any other question arising in social science—otherwise than from the point of view of society. The reason for this is that in taking the viewpoint of society we can the more easily discover why play occurs earlier than labour in the life of the individual; had we gone no further than the point of view of the individual we should have understood neither why play occurs

[1] "Another favourite amusement among the children is to practise the dances and songs of the adults." Eyre, *op. cit.*, p. 227.

[2] "The play of the girls consists in imitation of the serious work of their mothers . . . the boys play with small . . . bows and arrows." (*The Exploration of the Zambesi by David and Charles Livingstone*, London, 1865, p. 294.—TRANS.)

"The amusements of the natives are various but they generally have a reference to their future occupations." Eyre, p. 227.

[3] "These games are an exact imitation of later work." Klutschak, *op. cit.*, p. 222.

in his life earlier than labour, nor why he amuses himself with these particular games rather than any others.

This is true also of biology, except that instead of the concept "society," the concept "kind" (or rather, "species") is required. If play serves the purpose of preparing the young individual for the tasks of life awaiting it in the future, obviously to begin with the development of the species places before it a certain task demanding a definite form of activity. It is only afterwards, as a result of the existence of this task, that there takes place the selection of individuals according to the qualities demanded by it and the training up of these qualities in childhood. Here also, play is no more than the child of labour, or a function of utilitarian activity.

The difference between man and the lower animals in this case lies only in the fact that the development of inherited characteristics plays a much smaller role in his upbringing than it does in the upbringing of an animal. A tiger cub is born a beast of prey, but a man is not born a hunter or a farmer, a warrior or a trader: he becomes one or the other under the influence of environmental conditions. And this is true of both sexes. The Australian girl on her appearance in the world does not bring with her an instinctive urge to pull up roots from the ground or to carry out other similar economic tasks. This tendency arises from her inclination to imitate: in the course of amusing herself she tries to reproduce the work her mother does. But why should she imitate her mother and not her father? Because, in the society to which she belongs, a division of labour has already been established between man and woman. Neither has this, as you see, anything to do with the individual's instincts. It is a question of his or her social environment. But the greater the significance of social environment the less permissible it is to abandon the point of view of society and to adopt the point of view of the individual, as Buecher does in his consideration of the relations of play and labour.

Groos says that Spencer's theory does not take into account the *biological* significance of play. It can be said with far greater justification that Groos himself has failed to note its *social* significance. But then, he may possibly correct this oversight in the second part of his work, which will be devoted to play amongst human beings.

The division of labour between the sexes gives grounds for

looking at Buecher's arguments from a new angle. He depicts the labour of the adult savage as an amusement. This, of course, is in itself mistaken; to the savage hunting is not a sport, but a serious occupation necessary to the maintenance of life. Buecher himself remarks, quite rightly, that "savages often suffer cruel want, and the belt which constitutes their only clothing, actually does duty for a 'Schmachtriemen,' as the Germans call it, with which they tighten their bellies to lessen the pains of hunger that torment them."[1] Do the savages really, even in these instances ("frequent," as Buecher himself admits) still remain sportsmen, hunting only for amusement and not out of dire necessity? From Lichtenstein we learn that the Bushmen on occasions remain without food for periods of several days. These periods of hunger, of course, are occupied in an intensive search for food. Is this search, too, purely for amusement? The Redskins of North America dance their "bison dance" at precisely those times when they have met no bison for a long time and when death by starvation is threatening them.[2] The dance goes on until such time as bison are seen, and their appearance is held by the Indians to be causally connected with their dance. Leaving aside the question, which does not concern us here, of how such a connection could arise in their minds, we can say with assurance that under such circumstances as these neither the "bison dance," nor the hunt which begins on the appearance of the animals, can be regarded as an amusement. In this case the dance itself proves to be an activity pursued for utilitarian purposes intimately linked with the main economic activity of the Redskin.[3]

[1] *Four Essays*, p. 77. [2] Catlin, *op. cit.*, Vol. I, p. 127.

[3] Buecher thinks that primitive man could have lived without labour. "There is no doubt," he writes, "that man, in the course of countless ages, lived without working and, should one wish, it would be possible to find not a few localities on the earth where the sago palm, banana, bread-fruit, cocoa-nut, and date palms would even now permit of his existence with a minimum expenditure of energy on his part" (*Four Essays*, pp. 72–3). If, by countless ages, Buecher means the epoch when "man" was only in process of formation as a distinct zoological species (or genus), then I shall say that at this time our forebears were probably "working" no more nor less than the anthropoid apes were. And we have no right whatever to say that play takes up more of their life than activities necessary to support their existence. And so far as concerns certain special geographical conditions supposed to guarantee man's subsistence with a minimum expenditure of energy, it would also be wrong to exaggerate here. The luxuriant nature of hot countries demands of man no less energy than that of

Let us, further, take a look at our supposed sportsman's wife. During the hunting trek she carries heavy bundles, digs up roots, builds huts, kindles fires, scrapes hides, weaves baskets and, later on, tills the land.[1] Can all this possibly be play and not work? According to F. Prescott the male Dakota Indian does not work in summer more than one hour a day; this, if you like, may be called amusement. But in the same tribe and at the same time of year the women work about *six* hours a day; in this case it is more difficult to suppose that we are dealing with "play." And in winter both men and women have to work much harder than in summer: the men then work about six hours and the women about *ten*.[2]

Here there can be no question about it; it is no longer possible to talk of "play." We now have to do with labour *sans phrases*, and although this labour is less intensive and less exhausting than the labour of workers in civilised society, it does not, because of this, cease to be *economic activity of a quite definite kind*.

And so the theory of play put forward by Groos does not rescue Buecher's thesis, which I have been analysing. Labour turns out to be older than play in the same sense that parents are older than their children, or society older than its individual members.

But having once broached the subject of play, I must draw your attention again to another thesis of Buecher's with which you are already, in part, familiar.

It is his opinion that transmission of cultural acquisitions from generation to generation does not occur at the very earliest stages of human development,[3] a circumstance that deprives the savage's mode of life of one of the most essential features of an economy.[4] But play, even in Groos' view, serves in primitive society as a

the temperate zones. Ehrenreich even thinks that the sum of such energy required in the tropics is much more than in the temperate zones ("Ueber die Botocudos," *Zeitschrift fuer Ethnologie*, Vol. XIX, p. 27).

Of course, when the cultivation of plants for food begins, the rich soil of tropical lands can very considerably lighten man's labour, but such cultivation begins only at a comparatively high level of cultural development.

[1] "The principal occupation of the women in this village consists in procuring wood and water, in cooking, dressing robes and other skins, in drying meat and wild fruit and raising corn." Catlin, *op. cit.*, Vol. I, p. 121.

[2] *Vide* Schoolcraft, *Historical Information etc.*, Vol. III, p. 235.

[3] *Four Essays*, pp. 87 ff.

[4] *Ibid.*, p. 91.

preparation of the young for the fulfilment of their future economic tasks. It thus clearly forms one of the links that unite different generations and acts as a transmitter of cultural acquisitions from generation to generation.

"Of course," Buecher says, "it may be admitted that the latter (i.e. primitive man) treats the stone axe at which he has worked for a whole year perhaps, and which has cost him the greatest efforts, with particular fondness, and that this axe will seem to him to be a part of his very being; but it is a mistake to think that this valuable possession will pass on by inheritance to his children and grandchildren and serve as a basis for further progress." The assertion that such articles provide grounds for the development of first conceptions of "mine" and "thine" is as sound as the observations are numerous to indicate that these conceptions are linked only with the individual and disappear with him. "*Property is interred in the grave along with its owner* (Buecher's italics), whose personal possession it was during his lifetime. This custom is widespread in all parts of the world and vestiges of it are met with among many peoples, even in the cultural periods of their development."[1]

This is correct, of course. But does *the ability to make the article anew* disappear together with the article itself? No, it does not. Even among the lower hunting tribes we see how parents try to pass on to their children all the technical knowledge which they themselves have managed to acquire. "As soon as the son of an Australian aborigine starts to walk, his father takes him with him hunting and fishing, teaches him and tells him of various traditions."[2] And in this instance the Australians are no exception to the general rule. Among the North American Redskins the clan appointed special educators whose duties included the communication to the younger generation of all the practical knowledge of

[1] *Four Essays*, p. 88.

[2] Ratzel, *Voelkerkunde, zweite Ausgabe*, Vol. I, p. 339. Schadenberg says exactly the same of the Philippine Negritos, *Zeitschrift fuer Ethnologie*, Vol. XII, p. 136. On the upbringing of children among the inhabitants of the Andaman Islands see Man, in the *Journal of the Anthropological Institute*, Vol. XII, p. 94. If Emile Deschamps is to be believed, the Veddas are an exception to this general rule: they do not train their children in the art of manipulating a weapon (*Carnet d'un Voyageur au Pays des Veddas*), 1892, pp. 369–70. This is very unreliable evidence. As a whole Deschamps does not give the impression of being a reliable research worker.

which they might stand in need in the future.[1] Among the Caffres of Koossa all children above the age of ten were brought up together under the unflagging supervision of the chief of the tribe, the boys being trained for war and hunting, and the girls for various kinds of domestic work.[2] Is this not a living link between the generations? Is this not the transmission of cultural acquisitions from generation to generation?

Although articles belonging to the deceased are actually often destroyed on his grave, the knowledge of how to produce these articles is transmitted from generation to generation, and *this is much more important than the transmission of the actual articles.* Of course, the destruction of the deceased's possessions on his grave, does hinder the accumulation of wealth in primitive society, but it does not, in the first place, remove the living connection between the generations, as we have seen; and secondly, with the existence of social ownership of a great many articles the property of the individual is usually very inextensive. It consists primarily of weapons, and the weapon of a primitive warrior-hunter grows to be such an intimate part of his personality that it amounts, as it were, to a continuation of himself and for this reason appears little suited for other persons.[3] This is why its burial, together with the deceased owner comprises a lesser loss to society than might seem to be the case at first glance. When, later on, with the development of technique and of social wealth, the destruction of articles belonging to the deceased becomes a serious loss to those near to him, it is gradually limited, or even ceases altogether, giving place to a mere symbol of destruction.[4]

Since Buecher denies the existence among savages of any living link between the generations, it is not surprising that he is very sceptical as to their parental feelings.

"Modern ethnographers," he writes, "have devoted no small effort towards proving that the power of mother-love is a feature common to all stages of cultural development. It is, indeed, hard

[1] Powell, *Indian Linguistic Families,* Eleventh Annual Report, p. 35.

[2] Lichtenstein, *Reisen,* Vol. I, p. 425.

[3] One example from a great many: "The hunter must not use the weapon of another; those savages particularly who shoot with the blowpipe assert that this weapon is spoiled if it is used by a stranger and they will not let it out of their hands." *Marzius, op. cit.,* p. 50.

[4] *Vide* Letourneau, *L'Evolution de la Propriété,* pp. 418 ff.

for us to reconcile ourselves to the idea that an emotion which is evident in such attractive form in many species of animals, in all parts of the world, could be absent in human beings. However, a number of observations have been made indicating the spiritual link between parents and children to be in fact the fruit of culture. Such observations show that among peoples who are at the lowest level of development care for the preservation of the individual's own *ego* is stronger than all spiritual impulses, and even that this is the sole care they have. The same characteristic of unlimited egoism is seen in the merciless manner in which many primitive peoples, when on trek, cast their *sick* and *aged*, who might hinder those sound in health, to the whim of fate or abandon them in isolated places."[1]

Unfortunately Buecher quotes very few facts in support of his argument and we remain in almost complete ignorance as to precisely what observations he is referring. All I can do, therefore, is to verify what he says on the basis of those observations that are known to myself.

The Australians are quite justifiably regarded as belonging to the lowest hunting tribes. Their cultural development is insignificant. In view of this it might, perhaps, have been expected that the "cultural acquisition" which we call parental love would as yet be unknown to them. However, the reality does not bear out this expectation: *the Australians are passionately attached to their children; they often play with them and caress them.*[2]

The Veddas of Ceylon are also at the lowest stage of development. Buecher quotes them together with the Bushmen as examples of extreme primitiveness. Yet at the same time even they, according to Tennant's evidence, "are marvellously attached to their children and relatives. . . ."[3]

The Eskimos—those representatives of the culture of the ice-age—are also "extremely fond of their children."[4]

Again, Father Gumilla has spoken of the great love of the South American Indians for their children.[5] Waitz considered it

[1] *Four Essays*, pp. 81–2.

[2] Eyre, *op. cit.*, p. 241.

[3] Tennant, *Ceylon*, Vol. II, p. 445. Cf. *Die Weddas von Ceylon*, von P. und F. Sarasin, p. 469.

[4] D. Kranz, *Historie von Groenland*, Vol. I, p. 213. Cf. Klutschak, *Als Eskimo unter den Eskimos*, p. 234, and Boas, *op. cit.*, p. 566.

[5] *Histoire naturelle, civile et géographique de l'Orénoque*, Vol. I, p. 211.

one of the most oustanding features in the character of American natives.[1]

Among the dark-skinned tribes of Africa not a few can be designated as having drawn the attention of explorers by tender care for their children.[2]

In a word, the empirical material at the disposal of the modern ethnographer does not confirm Buecher's views in this case either.

How did he come to make his mistake? He misinterpreted a fairly widespread custom among savages of killing their children and old people. Of course, at first glance, to conclude from the killing of children and old men that there is an absence of mutual attachment between children and parents seems perfectly logical. But it only *seems* so, and indeed only *at first glance*.

Infanticide is indeed very widespread among the Australian aborigines. In 1860 a third of the new-born children of the Nerinaieri tribe were killed: every child born into those families where there were already small children was killed; twins were killed and so on. But this still does not mean that the Australians of the tribe in question were devoid of parental feeling. Quite the contrary; having decided that such and such a child should remain among the living they took care of him "with boundless patience."[3] As you see, the matter is not so simple as it appeared in the first instance; infanticide has not prevented the Australians from loving their children and taking patient care of them. And this is true not only of the Australians. Infanticide also took place in ancient Sparta. But does it follow from this that the Spartans had not yet reached that stage of cultural development at which parental love originates?

As far as concerns the killing of the sick and aged, the exceptional circumstances under which this takes place must, before all else, be taken into account. It is only done when the old people are exhausted and have become incapable of accompanying their

[1] *Die Indianer Nordamerikas*, Leipzig, 1865, p. 101. Cf. the work by Matilda Stevenson, *The Siou*, in the *Eleventh Annual Report of the American Ethnological Bureau to the Smithsonian Institution*. According to Matilda Stevenson, where there is a lack of food the adults go hungry themselves, but feed their children.

[2] See for example Schweinfurth on the Diurs: *Au Cœur de l'Afrique*, Vol. I, p. 210.

[3] Ratzel, *Voelkerkunde*, Vol. I, pp. 338–9.

clansmen on their expeditions.[1] Since the means of migration at the disposal of savages are insufficient for the transport of such exhausted members of the tribe, necessity dictates that they be left to the mercy of fate and, this being so, death at friendly hands seems to be the least of all the possible evils they might suffer. It must be remembered, moreover, that abandonment to the mercy of fate or the killing of the aged is put off until the last possible moment and for this reason very rarely occurs, even amongst the tribes that have become best known in this respect. Ratzel remarks that, despite Darwin's oft-repeated story of the Fuegians eating their old women, the old men and old women of this tribe enjoy great respect.[2] Earle tells us the same of the Negritos on the Philippine Islands[3] as does Ehrenreich (after Marzius) of the Brazilian Botocudos.[4] Heckewelder describes the North American Indians as a people which, more than any other, holds its old folk in respect.[5] The African Diurs are said by Schweinfurth not only to take the greatest care of their children but also to respect their old people, a circumstance that strikes the eye in any of their villages.[6] And according to Stanley, respect for old people is a general rule throughout the hinterland of Africa.[7]

Buecher takes an abstract view of a phenomenon that can only be explained if we adopt a quite practical point of view. It is not primitive man's natural characteristics which lead him either to kill the aged or to infanticide, it is not his supposed individualism nor the absence of a connection between the generations; it is the

[1] C. Lafitau, *Les Moeurs des Sauvages* . . . Vol. I, p. 490. Also Catlin, *Letters and Notes*, Vol. I, p. 217. Catlin asserts that, in such cases, the old men, pointing to their decrepitude, themselves insist that they should be killed (*ibid.*, same page). I admit that this latter circumstance for a long time seemed to me to be open to doubt. But tell me, Sir, whether you think the following passage from Tolstoy's story *Master and Workman* errs against the psychological truth: "Nikita died sincerely rejoicing in the fact that by his death he was ridding his son and daughter-in-law of the burden of an extra mouth to feed," etc. In my opinion, there is no psychological falsehood here. And if this is so, then neither is there anything psychologically impossible in the assertion by Catlin, which I have quoted.

[2] *Voelkerkunde*, Vol. I, p. 524.

[3] *Native Races of the Indian Archipelago*, p. 133.

[4] *Ueber die Botokudos*, etc., *Zeitschrift fuer Ethnologie*, XIX, p. 32.

[5] *Op. cit.*, p. 251.

[6] *Au Cœur de l'Afrique*, Vol. I, p. 210.

[7] *In Darkest Africa*, Vol. II, p. 368.

conditions in which the savage has to carry on his struggle for existence. In my first letter I reminded you of Darwin's suggestion that if people were to live under the same conditions as bees they would, without the slightest compunction and even with a sense of pleasure in a duty well done, destroy the unproductive members of their society. Savages, to a certain extent, do in fact live under conditions where the destruction of unproductive members is a moral duty towards society. And in so far as they are affected by such conditions they find themselves *compelled* to kill superfluous children and decrepit old men. But that they do not, because of this, become the individualists and egoists that Buecher depicts is proved by the abundance of examples from which I have quoted. The very same conditions of savage life that lead to infanticide and the killing of the aged lead also to the maintenance of intimate ties between those members of the union that remain alive. It is this which explains the paradox whereby the killing of children and old men is sometimes carried on amongst tribes whose members have, at the same time, a singularly strongly developed sense of parental affection and great respect for the aged. It is not a matter of the *psychology* of the savage, but of his *economy*.

Before finishing with Buecher's arguments as to the character of primitive man, I must make two more observations on this subject.

In the first place one of the most striking manifestations of individualism ascribed by him to savages is, in his view, their very widespread habit of eating their food alone.

My second observation is as follows: amongst many primitive peoples each member of a family has his movable property to which none of the other members of the family has the slightest right nor, usually, lays any claim. It often happens that individual members of one large family even live separately from one another in small huts. In this Buecher sees a manifestation of extreme individualism. He would not hold the same opinion did he know the state of affairs that obtained in the large peasant families, once so numerous in our Great Russia. The basis of economy in these families was one of pure communism; but this did not prevent their separate members, for instance, the *baba* and the *dievki*,[1] from having their own movable property, strictly preserved as a matter of custom from any infringement on the part of

[1] *Baba*—Russian peasant woman (married). *Dievki*—peasant girls.—TRANS.

even the most despotic *bolshak*.[1] In such large families separate cottages for the married members of the family were not infrequently built around the common *dvor*.[2] (In the province of Tambov these were called *khatki*.[3])

It is quite possible that you have long since had enough of this discussion of primitive economy. You will be bound to admit, however, that I simply could not avoid it. As I have already remarked above, art is a social phenomenon, and if the savage were really a complete individualist there would be no point in asking ourselves what kind of art he practised; we should have discovered no signs of any artistic activity whatever on his part. But this activity is not in the slightest doubt. Primitive art is by no means a myth. This fact alone may serve as a convincing, even if indirect refutation of Buecher's views on "primitive economic structure."

Buecher often repeats that "where there is constant nomadism care for his subsistence absorbs man completely and does not permit even the feelings we consider most natural to find a place alongside it."[4] And this same Buecher is firmly convinced, as you are already aware, that man lived through countless ages without working and that even at the present time there are many localities where geographical conditions permit of his existence with the minimum expenditure of energy. Added to this our author is convinced that art is older than the production of articles of use, just as he holds that play is older than labour. If all this were true, then:

Firstly, primitive man would have supported his existence at the cost of quite insignificant efforts;

Secondly, these insignificant efforts would nevertheless have completely absorbed all his energy and left no room for any other activity, not even for a single one of the emotions that seem natural to us;

Thirdly, man, whilst thinking of nothing but feeding himself, would have begun, not by producing articles, even those useful for providing food, but by satisfying his aesthetic requirements.

This is odd in the extreme! The contradiction is obvious; but how are we to get out of it?

[1] *Bolshak*—eldest of a family.—TRANS.

[2] *Dvor*—yard, area, around which homestead is built.—TRANS.

[3] *Khatki*—little huts.—TRANS.

[4] *Four Essays*, p. 82; cf. also p. 85.

There is no way out unless we have convinced ourselves of the erroneousness of Buecher's views on the relations of art and activities undertaken for the production of articles of use.

Buecher is very much mistaken in saying that the development of manufacture always begins with the adornment of the body. He did not quote—*nor, of course, could he quote*—a single fact to give grounds for thinking that painting the body or tattooing preceded the making of primitive weapons or primitive tools. The most important of the few ornaments worn amongst some of the Botocudo tribes is their famous *botoque*, i.e. a piece of wood inserted in the lip.[1] It would be very strange indeed to suppose that this piece of wood served the Botocudo as an ornament before he ever learnt to hunt, or at any rate before he learnt to dig up edible roots with a sharpened stick. Speaking of the Australians, R. Semon says that many of their tribes have no ornaments whatever.[2] This is probably not quite correct; in fact it is probable that all Australian tribes use ornaments of some sort, if only a few of the most simple design. But even here it must not be supposed that these few simple ornaments made their appearance with the Australian, at an earlier stage, or that they occupy a more important place in his activity than care for the provision of food or the corresponding implements of labour, that is, weapons and sharpened sticks used in obtaining plant foods. The Sarasins think that the men, women and children of those primitive Veddas, who had not yet experienced the influence of an alien culture, *had no ornaments whatsoever*, and that there may be found to this day in the mountains Veddas who are conspicuous by a complete absence of ornaments.[3] These Veddas do not pierce their ears, but at the same time they are, of course, already familiar with the use of weapons, which they do actually fashion. It is obvious that productive activity on the part of such Veddas, for the purpose of making weapons, preceded productive activity in the preparation of ornaments.

True, even hunters at a very low stage—for example, the Bushmen and the Australians—go in for pictorial art: they have regular picture galleries about which I shall have something to say

[1] Waitz, *Anthropologie der Naturvoelker*, Part Three, p. 446.

[2] *Im australischen Busche und den Kneusten des Korallenmeeres*, Leipzig, 1896, p. 223.

[3] *Die Weddas von Ceylon*, p. 395.

in my other letters.[1] The Chukchi and Eskimos are outstanding in their sculpture and carving.[2] The tribes inhabiting Europe during the age of the mammoth had no less marked artistic propensities.[3] All these are very important facts which no historian of art can ignore. But why should it follow from this that the artistic activity of the Australians, the Bushmen, the Eskimos or the contemporaries of the mammoth preceded the production of articles of use—that their art should be "older" than their labour? There are no grounds at all why it should follow. Quite the contrary. The character of the primitive hunter's artistic activity demonstrates, without the slightest ambiguity, that the production by him of articles of use and his economic activity in general preceded his earliest art and laid upon it the clearest of imprints. What do the Chukchi drawings depict? Various scenes from hunting life.[4] It is clear that the Chukchi began to take up hunting first and only afterwards started reproducing their hunting in drawings. In exactly the same way, when the Bushmen almost exclusively depict animals—peacocks, elephants, hippopotami, ostriches and so on[5]—they do so because animals play an enormous, a decisive role in their hunting life. First of all man came to stand in a particular relationship to animals (he began to hunt them), and only afterwards—and for the very reason that he stood in this particular relationship to them—did his urge to draw these animals arise. Which, then, came first? Labour before art or art before labour?

No, my dear sir, I am firmly convinced that we shall understand precisely nothing of the history of primitive art unless we become imbued with the idea that *labour is older than art* and that in

[1] On the drawings of the Australians see *Waitz, Anthropologie der Naturvoelker*, Part Six, pp. 759 ff. Cf. also the interesting article by R. H. Matthews, *The Rock Pictures of the Australian Aborigines*, in *Proceedings and Transactions of the Queensland Branch of the Royal Geographical Society of Australia*, Vols. X and XI. On the pictorial art of the Bushmen see the work by Fritsch, from which I have already quoted, on the natives of South Africa, Vol. I, pp. 425–7.

[2] Vide: *Die Umsegelung Asiens und Europas auf der "Vega,"* von A. E. Nordenskiöld, Leipzig, 1880, Vol. I, p. 463, and Vol. II, pp. 125, 127, 129, 135, 141, 231.

[3] See *Die Urgeschichte der Menschen nach dem heutigen Stande der Wissenschaft*, von Dr. M. Hoernes, first half-vol., p. 191 ff., p. 213 ff. Not a few facts with bearing on this question are given by Mortillet in his *Le Préhistorique*.

[4] Nordenskiöld, Vol. II, pp. 132, 133, 135.

[5] Fritsch, *Die Eingeborenen Sued-Afrikas*, Vol. I, p. 426.

general *man first looks on objects and phenomena from a utilitarian point of view and only afterwards takes up an aesthetic attitude in his relationship to them.*

I shall bring forward a great many—in my opinion completely convincing—proofs of this concept in my next letter. However, I shall have first to examine how far the old and well-known subdivision of peoples into *hunting*, *pastoral* and *agricultural* categories accords with the present state of our ethnological knowledge.

FOURTH LETTER[1]

HUNTING, PASTORAL AND AGRICULTURAL PEOPLES
(*A Fragment*)

DEAR SIR,—In my previous letters I have not infrequently used the expressions "hunting peoples," "lower hunting tribes" and so on. Had I any right to do so? In other words, is the old, well-known system whereby peoples are subdivided into hunting, pastoral and agricultural categories a satisfactory one?

Many people now think it quite unsatisfactory. Among those who do is Buecher. He argues that the system in question was based on the silent assumption that primitive man was carnivorous in the first place and only gradually changed to plant foods. But in actual fact man began by using plant foods: he ate fruit, berries and roots. The natural supplement to this plant food consisted of small organisms: shell-fish, grubs, beetles, ants and so on. "If we are to look for the transition to the following stage," Buecher goes on, "then, according to certain trends of thought, it may be supposed that primitive man found no difficulty in noticing how bulbs and seeds falling on the ground gave rise to plants and that to do so, in any case, was no harder than the taming of animals, the invention of the fishing-rod or of bows and arrows needed for hunting."[2] Buecher, moreover, expresses his conviction that nomadic pastoral peoples must be regarded as agricultural people who have turned wild, and he adds that, with the exception of the extreme north, there even now exists no people for whom plant foods do not compose a considerable portion of their diet. Elsewhere he states that the course of economic development amongst primitive tribes entirely depends upon geographical environment and that therefore it would be pointless to attempt to lay down a system of developmental stages "universally applicable to Negroes, Papuans, Polynesians and American Indians."[3]

[1] According to Plekhanov's heading, the "Third Letter"—Editorial Board of "Literary Heritage of Plekhanov."—TRANS. Further notes by this body will be referred to as "Russian Editors."

[2] *Four Essays*, pp. 111–12.

[3] *Ibid.*, p. 77.

Exactly the same view was put forward a few years ago by another German expert on primitive economy, Hellmuth Pankow, in an article entitled *Betrachtungen ueber das wirtschaftliche Leben der Naturvoelker*,[1] published in the third number of the *Journal of the Berlin Geographical Society* for 1896. In Pankow's opinion the system of dividing the peoples into hunting, pastoral and agricultural categories prevents a correct understanding of the economic life of primitive man. True, this life has always a very narrow basis, but it is nevertheless considerably wider than is supposed to be the case according to "the deeply rooted system" under examination. In it hunting is combined with agriculture and agriculture goes hand in hand with cattle-breeding. As a whole, human progress does not occur so simply and schematically as to subject the movement of all peoples to one and the same law. It is achieved in one way in one place and elsewhere quite differently. Pankow, moreover, believes that the "deeply rooted system" depicts the order of historical origin of the different manners of obtaining food incorrectly. Like Buecher he considers that *agriculture preceded the taming of animals for economic purposes.* Pankow's general conclusion is that the usually accepted system bears little resemblance to the real course of economic and cultural development and that the advances in our knowledge insistently demand its rejection.

This conclusion is fully shared by A. Firkandt who puts forward a new classification of the forms of development of primitive economy.[2] I think it would be an advantage, Sir, for you to be acquainted with this new classification.

Firkandt states that the tribes at the lowest level of all are those whose activities are confined to the simple *gathering* of the ready gifts of nature. He calls them *gatherers (die Sammler)*. The natives of the Australian mainland, for example, belong to the gatherers, supporting their existence by collecting the roots of wild plants and shell-fish, and also by hunting, with them in its most primitive form. To the same group belong the Bushmen, the Fuegians, the Botocudos, the inhabitants of the Andaman Islands, the Negritos of the Philippine Archipelago—in short, the same tribes which I have been calling *the lower hunting tribes.*

[1] *Notes on the Economic Life of Primitive Peoples.*

[2] *Vide Die Wirtschaftlichen Verhaeltnisse der Naturvoelker*, by the same author in *Zeitschrift fuer Sozialwissenschaft*, Nos. 2 and 3 for 1899.

At the next stage of development we find *hunting, fishing, cattle-rearing* and a special form of *agriculture*, to which German experts have recently applied the term *Hackbau* (tilling the soil with a pick). Pure hunters and fishers are met with only under exceptional geographical conditions "where cultivation of the soil is impossible for climatic reasons," for example, in the extreme north of the Old and New Worlds. To the south of this cold belt lies an exceedingly broad zone, where hunting, cattle-rearing and cultivation of the soil with the pick are combined—or were combined in the age preceding the appearance of the Europeans.

But with each separate people each of these separate means of obtaining food enters or entered into union with the others in various proportions. Among the Indians of North . . .[1]

[1] Here the manuscript breaks off.—RUSSIAN EDITORS.

FIFTH LETTER

ART AND UTILITY (1)

DEAR SIR,—At the close of my first letter I said that in the next I would show how readily the art of primitive peoples—in German terminology the so-called *Naturvoelker*,—is to be explained from the standpoint of the materialist conception of history. I must now do as I promised.

In undertaking this task I want, first of all, to come to an agreement with you again over terminology. What are primitive tribes? What are *Naturvoelker*?

The term usually covers all those many and various tribes which, in their cultural development, have not yet reached the level of *civilisation*. But where does the boundary dividing civilised from uncivilised peoples lie?

L. H. Morgan, in his well-known work, *Ancient Society*, accepts the age of civilisation as beginning from the time when the phonetic alphabet and the use of characters were invented. I find it hard to agree with him about this, except with certain fundamental reservations. But that need not concern us here. No matter how far back we move the boundary dividing civilised from uncivilised peoples, we shall have in any case to admit that a very large number of tribes, at very different cultural levels, belong to the latter category. Consequently the material we have to deal with is very extensive and varied. True, the influence of racial peculiarities in this case, if it exists at all, is so slight that it is almost impossible to determine it: the art of one race scarcely differs at all from the art of another. "Primitive art, this universal language of mankind," says Luebke, "covered the earth with uniform monuments, the remains of which are to be found over an area stretching from the islands of the Pacific Ocean to the banks of the Mississipi and from the shores of the Baltic to the Greek Archipelago."[1] We can, therefore, regard this influence as negligible in the overwhelming majority of cases. This, of course,

[1] Luebke, *History of Art*, Paris, 1892, p. 1.

makes our task much easier. Nevertheless it still remains a very complex one, for, after all, the uncivilised peoples include not only the Australian and Polynesian tribes, but also the overwhelming majority of the inhabitants of Africa, tribes at quite different levels of savagery and barbarism. How, then, are we to cope with this material?

Why do we examine the art of primitive peoples separately from that of civilised peoples? Because, in the art of civilised peoples, the influence of technique and economics is pushed into the background by the division of society into classes and the resulting class antagonisms. And so the further any tribe is removed from the stage of social evolution when such divisions arise, the more suitable material will it provide for my research. But which tribes are furthest from possessing the social structure characteristic of civilised peoples, that is, the division of society into classes? Those which have the least developed productive forces. But it is the so-called *hunting* tribes that are distinguished by the least developed productive forces, their existence being maintained by fishing, hunting and gathering the fruits and roots of wild plants. It is, therefore, to these tribes, and to those closest to them in cultural development, that I shall turn in the first place. I shall refer to tribes at a higher level, the African Negroes, for example, only in so far as the data which they present modify or confirm the results obtained by our study of hunting tribes.

I shall begin with the dances, which occupy a very important place in the life of all primitive tribes.

"A distinguishing feature of the dance is the rhythmical order of its movements," writes E. Grosse. "There is not a single dance without rhythm."[1] We have already seen in the first letter that the faculty for perceiving and enjoying the music of rhythm is inherent in human nature (and not only in human nature). But how is this faculty manifested in dances? What do the rhythmical movements of the dancers *signify*? How are the dances connected with their mode of life, with their mode of production?

Sometimes dances are simply an imitation of the movements of animals. Such, for example, are the Australian frog, butterfly, emu, dingo and kangaroo dances. The North American bear and bison dances are similar. And such dances as the Brazilian Indian

[1] *Die Anfaenge der Kunst*, p. 198.

"fish" dance and the Bakairi *bat* dance[1] should probably be included in this category.

These dances reveal an imitative faculty. In the kangaroo dance the Australian so well imitates all the movements of this animal that, as Eyre remarks, his performance would be applauded enthusiastically in any European theatre.[2]

. . .[3] how she climbs a tree to catch an opossum; or how she dives to bring up a shell-fish; or how she grubs up edible plants. The men also have similar dances. Such, for example, is the Australian rowers' dance or the dance depicting the making of a boat, which the New Zealanders used to perform. All these dances amount to simple depictions of productive processes. They deserve great attention, since they serve as remarkable examples of the intimate connection between primitive artistic and productive activity.

But there are evidently social formations, too, corresponding to such dances. Among primitive hunters such formations cannot be at all stable, if only because of the very conditions of hunting life, that is, because the means of existence provided by hunting are extremely meagre and insecure.[4] Eyre says that the number of Australians wandering together varies at different times of the year and depends upon the quantity of food which can be obtained by them.[5] But in general, the Australian hordes consist of not more than fifty individuals. On the Philippine Islands the Aeti live in hordes numbering from 20 to 30 individuals; a horde of Bushmen comprises 20 to 40 families; a horde of Botocudos sometimes runs into hundreds of members, and so on.[6] A horde embracing forty families, i.e. up to 200 persons, is nevertheless still of insignificant size. These same conditions of life lead to frequent clashes between separate hordes of primitive hunters.

[1] Von den Steinen, *Unter den Naturvoelkern Brasiliens*, p. 300.

[2] *Journal of Expeditions of Discovery*, Vol. II, p. 223.

[3] Pp. 9–11 of the MS. are missing. They are made good in part by the extracts from lectures on art printed at the end of this letter (pp. 128–9).—RUSSIAN EDITORS.

[4] "The number travelling together depends in a great measure upon the period of the year and the description of food that may be in season." Eyre, *Journal of Expeditions*, etc., Vol. II, p. 218.

[5] *Ibid.*, Vol. II, p. 218.

[6] See G. Kunov's interesting and important work: *Les bases économiques du matriarcat* in *Le Devenir Social* for January, February and April, 1898.

According to T. Waitz, most of the wars among the Redskin tribes of North America arose over the hunting rights on certain territories.[1] How such wars are brought about is well demonstrated by the following conversation between Stanley and the representatives of a certain Central African negro tribe. "Do you always fight your neighbours?" he asked them. "No; some of our young men go into the woods to hunt game and they are surprised by our neighbours; then we go to them and they come to fight us until one party is tired or one is beaten."[2] Frequent repetition of hostile encounters among primitive tribes results in feelings of mutual hatred and unrequited vengeance which, in turn, serve as a ground for further clashes.[3] As a result, the primitive hunting tribe must be always on the alert against hostile attacks.[4] And since the tribe is too short of men and means to afford to maintain a body of military specialists, every hunter has to be at the same time a warrior, and for this reason the *ideal warrior* becomes the *ideal man*. According to Schoolcraft, the whole force of social opinion among the Redskins of North America is directed towards making their young men dauntless warriors and arousing in them a thirst for military glory.[5] Many of their religious ceremonies have the same aim in view; it is not surprising that the art of the dance has the same purpose. This is how . . .[6]

If full accordance of form with content is the first and principal sign of a genuine work of art, it cannot but be admitted that the war dances of primitive peoples are artistic in the full sense of the

[1] *Die Indianer Nordamerikas*, p. 115.

[2] *In Darkest Africa*, London, 1890, Vol. II, p. 92. True, Ratzel remarks that the desire to taste human flesh not infrequently gave rise to war between the New Zealanders (*Voelkerkunde*, Vol. I, p. 93). But in that case war must be regarded as an aspect of hunting. It should be noted that primitive peoples often go to war over issues which with us would be referred to a magistrate's court. But for the parties in dispute to accept the authority of a magistrate, an organisation of social government is required of a character quite impossible for the hunting period.

[3] (From Sieber). Plekhanov here has in mind N. I. Sieber's book, *Studies in Primitive Culture*.—RUSSIAN EDITORS.

[4] This is from Marzius.

[5] *Op. cit.*, Vol. II, p. 57.

[6] Pages 15–19 are missing. On p. 20 in all only a few lines have been written. These do not fully link up with the text and for this reason are quoted as a footnote: "I do not think that anyone at present will dispute the fact that the military organisation of any society is determined by the state of its productive forces and its economy."—RUSSIAN EDITORS.

word. The truth of this is demonstrated by the following description of a war dance seen by Stanley in Equatorial Africa:[1] ". . . Thirty three lines of thirty three men each . . . each man was forcefully stamping the ground . . . the thousand heads rose and drooped together, rising when venting the glorious volume of energy, drooping with the undertone of wailing murmur of the multitude. As they shouted with faces turned upward and heads bent back to give the fullest effect to the ascending tempest of voices, suggestive of quenchless fury, wrath and extermination, it appeared to inflate every soul with the passion of deadly battle and every eye of the onlookers glowed luridly, and their right arms with clenched fists were shaken on high as though their spirits were thrilled with the martial strains. But as the heads were turned and bowed to the earth we seemed to feel war's agony, and grief, and woe, to think of tears, and widow's wails, and fatherless orphans' cries, of ruined hearths and a desolated land." Stanley adds that this was one of the "best and most exciting exhibitions" he saw in Africa.[2]

Thus the war dances of primitive hunting peoples are in themselves works of art expressing feelings and ideas which are necessarily and naturally bound to develop among them, given their particular mode of life. And as their mode of life is wholly

[1] The following words in the text are deleted: "However, it is not always only victories that spring to the imagination of the dancing warrior."—RUSSIAN EDITORS.

[2] *In Darkest Africa*, Vol. I, pp. 413 and 414. [Plekhanov's Russian version taken from a French edition differs considerably in detail from the original passage quoted here.—TRANS.]

Eight further lines of text are deleted, as also their continuation, which is on the reverse of p. 44 of the MS., and numbered 19 (see double numbering of p. 23). We quote this passage:

"The war dances of primitive peoples amount to no less than a school of warfare. And although primitive war very closely borders on primitive hunting, it nevertheless cannot be in any way called a productive occupation. It is, therefore, evident that you, Sir, not without reason, may tell me that the dances, both in their origin and character, are divorced from all connection with the productive forces of primitive society and with its economy.

"But is this so? It would be if war itself were not causally connected with economy; but in fact this connection with it is not subject to the slightest doubt, and for this reason . . .

"Every war is a hostile encounter between two independent political organisms sometimes . . ."—RUSSIAN EDITORS.

conditioned by the state of their productive forces,[1] we are bound to admit that in the last resort the character of their war dances, too, is conditioned by the state of these productive forces. This is all the more evident because, as I have already said, every warrior is at the same time a hunter and uses the very same weapons in war as in hunting.

An intimate connection is to be found between the mode of life of hunting tribes and their incantational and funeral dances. Primitive man believes in the existence of a greater or lesser number of spirits, but his relationship to these supernatural forces is limited to various attempts to exploit them to his own advantage.[2] In order to propitiate a spirit, the savage tries to do him a good turn. He bribes him with some favourite food ("a sacrificial offering") and he dances in his honour those dances from which he himself derives the greatest pleasure. In Africa, the negroes, when they succeed in killing an elephant, often dance around it in honour of the spirits.[3] The connection of such dances with hunting life is obvious. The dependence of *funeral* dances on hunting life will become just as obvious when we remember that the deceased becomes a spirit whom the living try to propitiate in exactly the same way as they do other spirits.[4]

The *love* dances of primitive peoples seem very indecent, from our point of view. It goes without saying that this kind of dance has no *direct* relation at all to any sort of economic activity. Their mimicry serves as the undisguised expression of elementary physiological requirements and probably has not a little in common with the love mimicry of the great anthropoid apes. The hunting mode of life, of course, is not without its influence even on these dances; but it has influenced them only in so far as it has

[1] The following is here deleted: ". . . it is not hard to discern the causal connection existing between the state of these forces on the one hand and the war. . . ."—RUSSIAN EDITORS.

[2] A similar relationship is also often found among African negroes, who have, however, considerably progressed in culture beyond the *hunters* in the strict sense of the word.

[3] *Voyages et Aventures dans l'Afrique Equatoriale*, par Paul du Chaillu, Paris, 1863, p. 306.

[4] The Brazilian Indians sing their *hunting* songs at burials (Von den Steinen, *Among the Primitive Peoples of Brazil*, p. 493)—at the burial of a hunter other songs would be far less appropriate.

constituted a factor in determining the *mutual relations of the sexes in primitive society*.

I can see you, my dear Sir, rubbing your hands with satisfaction. "Aha!" you say, "So even primitive man's requirements are far from being all connected with his particular mode of production or his economy. The sex instinct proves this with extreme clarity. But once we allow a single exception to the general rule, we are bound to admit that, no matter how great the significance of the economic factor, it cannot be accepted as exclusive, and upon this your whole materialist conception of history falls to the ground."

I must hasten to point out that no supporter of this conception has ever dreamt of asserting that men's economic relationships create or help to determine their basic physiological requirements. The sex instinct was, of course, present in our anthropoid forbears back in those remote times when not even the barest rudiments of *productive* activity had arisen.[1]

The mutual relations of the sexes are conditioned precisely by this instinct. But at different stages of human cultural development these relations assume a different *form*, dependent upon the development of the family, which in its turn is determined by the development of the productive forces and the character of social-economic relationships.

The same must also be said of *religious* ideas. In nature nothing happens without reason. This circumstance finds its psychological reflection in man, in his always wanting to find the reason for those phenomena which interest him. Primitive man, having at his disposal only an extremely meagre store of information, "*judges according to his own lights*" and ascribes the phenomena of nature to the premeditated action of conscious forces. Such is the origin of *animism*. The relationship of animism to the productive forces of primitive man is such that its domain contracts in direct proportion to the growth of man's power over nature. But, of course, this still does not mean that animism owes its origin to the *economics* of primitive society. No, the origin of animist ideas is to be found in the nature of man; but their development, as well as the influence they acquire over the social behaviour of men, is determined in the last resort by economic relationships. Indeed,

[1] The following is deleted in the text: "But the same must be said of this instinct that I said in my first letter of the aesthetic sense: this sense is the gift of nature, but its manifestation. . . ."—RUSSIAN EDITORS.

animism and, in particular, belief in life beyond the grave, has at the outset no influence at all on men's mutual relationships, since it is in no way connected with the expectation of punishment or reward for bad or good actions. Only gradually does this belief become associated with the practical morality of primitive people. Men begin, let us say, to believe—as, for example, the inhabitants of the islands in the Torres Straits do—that the spirits of their bravest warriors have a happier existence beyond the grave than the spirits of ordinary people. This belief has a most marked and at times extremely strong influence on the behaviour of those who entertain it. And in this sense primitive religion is an indisputable "*factor*" in social development. But the whole practical significance of this factor depends upon what precisely are the actions prescribed by those rules of practical reason with which animist ideas are associated, and this is wholly conditioned by the social relationships arising from a given economic basis.[1] And so, if primitive religion acquires significance as a factor in social development, this significance is wholly rooted in economics.[2]

This is why examples showing that the development of art often takes place under a strong religious influence, do not in the least undermine the correctness of the materialist conception of history. I have considered it necessary, Sir, to draw your attention to this, because those who forget it become victims of the most ridiculous misconceptions and naturally behave like Don Quixotes tilting at windmills.

I will also make an additional remark. The first permanent division of social labour is the division of labour in primitive society between men and women. Whereas men engage in hunting and war, it falls to the lot of women to collect the roots and fruits

[1] Probably Emile Burnouf had this in mind when he wrote: "If the morality of a nation is the product of its customs, a fact which is indisputable, the cause of religious diversity must be sought in the social condition of man." In notebook No. 38 in the G. V. Plekhanov archives, this quotation from Burnouf is completed: ". . . since customs have their genesis in social conditions." *Vide* Burnouf, *La Science des Religions*, Paris, 1872, p. 287.

[2] I must remark, however, that I am most reluctant to make use, in this instance, of the term "factor." Strictly speaking there is only one factor in historical development—to wit, social man, who acts, thinks, feels and believes in one way or another according to how his economy is formed in the course of development of his productive forces. Participants in disputes about the historical importance of various "factors" often, without knowing it, *hypostasise* abstract concepts.

of wild plants (and shell-fish, too), to look after the children and in general all matters of domestic economy. This division of labour is also reflected in dances: each sex has its special dances: it is only on rare occasions that both sexes dance together. Describing the festivals of the Brazilian Indians, Von den Steinen remarks that if the women take no part in the hunting dances that accompany these festivals it is because hunting is not a feminine occupation.[1] This is quite true, and it should be added, again according to Von den Steinen, that during such festivals the women are even more occupied with domestic matters, providing hospitality for guests, than at other times.

I have said that animist ideas only gradually become associated with primitive morality. Today this is a generally accepted fact.[2]

But this generally accepted fact stands in sharp contradiction to the opinion of Count L. Tolstoy, to which I drew your attention in my first letter and according to which the consciousness of good and bad, characteristic of all members of society, no matter when or where ("in every society") is a *religious* consciousness. The various picturesque dances of primitive peoples, which occupy so important a place in their art, express and depict those emotions and actions that are of essential significance in their life. And this is why they have a direct relation to "what is bad and what is good." But in the overwhelming majority of cases they are devoid of all connection with primitive "religion." Count Tolstoy's argument is mistaken, even in its application to the Catholic peoples of the Middle Ages, amongst whom the association of religious concepts with practical morality was incomparably closer and extended over a far wider field. Even among these peoples, the consciousness of "what is bad and what is good" was far from being always religious consciousness, and for this reason also, the emotions conveyed by art had often not the slightest relation to religion.[3]

But whilst consciousness of what is good and bad is far from

[1] *Op. cit.*, p. 298.

[2] *Vide* Taylor's *Primitive Culture*, also Mariller's *La survivance de l'âme et l'idée de justice chez les peuples noncivilisés*, Paris, 1894.

[3] The following has been erased from the text by Plekhanov: "Nevertheless this idea of Count Tolstoy's does bring us face to face with the question of the role of art in the history of mankind, a question which I raised in my first letter. In disputes as to whether art *ought* or *ought not* to be an end in itself, as in all. . . ." —RUSSIAN EDITORS.

being always a *religious* consciousness, there can be no doubt that art acquires a social significance only in so far as it depicts, evokes or conveys *actions, emotions and events that are of significance to society.*[1]

We saw this in the case of the dances: Brazilian *fish-dances* are as intimately connected with the phenomena upon which the life of the tribe depends as the North American *scalp-dance* or the *dance of the shell-fish gatherers* performed by Australian women. True, none of these three dances is of any direct utility at all, either to the dancers themselves or to the spectators. Here, as always, the beautiful appeals to people independently of any utilitarian considerations whatsoever. But the *individual* can quite disinterestedly enjoy something which is very useful to his *kind* (to society). What we have seen in the case of morality is repeated here: if those acts of the individual are moral which he performs irrespective of all considerations of self-interest, this still does not mean that morality has no relation to social interest. Quite the contrary: self-abnegation on the part of the *individual* has a meaning only in so far as it is useful to the kind. For this reason the Kantian thesis, that the beautiful is that which pleases us independently of all interest, is wrong. But with what can we replace it? Can we say, for instance, that the beautiful is that which pleases us independently of all personal interest? No, that will not do. If the work of an artist, even of a group of artists, is for him an end in itself, those who enjoy a work of art (be it the *Antigone* of Sophocles, Michelangelo's *Night* or the dance of the rowers) forget, when they see it, all practical aims in general and the interest of their kind in particular.

Consequently the enjoyment of a work of art is *enjoyment* of the depiction (of an object, phenomenon or state of mind) advantageous to the kind, *independently* of any conscious consideration whatsoever of such advantage.

A work of art executed in images or sounds acts upon our *contemplative faculty* and not upon our *logical* faculty; and it is for this reason that there is no aesthetic enjoyment where a work of art arouses in us only considerations of social good: in such an instance there is only a *substitute* for aesthetic enjoyment: the pleasure afforded us by such a consideration. But since it is the artistic image in question that leads us to these considerations, a psychological aberration takes place, as a result of which we

[1] For note on the Spencerian definition see pp. 77 ff. and pp. 84 ff.

consider this image to be the cause of our enjoyment, whereas in actual fact it is caused by the *thoughts* evoked by the image and, consequently, has its roots in the functioning of our *logical faculty*, and not in that of our *contemplative faculty*. It is to this latter faculty that the true artist always turns, whereas tendentious work always seeks to evoke in us considerations of common good, in other words it acts in the last analysis, upon our logical faculty.

It must be remembered, however, that *historically* speaking a consciously utilitarian standpoint towards objects usually precedes the aesthetic standpoint. Ratzel, who does not at all approve the tendency of many students of primitive customs to infer consciousness where it cannot exist,[1] is himself, however, compelled to appeal to it in certain important instances. For example, we know that savages almost universally rub their bodies with fat, with the juice of various plants or, in the last instance, simply with clay. This custom plays an important role in the primitive adornment of the body. But what gave rise to it? Ratzel thinks that the Hottentots, who smear their bodies with the juice of an aromatic plant called *buchu* do so *in order to protect themselves from insects*. And, he adds, the fact that these same Hottentots take special pains in greasing their hair is only to be explained by their *need to protect themselves from the sun*.[2] The well-known Jesuit, Lafitau, accounted in a similar way for the North American Redskins' custom of rubbing themselves with *fat*.[3] In our own time this view has been supported with particular force and conviction by Von den Steinen. Speaking of the Brazilian Indians' custom of daubing themselves with coloured clay, he remarks that they must first have noticed that the clay cools the skin and is a protection from mosquitoes and only afterwards turned their attention to the fact that the body, thus daubed, was more beautiful. "I myself hold the view," he adds, "that it is pleasure which lies at the root of adornment, in just the same way as a surplus of accumulated strength forms the basis for play; but the objects employed for adornment originally become known to men because of their use. Among our (Brazilian) Indians, the useful goes hand in hand with

[1] *Voelkerkunde*, Vol. I, Einleitung, p. 69. [2] *Ibid.*, Vol. I, p. 92.

[3] *Les Moeurs des Sauvages Américains*, Paris, 1724, Vol. II, p. 59: "The oils with which the savages smear themselves make them extremely smelly and filthy. . . . But these oils, without which they are devoured by insects, are an absolute necessity for them."

the ornamental, and we have every ground for believing that the former arose before the latter."[1]

Thus man originally rubbed himself with clay, fat or plant juices because it was *useful*.[2] Afterwards the body, smeared in this way, began to seem *beautiful* to him, and he began smearing himself for *aesthetic pleasure*. This point once reached, a number of the most varied "factors" arise, whose influence conditions the *further evolution* of primitive cosmetics. Thus, according to Burton, for example, negroes of the Wajiji tribe (in East Africa) are fond of covering their heads with lime, the whiteness of which beautifully sets off the darkness of their skin. The same Wajiji, and for the very same reason, love ornaments made from the teeth of the hippopotamus, which are remarkable for their dazzling whiteness.[3] In exactly the same way the Brazilian Indians, according to Von den Steinen, prefer buying *light blue* beads that show up more beautifully against their skin than other colours.[4] In general the effect of *contrast* (the principle of antithesis), is of great significance here.

As great, if not greater, of course, is the influence of the *mode of life* of primitive peoples. Besides what we have already pointed out, another explanation for the origin of smearing and painting the body can be found in the desire to appear as terrible as possible to one's enemies. "When a savage in hunting or in victorious battle with his enemy happened to get spattered with mud and blood, he could not but notice," says Joest, "the expression of horror mingled with fear which this produced on the faces of those around him, who in turn began trying to produce the same impression for their own purposes."[5]

Indeed, we know that some savage tribes, after a successful hunt, smear themselves with the blood of the animals they have killed.[6] We also know that primitive warriors paint themselves

[1] *Unter den Naturvoelkern Brasiliens*, p. 174. Cf. also p. 186.

[2] Joest rightly remarks: "Examples of this kind are provided by animal life. Buffaloes, elephants, hippopotami, etc., frequently wallow in slime with the obvious intention of protecting themselves from the stings of flies, mosquitoes, etc., by means of an armour of mud. Men have done the same and still do so" (*Taetowieren, Narbenzeichnen und Koerperbemalen*, Berlin, 1887, p. 19).

[3] Burton, *The Lake Regions of Central Africa*, London, 1860, Vol. II, p. 63.

[4] *Loc. cit.*, p. 185.

[5] Cf. Ratzel, *Voelkerkunde*, Vol. I, *Einleitung*, p. 69, Grosse, *Anfaenge der Kunst*, pp. 61 ff.

[6] *Loc. cit.*, p. 19.

with red paint when setting off to war or getting ready for a war dance. The gradual emergence and perpetuation among warriors of this custom of painting themselves red—the colour of blood—was probably also due to a desire to please their women-folk at home, who would have treated with contempt any man deficient in warlike behaviour.[1] There were other causes behind the use of other colours: certain Australian tribes in token of grief for the deceased smear themselves with *white* clay. Grosse[2] makes the interesting point that the colour for mourning amongst white Europeans is *black*, while with the black Australians it is *white*. What is the explanation? I think it is as follows.[3] Primitive tribes are usually proud of all the physical peculiarities of their race. A white skin appears ugly to dark-skinned peoples.[4] In the ordinary course of life, therefore, they strive, as we have already seen, to show off, to accentuate the darkness of their skin. And if grief drives them to adorn themselves with *white*, this probably happens thanks to the principle of antithesis, with which we are familiar. But a different explanation is possible. Joest thinks that primitive man paints himself on the death of a relative, solely to prevent the soul of the deceased from recognising him, in the event of its conceiving the inopportune desire to drag him away to the realm of spirits.[5] If this supposition is correct—and there is nothing improbable about it—white colouring is preferred by dark-skinned tribes simply as the best means of making themselves unrecognisable.

[1] "The fights are sometimes witnessed by . . . the women and the children. The presence of the females may be supposed probably to inspire the belligerents with courage and incite them to deeds of daring." Eyre, *loc. cit.*, p. 223.

"Custom demands also that, before taking a wife, the young Caffre should have performed certain acts of bravery or have received his baptism in blood: until his assagai has been washed in the blood of the enemy he cannot marry; hence the veritable frenzy which carried the Zulu warriors right to the mouths of the English cannon during the recent war and made them perform acts of incomparable daring and recklessness." *Du Cap au Lac Nyassa*, par Edouard Foà, Paris, 1897, pp. 81–2.

[2] *Anfaenge der Kunst*, p. 54.

[3] "It is well known that almost everywhere mothers seek by external means to make their children's nationality as obvious as possible." Schweinfurth, *op. cit.*, Vol. II, p. 256.

[4] "What should you think of these Whites as husbands?" asked Burton's Negro interpreter. "*Sivyo!* Not by any means," was the unanimous reply, accompanied by peals of merriment. *Op. cit.*, p. 58.

[5] *Loc. cit.*, p. 22.

However this may be, there is no doubt that *smearing* of the skin is very soon complicated by *painting*.[1] And the smearing itself ceases to be such a simple affair as it was originally. Certain negro tribes in Africa, who go in for cattle rearing, consider it good form to grease the body with a whole coating of butter;[2] others, for the same purpose, prefer cow dung reduced to ashes and mixed with the animal's urine. Butter, dung and urine serve in these cases as a sign of wealth, since only the owners of cattle can afford to smear themselves in this way.[3] Perhaps butter and cow dung protect the skin better than wood ash. If this really is so, the change over from ashes to butter or dung, which took place with the development of cattle rearing, came about under the influence of *purely utilitarian* considerations. But once it had come about, a body smeared with butter or ashes of cow dung, began to arouse in men's aesthetic sense more pleasure than a body smeared with bark. Nor is this all. By rubbing his body with butter or dung a man gave visible proof to his neighbours that he was not without a certain affluence. Evidently, the prosaic satisfaction of this demonstration here again preceded the aesthetic satisfaction of seeing his body coated with dung or butter.

But primitive man does not only *smear* and *paint* his skin. He also incises certain patterns upon it, often extremely intricate ones; he *tattoos* himself, and does this with the evident aim of beautifying his person. Can it also be said, in the case of tattooing, that he regarded it from the standpoint of its *use* before he took *aesthetic pleasure* in it?

You are of course aware, Sir, that there are two kinds of tattoo: (1) a tattoo in the proper sense of the word, and (2) an ornamentation of the skin by means of *scars*. The introduction of certain colouring materials into the skin by mechanical means constitutes tattooing in the proper sense. The colours, introduced in a definite order, form a more or less permanent design.[4] The ornamentation

[1] "The Oyampi of South America not only like painting themselves red and yellow, but paint their dogs and tame monkeys in the same way."—Ratzel, *Voelkerkunde*, Vol. II, p. 568.

[2] ". . . the skin . . . drips with ghee, the pride of rank and beauty."—Captain Burton, *op. cit.*, Vol. I, p. 305.

[3] Schweinfurth says that among the Shilluks the poor rub themselves over with *wood ash*, whereas the well-to-do smear themselves with cow dung (*Au Cœur de l'Afrique*, Vol. I, p. 82).

[4] Cf. F. Joest, *loc. cit.*, p. 8.

of the skin by means of scars, effected by incisions or burning, is sometimes designated by the Australian word, *manka*,[1] as distinct from tattooing. The tribes which practise scarring for the most part do not practise tattooing, and vice versa. But why do some tribes prefer scarring themselves and others tattooing? This question is easily answered when we learn that scarring is widespread among *dark-skinned* peoples, and tattooing among *light-skinned* peoples. Thus, if incisions are made in the skin of a negro, and the healing process is artificially delayed so that festering takes place, the pigment destroyed during the period of festering is not restored and white scars are finally formed.[2] These scars stand out sharply on a dark skin, in such a way that the skin can be ornamented in any pattern desired. Dark-skinned tribes, therefore, find it more satisfactory to scar themselves, since tattooed designs do not stand out so well on a dark skin. Light-skinned tribes are in a different position. Scars do not stand out so well on their skin, which is better adapted for tattooing. So everything here depends on the colour of the skin.

But we have still not explained the *origin* of the custom of *manka* and tattooing. What could have induced dark-skinned tribes to decorate their skin with scars, and why did light-skinned tribes find it necessary to tattoo themselves?

Certain tribes of North America tattoo on their skins pictures of their imaginary animal ancestors.[3] Brazilian Indians of the Bakairi tribe *paint* black dots and circles on their children's skins, to make them look like jaguars, this animal being supposed to be the tribe's ancestor.[4] Here the course of development is quite clear: originally the savage used to *draw* certain signs on his skin, and afterwards he began, so to speak, to *carve* them. But why did he need them at all? So far as pictures of supposed tribal ancestors are concerned, the most natural answer would be the following: the desire to draw or carve such pictures on his skin arose from the savage's attitude towards his tribal ancestor and by his

[1] Cf. paper by M. Gaberland: *Ueber die Verbreitung und den Sinn der Taetowierung* in the fifteenth volume of *Mitteilungen der Anthropologischen Gesselschaft in Wien.*

[2] See von Langer's explanation at the monthly meeting of the Vienna Anthropological Society, 10th February, 1885. (*Mitteilungen der Anthropologischen Gesellschaft in Wien.*)

[3] J. G. Frazer, *Totemism*, Edinburgh, 1887, p. 28.

[4] P. Ehrenreich, *Mitteilungen ueber die zweite Xingu-Expedition in Brasilien, Zeitschrift fuer Ethnologie*, 1890, Vol. XXII.

conviction that a mysterious bond existed between the ancestor and all his descendants. In other words, the natural thing to suppose would be that tattooing arose as a result of primitive *religious* feelings. If this hypothesis were correct, we could say that the hunting life gave birth to hunting *mythology* which, in its turn, became the basis for one of the forms of primitive ornamentation. This, of course, would not only not contradict the materialist conception of history, but would be a clear illustration of the thesis that the development of art is causally connected—even if not always *directly*—with the development of the productive forces.

But this hypothesis, which appears at first glance so natural, is not fully confirmed by observation. The North American Redskins carve or draw pictures of their supposed ancestors on their weapons, their boats, their wigwams and even on their domestic utensils.[1] Can it be allowed that they do all this from religious motives? I think not. It would be truer to say that they are prompted by the simple desire to designate that the objects concerned are owned by members of a certain gens. But if this is so, we may also believe that the Brazilian Indian woman, when she paints her child's skin to look like a jaguar's coat, desires, quite simply, to give a visible indication of his *relationship to the gens*. This indication of the individual's gentile relationship is useful even in his childhood—for instance, in the event of his abduction—and becomes absolutely essential on his reaching sexual maturity. We know that amongst primitive peoples there exists a complicated system of strict provisions determining the mutual relations of the sexes. Violation of these provisions is severely dealt with, and, to avoid possible mistakes, appropriate marks are made on the skin of persons reaching puberty. If a woman lacks these marks, her children are considered illegitimate and, in some cases, are put to death.[2] It is understandable, therefore, that on reaching the age of puberty the young people are eager to be tattooed despite the pain caused by the tattooing operation.[3]

[1] Frazer, *loc. cit.*, p. 45.

[2] J. S. Kubary, *Das Taetowieren in Mikronesien, speciell auf den Carolinen*, and the book by Joest already cited: *Taetowieren, etc.*, p. 86.

[3] "The girls . . . are always anxious to have this ceremony performed."—Eyre, *op. cit.*, p. 343.

"On the Caroline Islands, as soon as the time comes for a girl to enter into relations with men she endeavours to get the indispensable 'telengekel'—to become tattooed—since without it no man will look at her." *Op. cit.*, p. 75.

Nor is this all, of course. By means of tattooing the savage depicts not only his gens relationship but, it might also be said, his whole life. This is how Heckewelder describes the tattooing he saw on one old Redskin warrior: "On his face, his neck, his shoulders, his arms, his legs, and likewise his back and his chest, were depicted various scenes of actions and skirmishes in which he had taken part. In a word, his whole life was etched upon his body."[1] And not only his own life. Tattooing also reflects the life of the whole community, or, at any rate, all the relationships existing within it. I will leave aside the fact that the tattooing of women always differs from that of the men. But the men are by no means all tattooed in the same way either: the rich like to be distinguished from the poor, the slave-owners from the slaves. Little by little things reach a point where, *in accordance with the principle of antithesis*, the most highly placed persons *cease to be tattooed*, in order thereby to stand out in greater contrast to the crowd.[2] In a word, Lafitau, the Jesuit, was perfectly correct when he said that the different signs "engraved" by the North American Indians on their skins served them instead of "written memoirs."[3] And if such "engravure" has become a universal custom, this has been due to its practical use and even necessity in primitive society. In the first place the savage perceived the usefulness of tattooing, and only later—much later—did he find aesthetic enjoyment in the sight of a tattooed skin.

Thus—following Gaberland[4]—I decisively reject the idea that the original purpose of tattooing was adornment. But that does not solve the problem of what specific practical requirement led the primitive hunter to practise it. I am firmly convinced that his need of "characters and memoranda" greatly influenced the *extension* and *perpetuation* of the custom of "engraving" certain signs on the skin. But the *origin* of this custom may have been due to other causes. Von den Steinen believes that it is rooted in the *skin incisions* practised to this day by medicine-men *in order to reduce inflammation*. In his remarkable book *Unter den Naturvoelkern Brasiliens*, which I have already repeatedly quoted, he included a picture of a woman of the Katayu tribe, on whose skin incisions

[1] *Op. cit.*, p. 328.

[2] Cf. Joest, *op. cit.*, p. 27.

[3] *Moeurs des Sauvages Americians*, Vol. I, p. 44.

[4] Cf. the above-quoted paper in *Mitteilungen der Anthropologischen Gesellschaft in Wien*.

had been made for purely medical purposes. There is nothing easier than to confuse these incisions with those the Brazilian Indians make for adornment. It is quite possible, therefore, that tattooing developed from primitive surgical practice and only afterwards began to play the role of birth-certificate, passport, "memoranda" and so forth. If this is the case, the fact that "engravure" of the skin is accompanied by religious ceremonies would become perfectly comprehensible: primitive doctors and surgeons are often at the same time magicians and exorcisers. But whether this is so or not, it is clear that all the tattooing known to us confirms the correctness of the general rule I have indicated: the utilitarian standpoint preceded the aesthetic standpoint.

The same thing may be seen in other branches of primitive ornamentation. The hunter originally killed birds, like other game, for food. Those parts of the kill—the bird's feathers, or the skins, prickles, teeth and claws of beasts—which could not be eaten or used to satisfy any other requirement could, however, act as evidence and as a sign, as it were, of strength, bravery or skill. He therefore began covering his body with *skins*, fastening *horns* on his head, hanging *claws* and *teeth* round his neck, or even sticking feathers through his lips, his ears and his nose. Besides the desire to boast of his successes, there must have been a further "factor" at work when he stuck feathers into himself—his desire to demonstrate ability to bear physical pain which, of course, constitutes a very valuable quality in the hunter, who is also a warrior. "When wearing his treasure in the aperture pierced in his nose, lip or ear," Von den Steinen rightly remarks, "a young man must have felt himself to be much more of a fine fellow than if he simply had it suspended on a string."[1] And so the custom of piercing the nose and ears gradually developed and became established, whilst failure to observe it must have made an unpleasant impression on the *aesthetic sense* of primitive hunters.

The correctness of this supposition is demonstrated by the following. As I have already said, uncivilised peoples wear masks meant to depict animals for their dances. Von den Steinen[2] found many masks depicting birds and even fish among the Brazilian Indians. But note that when the Brazilian Indian reproduces the features of a pigeon, for example, he does not forget to

[1] Von den Steinen, *op. cit.*, p. 179.

[2] *Ibid.*, *op. cit.*, p. 305.

pierce its beak with a feather: evidently the gentle bird seems more beautiful to him with this hunting trophy.[1]

When the sight of a hunting trophy begins to evoke a sense of pleasure independently of any sort of *conscious* consideration as to the strength or skill of the hunter whom it adorns, it becomes an object of aesthetic enjoyment, and then its colour and its form take on a considerable independent significance. The Redskin tribes of North America used sometimes to make most beautiful headgear from brightly coloured feathers.[2] On the Friendship Islands the most important objects of exchange were the red feathers of one of the Polynesian birds.[3] A great many such examples can be quoted, but they must all be regarded as secondary phenomena, to which the basic conditions of hunting life have given rise.

For a very understandable reason, i.e. because hunting is not a feminine occupation, the women never wear hunting trophies. But the custom of wearing hunting trophies in the ears, lips or nose led at an early stage to the habitual insertion of bones, pieces of wood, straws or even stones in these parts of the body. The Brazilian *botoque* has evidently evolved from this kind of ornament. As this new kind of ornament had no definite connection with the exclusively male occupation—hunting—there was nothing to stop the women from wearing it as well. Nor is this all. It is very probable that it was the women who introduced such ornaments. In Africa, every woman of the Rongo tribe when she marries, pierces her lower lip and inserts a wooden stick in it. Others

[1] On the reverse of p. 72 (54) there is the following excerpt, which evidently formed part of the original version:

How great the influence of the division of labour is can be seen from what F. Prescott says: "The men make all the arms and implements of war, and the women are not allowed to touch them, nor go near them—(sic!), particularly when menstruating." (Schoolcraft, *op. cit.*, Vol. III, p. 235.)

At a higher level of productive forces, among pastoral tribes, the women are often forbidden to look after the cattle and even to enter the enclosures where they are fastened in for the night. (Cf. Ratzel, *op. cit.*, Vol. I, p. 252 and Casalis, *Les Bassoutos*, p. 131.)—RUSSIAN EDITORS.

[2] Schoolcraft, *op. cit.*, Vol. III, p. 67. I have already mentioned in my first letter that the favourite adornment of the North Western American Redskins consists of the claws of the grey bear. This fact shows very well how primitive hunting adornment serves as a sign of hunting "skill," just as the scalp bears witness to warlike prowess.

[3] Ratzel, *Voelkerkunde*, Vol. II, p. 141.

make holes in their nostrils as well, in which they insert straws.[1] This custom probably arose at an earlier stage, when the manufacture of metals was as yet unknown and when the women, wanting to imitate the men, but having no right to adorn themselves with the trophies of war or of the hunt, still knew nothing of metal ornaments.

The manufacture of metal was the starting point for a new period in the history of ornamentation. Metal embellishments gradually began to exclude those provided by the hunt.[2] Men and women began to cover their extremities and their necks with metal bracelets and necklaces. Feathers, small sticks and straws, which were inserted in the lips, nose or ears, gave place to metal rings and earrings. The beauties of the Bongo tribe, mentioned above, often stick iron rings in their noses, in the same way as Europeans do with a bull that is difficult to manage.[3] Many of the Senegambia women also wear rings.[4] As for iron earrings, the women of the Bongo tribe wear them in their ears almost by the dozen, and for this purpose not only pierce the lobe in a number of places, but also the auricle. "One comes across smart women," says Schweinfurth, "whose bodies are ornamented like this in as many as a hundred places. There is not a single prominence of the body, not a fold of skin where an aperture has not been made."[5] But it is no far cry, either, from the ring in the nose to the ring through the upper lip, i.e. to the *pelelé*, of which we spoke in the first letter. When the old chief of the Makololo told David and Charles Livingstone that the women of his tribe wore the *pelelé* for *beauty's* sake, he was, in his own way, perfectly right; but he could not, of course, explain *why* the ring through the upper lip had come to be considered by his fellow tribesmen as an object of adornment.

[1] Schweinfurth, *op. cit.*, Vol. I, pp. 283–4.

[2] These ornaments, however, are remarkable for their great viability. We find them in the ancient civilisations of the East, in the costumes of priests and kings. Thus the Assyrian kings wore crowns decorated with feathers and some Egyptian priests, at the time of worship, covered themselves with tiger skins.

[3] Schweinfurth, *op. cit.*, Vol. I, p. 284. It is remarkable that the wearing of iron rings in the nose is left to the personal discretion of the dark-skinned beauty, while the wearing of a wooden stick in the lower lip is compulsory for all women of the Bongo tribe. From this alone it is clear that the second custom is more ancient than the first.

[4] Bérenger-Féraud, *Les Peuplades de la Sénégambie*, Paris, 1879, p. 187.

[5] *Loc. cit.*, Vol. I, p. 284.

In actual fact this is to be explained by tastes inherited long since from a strictly hunting epoch and by changes corresponding to the new state of productive forces.

The position is, in my opinion, also explained by the fact that in this new period the men no longer prevent the women from wearing the same kind of ornament as they themselves originally wore.[1] The feather inserted in the nose or in the ear bore witness to hunting skill, and it was displeasing to a man to see it on a woman who had never taken part in hunting. Metal ornaments, however, were evidence, not of skill, but of *wealth*. Vanity would have prompted the wealthy property owner to make the woman wear as many of these ornaments as possible, for at that time—in some places at least—she was herself becoming *more and more* the property of the man.

"I believe," says Stanley, "that Chumbiri [a certain African chieftain—G. V. P.] . . . as soon as he obtained any brass wire melted it and forged it into brass collars for his wives. . . . He boasted to me that he possessed 'four tens' of wives, and each wife was collared permanently in thick brass. I made a rough calculation, and I estimated that his wives bore about their necks until death at least 800 lb. of brass; his daughters—he had six—120 lb.; his favourite female slaves about 200 lb. Add 6 lb. of brass wire to each wife and daughter for arm and leg ornaments, and one is astonished to discover that Chumbiri possesses a portable store of 1,396 lb. of brass."[2]

[1] Whereas among the Makololo tribe the *pelelé* was a special feminine adornment, the Livingstones saw it worn in men's lips on the banks of the Rovuma river, *The Zambesi and its Tributaries*, London, 1865, p. 116. This shows that the head of the Makololo was mistaken when he supposed that the *pelelé* was meant to serve in place of a moustache for women. Nor are rings passed through the nose by any means universally worn by women alone. "Thus, for instance, in certain parts of Upper Nigeria the inhabitants of both sexes—Sarakole, Bambara—often wear metal rings passed through the nose (Bérenger-Féraud, *op. cit.*, p. 384). Fondness for metal ornaments sometimes has unexpected results. In Africa, wealthy members of the pastoral tribe of *Herero* cover their legs with rings of bronze wire and "fashion demands that, as he walks, a man should lean from side to side, as though he found it an effort to lift his legs" (Elisée Reclus, *Nouvelle Géographie Universelle*, Vol. XIII, p. 664).

[2] *Through the Dark Continent*, London, 1899, Vol. II, p. 249. The enslavement of women is not without its influence on the growth of the population. Among the Makololo "the wealthy old men who have plenty of cattle, marry all the pretty young girls. . . . The young men of the tribe who happen to have no

Thus, feminine ornamentation developed and changed under the influence of certain "factors." It should be noted that, without exception, these "factors" arose, in part simply as the result of a given state of the productive forces of primitive society (one such "factor," for example, was the enslavement of woman by man), and in part as permanent features of human nature which acted in a given way thanks to the direct influence of "economics": such, for example, was the vanity which prompted men to display their own riches in the opulent attire of their women; and other psychological traits manifest themselves in other ways.

We need not prove that love of metal ornaments could arise only after men had begun to manufacture metals. It is also quite clear that it was the man's desire to boast of his wealth that led him to adorn himself or his wives and concubines with metal ornaments. This could be proved from a number of examples. Do not imagine, however, that there is no evidence of other motives prompting men to wear such ornaments. On the contrary it is highly probable that metal rings were first worn on the legs and arms, for example, from certain practical considerations; afterwards they began to be worn not only from practical considerations, but to boast of wealth as well, and *parallel with this* people's tastes gradually began to form, so that arms and legs came to *appear beautiful* when decorated with metal rings.

Here again, the utilitarian standpoint precedes the aesthetic standpoint.

You will perhaps ask what practical considerations led to wearing metal rings. I am not going to enumerate them all, but I will point out a few of them.

First of all, we already have seen the important role of rhythm

cattle must get on without a wife, or be content with one who has few personal attractions. This state of affairs probably leads to a good deal of immorality, and children are few." (David and Charles Livingstone, *op. cit.*, p. 284.) The German writer (Karl Marx.—TRANS.) who said that it is only for plants and animals that there is a law of population in the abstract, was right. (See *Capital*, Vol. I, English edn., Allen & Unwin, p. 698.—TRANS.) But we are forced to believe that even this correct view of his will, like so many others, be thrown overboard by the gentlemen who have set themselves the praiseworthy task of "revising" his teachings. This "revision" consists in abandoning his teachings, one after the other, and substituting the teachings of bourgeois economists. The gentlemen engaged on this "revision" are "making progress" backwards.

in primitive dances. The measured stamping of feet and clapping of hands provides a way of beating time for these dances. But primitive dancers demand something more. They often festoon themselves with whole garlands of rattles to achieve the same purpose. Sometimes, as in the case of the Caffres of the Basuto tribe, for example, such rattles are no more than little sacks made of dried skin and filled with pebbles.[1] But it is obvious that *metal* rattles are better. And iron rings worn on legs and arms can do good service as metal rattles. In fact, we find these same Basuto Caffres very ready to wear these rings for their dances.[2] But it is not only in dancing that the metal rings clank as they strike each other; they do so, too, when the wearer is walking. The women of the Niam-Niam tribe wear so many rings on their legs that, whenever they walk, clanking can be heard a long way off.[3] Such a noise facilitates walking by beating time, and this may be another reason promoting the use of rings: negro porters in Africa sometimes hang bells on their loads, and are encouraged by their constant, regular tinkling.[4] The measured clink of metal rings would undoubtedly have eased much of the work done by women—for instance, the grinding of grain in handmills.[5] This was probably also one of the original reasons why they were worn.

In the second place, the custom of wearing rings on legs and arms preceded the use of metal ornaments. Among the Hottentots these rings were made of ivory.[6] Other primitive tribes sometimes make them from hippopotamus skins. This custom is preserved to this day by the Dinka tribe, although, as our first letter intimated, this tribe, to use Schweinfurth's words, is now experiencing a real iron age. Originally such rings may

[1] *Les Bassoutos*, par E. Casalis, Paris, 1859, p. 158. "Among the Guiana Indians the coryphaei sometimes equip themselves with bamboo sticks that have been filled with pebbles. They beat these sticks on the ground and the noises thus produced control the movements of the dancers." O. A. Schomburg, *Reisen in Guiana und am Orinoko*, Leipzig, 1841, p. 108.

[2] Casalis, *ibid.*, p. 158. The glint of the rings is probably of significance here, throwing all the movements of the dancers into vivid relief.

[3] *L' Afrique Centrale, Expéditions . . .*, by Colonel C. Chaille-Long, Paris, 1882, p. 282.

[4] Burton, *op. cit.*, Vol. II, p. 312.

[5] Casalis, *op. cit.*, p. 150. I have already referred to this in my first letter, though in a different context.

[6] Ratzel, *Voelkerkunde*, Vol. I, p. 91.

have been worn with the practical aim of protecting the exposed extremities of the body from thorned plants.[1]

When the manufacture of metals had begun and had become firmly established, skin and bone rings were gradually replaced by metal ones. Since the latter became a sign of affluence, it is not surprising that rings made from skins and bones became less sought after as a form of adornment.[2] This less *sought after* adornment also came to seem less *beautiful*. The sight of it evoked less pleasure than the sight of metal rings, quite apart from any utilitarian considerations whatever. And so here also the practically *useful* preceded the aesthetically *pleasant*.

Finally, iron rings covering the extremities and particularly the arms of the warrior, protected him from injury in battle, and were therefore of use in this way too. In Africa the fighting men of the Bongo tribe cover both arms from the wrist to the elbow with iron rings. This decoration, called *danga-bor*, can be regarded as the rudiment of iron armour.[3]

And so we find that if certain metal products were gradually transformed from *useful* objects into objects whose appearance provided *aesthetic pleasure*, this was due to the effect of a great variety of "factors." Here, however, as indeed in all the cases I have examined, certain of these factors were themselves created by the development of the productive forces, while the others could take effect in the particular manner indicated, for the very reason that the productive forces of society were at a particular stage of development.

In 1885 the well-known expert, Inama-Sternegg, read a paper before the Vienna Anthropological Society on "the politico-economic ideas of primitive peoples" in which, amongst other things, he posed the following problem: "Do they (primitive peoples) like the objects they use as ornaments because (they) have a certain value or, on the contrary, do these objects acquire a

[1] Note that here it is not a question of rings worn on the fingers, but of arm and leg *bracelets*. I realise that "leg bracelet" is a truly barbaric expression, but for the moment I can find no other.

[2] Cf. Schweinfurth, *op. cit.*, Vol. I, pp. 150–1. Among the Wakonju tribe the wearing of rings made from palm bark on arms and legs is very widespread. But for the leading members of the tribe metal rings have already superseded those of palm, and are probably now considered more beautiful. (See Stanley, *In Darkest Africa*, Vol. II, p. 262.)

[3] See Schweinfurth's description of this, *op. cit.*, Vol. I, p. 271.

certain value only because they serve as ornaments?"[1] The speaker did not give a categorical answer to this question. And it would indeed be difficult to do so, because the question is quite wrongly posed. The first thing necessary is to define *what value* we are talking about: use value or exchange value. If we have use value in mind, it can be confidently asserted that objects used by primitive peoples as ornaments were first *accepted as useful* or as signifying *attributes of their owner useful to the tribe, and that only later did they come to be regarded as beautiful.* The use value preceded the *aesthetic* value. But once the objects in question have acquired a certain value in the eyes of primitive man, he will seek to obtain them for the sake of their aesthetic value alone, forgetting the origin of their value and in fact not thinking about it at all. When exchange between different tribes arises, ornaments become one of the chief objects of exchange and then the capacity of a given article to serve as an ornament sometimes (though not always) provides the sole psychological motive for its acquisition by the purchaser. As far as concerns *exchange* value, this, as we know, is an *historical category* that develops very slowly and of which primitive hunters—for perfectly understandable reasons—have only the vaguest conception. This is why the quantitative relationship of the objects exchanged against each other is, to begin with, for the most part accidental.

If the state of the productive forces of primitive peoples is the factor which determines the particular form of ornamention they practise, the character of the ornaments used by a tribe must, for its part, indicate the state of its productive forces.

And in fact this is so. Here is an example.

The Niam-Niam negroes like best of all ornaments made from the teeth of human beings or wild beasts. Lions' teeth are highly valued by them. But obviously, the demand for these teeth exceeds their supply and for this reason the Niam-Niam use imitation lions' teeth made of ivory. Schweinfurth says that the necklaces they make of them look extremely striking against their dark skin. But you will understand, Sir, that the main point here is not a contrast of colours but the fact that the pieces of ivory which stand out so beautifully against their dark skins actually depict *lions'* teeth. And so if any question arises as to the mode of life of the Niam-Niam negroes, you can reply quite confidently.

[1] *Mitteilungen der Anthropologischen Gesellschaft in Wien*, XV Band.

Without demurring or hesitating for a moment you will say that they live by hunting. And you will be right. The men of this tribe are for the most part hunters, nor do they deny themselves the pleasure of partaking of human flesh. Agriculture is not unknown to them either, but the women are left to look after this.[1]

But these same Niam-Niam, as we know, also wear metal ornaments. This is already a significant step forward in comparison with such hunters as the Australians or the Brazilian Bakairi, who have no metal ornaments. But what does this step forward in ornamentation imply? It implies an advance made in the first place by their productive forces.

Here is another example. A dandy of the Fans tribe will adorn his hair with feathers of the brightest hue, paint his teeth black (the principle of antithesis: contrasting himself with animals which always have white teeth), sling a leopard skin or the skin of some other beast of prey over his shoulder, and fasten a large knife at his belt. A smart woman of the same tribe will go about stark naked, but her arms, on the other hand, will be ornamented with copper bracelets and her hair done with a quantity of white beads.[2]

Is there any connection between such ornaments and the productive forces at the disposal of the Fans tribe? Not only is there a connection, but it is obvious at first sight. The masculine attire of this tribe is the typical *attire of the hunter*. The feminine adornment—the beads and bracelets—are not directly connected with hunting, but are obtained in exchange for one of the most valuable products of the hunt, in fact for ivory. The man does not allow the woman to adorn herself with hunting trophies, but in exchange for the products of his hunting he obtains ornaments for her, which have been made by tribes (or peoples) whose productive forces are at a higher level of development. And so it is this higher level of productive forces which determines the aesthetic tastes of his better half.[3]

A third example. The inhabitants of the northern part of the

[1] Cf. Schweinfurth, *op. cit.*, Vol. II, pp. 5, 7, 9, 15, 16.

[2] Cf. Du Chaillu, *Voyages et Aventures dans l' Afrique Equatoriale*, p. 163.

[3] Since the male in primitive society sets great store by the trophies of the hunt and of war, he often turns out to be more conservative in his get-up than the woman, who "has nothing to lose."

island of Ubwari, on Lake Tanganyika (in Africa), wear a kind of cloak made from the bark of trees, finished in such a way as to resemble the skin of the leopard. The metal bracelets used by all the neighbouring tribes are here worn only by the wives of rich men, while the poor make do with bracelets of bark. Finally, in place of the metal wires with which the neighbouring tribes support their coiffure, here they make do with *grasses*. How does all this connect with the productive forces of the inhabitants of the island of Ubwari? Why do they paint their cloaks to resemble leopard skins? Because, while there are no leopards on their island, the skins of these beasts are nevertheless considered the best adornment for a warrior. And so the peculiarities of geographical environment have led to a change in the material from which the cloaks are made, though it could not alter the aesthetic taste with which the finish of the material accords.[1] Other peculiarities of this same environment—the absence of metal on the island of Ubwari—have delayed the spread of metal ornaments among the inhabitants of the island, but could not prevent them developing a liking for them: even on the island the wives of rich men wear them. Developments which elsewhere occur more rapidly, here take place at a slower pace as a result of the peculiarities of the geographical environment, though in both cases the development of aesthetic tastes occurs alongside the development of productive forces, since in both cases the state of the latter serves as a reliable index of the state of the former.

I have already more than once remarked that technique and economy are not always, even in primitive hunting society, the *direct* determining factor in aesthetic taste. Not infrequently we find fairly numerous and diverse intermediate "factors" at work. But indirect causal connection does not cease to be causal connection. If in one case *A* directly gives rise to *C*, while in another it gives rise to it through the mediation of *B*, to which it gave rise in the first place, surely it does not follow from this that C does not owe its origin to A? If a given custom has arisen—

[1] A question not without interest is whether these tastes have been acquired from their ancestors who inhabited places where beasts of prey were to be found, or whether the inhabitants of Ubwari Island submitted in this matter to the influence of their neighbours who still engaged in hunting? I do not know which of these two suppositions is the more probable, but I do know that neither of them contradicts my argument.

shall we say, from superstition or vanity, or a desire to frighten the enemy—this circumstance still does not give a final answer to the question of the origin of the custom. We still have to ask whether the superstition which gave rise to it was in fact a superstition peculiar to the mode of life in question, for example, hunting life—and whether the means by which man satisfied his vanity or frightened his enemies did not depend on the state of the productive forces of the society and its economy?

But it is sufficient to ask ourselves this question for the irrefutable logic of the facts to compel us to answer it in the affirmative.

The decorations made by primitive man on his weapons, on his implements of labour and on . . .[1]

FROM A LECTURE "ON ART"

Excerpt from the Conspectus of a lecture entitled "On Art," one of two from a series delivered at Brussels, Liège and Paris in 1904

From the First Lecture (1st Edition)

DANCES

NOWADAYS nobody calls the young man who dances a waltz or mazurka to perfection a *great artist*. But in these times dancing as a whole is not of great significance. It is confined to facilitating the bringing together of young people of both sexes, a process which not infrequently has matrimonial consequences. Dances nowadays are for the most part an expression of *elegance*. Elegance is a pleasant characteristic, but it is not among those without which society could not exist. The primitive dancer does not reveal *elegance alone*. The Australians, for example, express in their dances absolutely all those characteristics which are of importance for society, both in men and in women.

Women's dances. The woman depicts how she climbs a tree to catch the opossum, how she dives to get shell-fish, how she tears up the roots of certain nutritive plants, or how she feeds her children or even (a satirical dance), how she quarrels with her husband. Straightforward love dances do exist, but of these later.

Men's Dances: the rowers' dance; the kangaroo dance; dance depicting the abduction of cattle from white men, and so on. As

[1] Here the manuscript breaks off.—RUSSIAN EDITORS.

the time arrives for the collection of fruits they dance; a successful hunt, and they dance. These are the so-called mimetic dances. Their connection with the mode of production does not need explanation: *it is clear, evident. Here the economic factor* strikes the eye. There are other dances, also in close evident connection with the Australians' mode of life: the imitation of *various beasts*. Here the connection with economics is also obvious. The man who imitates a beast knows its habits well, and the man who knows its habits well will be a good hunter.

Gymnastic Dances. Corroborees. These are intertribal dances at which sometimes up to four hundred participants are gathered. For example, they dance on the conclusion of peace, at night, by moonlight. Sometimes these gymnastic dances are performed when the time draws near for gathering fruits, after successful hunting and so on. The gymnastic dances are often performed by both sexes. The skilled warrior dances the best.

Finally, there are *incantational dances*. It is supposed that the spirit finds it pleasant to watch the dance. These dances have no direct relationship to economy. But, in the first place, we shall see that the spirit is often asked for purely material benefits. In the second place, what kind of dance is it that pleases the spirit? The same as pleases the Australian in general. Here, obviously, there is an indirect relationship to it.[1] But these dances are *rare*. Remark to Tolstoy. Here men's views as to what is good and what is bad are expressed in art, but, generally speaking, these views are *not religious*.[2]

Excerpt from the 2nd Edition of the Foregoing Lecture.

Dances

Dances are the most important art of the savage. Nowadays no one will call a superb dancer a great artist. But dancing is now a rudimentary art, in the same way as there are rudimentary organs. At present, for the most part, dances express *elegance*. But *elegance* is not of great significance for society *as a condition* of its existence. The Germans in fact manage to get along very well without it;

[1] i.e. to the economy.—RUSSIAN EDITORS.

[2] This idea, as a "remark to Tolstoy," is developed by Plekhanov in more detail in the second edition of this lecture.—RUSSIAN EDITORS.

lack of elegance did not prevent them from beating the elegant French. Savages, in their dances, *are far from expressing elegance alone.* In them they express *absolutely everything*, all the most important characteristics for society both in men and in women.

Women's Dances

A woman will depict how she climbs a tree to catch an opossum; how she collects shell-fish; how she grubs up the roots of certain nutritive plants; how she feeds her child; how she declares her love and even how she quarrels with her husband.

Men's Dances

The dance of the rowers; dance of the kangaroo hunters; dance depicting the theft of cattle from white men; dance celebrating the approach of the gathering of wild fruits; dance celebrating a successful hunt. There are other dances: the imitation of *various beasts.* All these dances reveal and develop those qualities of the savage without which he would be unable to exist. The connection of these dances with his economy is direct. Here art, in part only, reproduces the movements which man makes when engaged in economic activity; in part it cultivates the qualities of the hunter; the man who imitates a beast knows its habits well; the man who knows its habits will be a good *hunter.* These are the *mimetic dances.* Besides these, there are the so-called *gymnastic dances* (all our dances). Love dances. *Corroborees.* The best dancer is usually also the skilled warrior. There are, finally,

Incantational Dances

It is supposed that a spirit also likes seeing a good dance, just as the hunter does.

Indirect relationship to economy. But these dances are very rare.

Remark to Tolstoy

In the hunters' dances men's views as to what is good and what is bad find expression, but this is not religious consciousness. Later on all men's social views are coloured by religious consciousness. But this is only considerably later, when the priesthood becomes the ruling class. *This for a start, is the first correction to be made to Tolstoy's view.*

SIXTH LETTER

ART AND UTILITY (2)

HAVE you ever happened, Sir, to see a picture of the hair-combs used by the Indians of central Brazil, for example, or by the Papuans of New Guinea? These combs consist purely and simply of a few sticks fastened together. It is, so to speak, the first step in the development of the comb. The next step in its evolution is the practice of making it from a whole piece of wood in which teeth are cut. Combs of this kind are used, for example, by the Monbuttu Negroes and the Borotse Caffres. At this stage of development the comb is sometimes decorated with meticulous care. But most characteristic of its ornamentation are the mutually intersecting rows of parallel lines made on the wooden back, evidently depicting the fastenings formerly joining together the sticks of which the comb was made. The *decoration* is in this case an image of what formerly served a *utilitarian* purpose. The standpoint of *use* preceded that of *aesthetic pleasure*.

What we find here in the instance of the comb can be observed in a very large number of other cases. You are of course aware, Sir, that stone provided primitive man with the material for making his weapons and tools. You are also probably aware that originally stone axes had no *handles*. Pre-historic archaeology shows quite convincingly that the handle was a fairly complex and difficult invention for primitive man and that it makes its appearance at a comparatively late period of the quaternary era.[1] Originally the handle was joined to the axe by means of a more or less durable ligature. Later on this became unnecessary because men had learnt, even without such aids, to make a firm joint between axe and handle. Ligatures then ceased to be used, but on the spot they had formerly occupied a depiction of them appeared, consisting of mutually intersecting rows of parallel lines and acting as a decoration.[2] The same also occurred in the

[1] *Vide* G. de Mortillet, *Le Préhistorique*, Paris, 1883, p. 257.

[2] These decorations can be seen on Polynesian axes illustrated in Hjalmar Stolpe's book, *Entwicklungserscheinungen in der Ornamentik der Naturvoelker*, Vienna, 1892, pp. 29–30.

case of other tools, parts of which, originally bound together, were later on joined by other means. They were also ornamented with depictions of the ligatures that had formerly been necessary. It was in this way that those "*geometric*" designs arose, that are such an outstanding feature of primitive ornamentation and which can already be observed upon implements of the quaternary era.[1] The further development of productive forces gave a new impetus to the development of this type of design. A very important role was played here by the art of pottery. We know that *wicker-work* preceded this art. To this day the Australians do not know how to make clay vessels and are content with wicker ones. When clay articles were first made they were given the shape and appearance of the wicker vessels that had formerly been in general use, bearing on their outer surface rows of parallel lines, similar to those I have already mentioned in the case of combs. This decoration on clay vessels, which came into use at the very earliest stages of the potter's art, is very widespread to this day, even among civilised peoples. The art of weaving has also provided this art with a great many designs.

The fruits of certain plants, pumpkins for example, were also used as vessels by primitive man and still are to this day. For convenience in carrying, these vessels were bound round with strips of leather and plant fibres.

When men had learned to manufacture metals, curved lines, sometimes very intricate, began to appear on clay articles, together with the *straight* lines. In short, the development of ornamentation in this case was obviously most intimately connected with the development of primitive technique or, in other words, with the development of the productive forces.

Of course, the application of geometrical designs or of designs from textile ornamentation is not completely limited to clay vessels: they are also applied to articles of wood and even of hide.[2] Generally speaking, once they had arisen, they soon became very widespread.[3]

[1] G. de Mortillet, *op. cit.*, p. 415.

[2] See illustration of an Algerian bottle made of camel hide on p. xviii of the Preface by R. Allier to Christol's book, *Au Sud de l'Afrique*.

[3] The passage which follows at this point is crossed out: "I hasten to note, Sir, however, that by no means all 'geometrical' designs can be referred to the source I have indicated. Ehrenreich's and Von den Steinen's observations on the art of the Brazilian Indians show that here yet another 'factor' played no less important a role, if not a greater one—to wit, 'nature.' "—RUSSIAN EDITORS.

In his report to the Berlin Anthropological Society on the second expedition to the Xingu River, Ehrenreich says that in native ornamentation "all drawings representing geometric figures turn out in actual fact to be abbreviated, in part even directly stylised depictions of perfectly tangible, familiar objects, in the majority of cases animals."[1] Thus, an undulating line accompanied by dots on each side depicts a snake, a rhomboid figure with blackened corners a fish, while an equilateral triangle is a depiction, so to speak, of the national costume of the Brazilian Indian women, which, as is well-known, consists entirely of certain variations of the famous "fig-leaf."[2] It is the same in North America. Holmes has shown that the geometrical figures with which Indian pots in those parts are covered are depictions of animal integuments. The clay vessels from Senegambia, preserved in the Paris Maison des Missions are ornamented with depictions of snakes and it is very easy to observe the manner in which the drawings representing animal integuments can turn into geometrical figures.[3]

Finally, if you happen to have in your hand Hjalmar Stolpe's work, *Entwicklungserscheinungen in der Ornamentik der Naturvoelkern* (Vienna, 1892),[4] examine carefully pp. 37-44 and you will see a striking example of the gradual development of the purely geometrical figure from figures representing a man.[5]

[1] *Zeitschrift fuer Ethnologie*, Vol. XXII, p. 89.

[2] This variation of the fig-leaf is called *uluri*. Whenever Von den Steinen drew an isosceles triangle in the presence of Indians of the Bakairi tribe, they would laugh and exclaim: "Uluri!" Not without humour Von den Steinen remarks: "Nowadays, of course, there is no point in the geometry teacher deriving special inspiration from the uluri in order to be able to draw a triangle. Thus, the uluri is a kind of archaeopteryx in mathematics."—*Unter den Naturvoelkern Zentral-Brasiliens*, p. 270.

[3] *Vide* p. xxi of the preface by R. Allier, already quoted. Having pointed to the fact that the simplest ornamentation of the final period of the quaternary era consists of "straight lines," in various combinations, Mortillet remarks that "behind this extremely simple decoration run series of undulating lines and other products of fantasy" (*Le Préhistorique*, p. 415). After what I have said above it is permissible to doubt whether we have to do, in this instance, with the products of fantasy. The undulating lines of the quaternary era probably signified approximately the same as they do now with the Brazilian Indians.

[4] *Phenomena in the Development of Ornamentation among Primitive Peoples.*

[5] According to Stolpe: "Purely geometrical ornaments have originated from figures depicting men or animals. The plant world, however strange this may

Australian ornamentation, it may be said, has not been studied at all as yet. But in view of what we know about ornamentation among other peoples we are perfectly justified in supposing that the rows of lines that act as decorations on their shields also depict animal integuments.[1]

In certain instances, however, the lines decorating Australian weapons have a different significance: they act as *geographical maps.*[2] This may seem strange and even quite improbable, but I would remind you that the Siberian Yukagirs also draw maps of this kind.[3]

People who live by hunting, and those who lead a wandering life, stand in far more need of such maps than, say, our own peasant-farmers of the good old days, who sometimes never went beyond the boundaries of their *volost*[4] in the whole course of their lives. And necessity is the mother of invention. She taught the primitive hunter to sketch maps, and it was she who taught him other arts as well, arts which are also completely unknown to our own peasant farmer: *painting and sculpture.* Indeed, the primitive hunter almost always, in his own way, turns out to be a skilful and sometimes keen painter and sculptor. Von den Steinen says that the favourite evening amusement of the natives who accompanied him on his journeys was to draw various animals and scenes from hunting life in the sand.[5] The Australians, in this respect, are by no means inferior to the Brazilian Indians. They are fond of cutting drawings of various kinds into the kangaroo skins which they use to protect themselves from the cold, and in the bark of trees. Near Port Jackson, Philipp saw a number of figures depicting a weapon, shields, people, birds, fish, lizards, etc. All these figures were cut on rocks, and some of them bore witness to quite considerable skill on the part of the primitive artists.[6] On

seem, appears to have provided primitive peoples with considerably less material for stylisation" (p. 23).

We are already aware of the degree to which this truly remarkable phenomenon is connected with the development of the productive forces of primitive society.

[1] On this see Grosse, *Anfaenge der Kunst*, pp. 118–19.

[2] Grosse, *ibid.*, p. 120. [3] *Vide* V. I. Jochelson, *Po rekam Yasachnoi i Korkodonu.*

[4] Small administrative area consisting of several villages.—TRANS.

[5] *Op. cit.*, p. 249.

[6] Waitz-Gerland, *Anthropologie der Naturvoelker*, Part Six, Leipzig, 1872, p. 759.

the north-western shores of Australia Grey came across figures depicting human arms, legs and so on, carved on rocks and on trees. These figures were rather badly done. But at the sources of the Glenelg he found several caves, the walls of which were covered this time with drawings which were far more life-like.[1] Some research workers believe that these drawings were not done by the Australians, but by Malays who sometimes go there to trade. But in the first place it is difficult to find any clear arguments in support of this opinion.[2] And secondly it is of no importance at all, in this instance, for us to know who it was that did the Glenelg cave drawings. The only fact we need to be convinced of is that the Australians in general are fond of making drawings of this kind, even though they are perhaps more crude. And about this there can be no doubt whatsoever.

The same characteristic has been noted among the Bushmen. For a long time now they have been well-known for their painting and bas-reliefs. On some rocks not far from Hopstone, Fritsch saw literally thousands of figures depicting various animals. In the caves where the Bushmen live Hutchinson found a number of drawings on the walls. In the Transvaal, Huebner saw hundreds of figures cut in the soft slate schist.[3] Sometimes the Bushmen's drawings depict individual animals and sometimes whole scenes: hunting the hippopotamus or elephant, shooting with the bow and skirmishes with enemies.[4] The wall painting (fresco) found in one cave near Hermon and depicting the abduction of cattle by Bushmen from the Matabele Caffres, is particularly famous and deservedly so. So far as I know, nobody has expressed any doubt whatever as to the origin of this fresco: it is accepted by everyone as the work of none other than the Bushmen. To doubt this would indeed be strange, since all the dark-skinned neighbours of the Bushmen are very bad at painting. But the undoubted and universally accepted ability of the Bushmen is a fresh argument in favour of the assumption that the drawings found by Grey in the caves by the banks of the Glenelg are the work of Australian

[1] Waitz-Gerland, *Anthropologie der Naturvoelker*, Part Six, pp. 760, 761, 762. *Vide* Grosse, *Anfaenge der Kunst*, pp. 159 ff., reproduction of these drawings.

[2] For the arguments against it Grosse, *vide op. cit.*, pp. 162 ff.

[3] Grosse, *ibid.*, p. 173.

[4] *Vide* reproduction of these drawings in F. Christol's book, *Au Sud de l'Afrique*, pp. 143, 145, 147.

artists: after all, in cultural respects the Australians differ scarcely at all from the Bushmen.

A strong bent towards the plastic arts is also displayed by polar fishing and hunting peoples. The Eskimos and Chukchi decorate their weapons and their tools with figures of birds and beasts, outstanding for their fidelity to nature.[1] Not content with this, however, they sometimes depict whole scenes taken, of course, entirely from the sole mode of life known to them, that of hunting and fishing.[2] The sculptural works of the Eskimos are truly remarkable.[3] There are positively none that can equal them in this respect amongst tribes existing at the present time. Only the tribes which inhabited Western Europe towards the end of the quaternary era can be mentioned as worthy to be considered their rivals.

These tribes, who as yet knew neither cattle breeding nor agriculture, have left numerous monuments of their art in the form of engraved and sculptured articles. As in the case of the tribes existing at present, they borrowed the themes for their artistic activity almost exclusively from the animal world. Mortillet knows of only two instances where a plant was portrayed. Of the animals, they depicted for the most part mammals, and of the mammals most frequently the northern reindeer (which was then to be found throughout Western Europe) and the horse, at that time still not tamed; then come wild oxen, wild goats, steppe antelopes, chamois, reindeer, mammoth, wild boar, foxes, wolves, bears, lynxes, martens, rabbits and so on. In short, as Mortillet puts it, the whole of the mammalian fauna of that time is passed in parade before us . . .[4] naturally the question arises, in which of the following phases of its development, under what historical conditions and for what reasons, art first becomes idealistic. This question up till now has been very unsatisfactorily explained by science. I will return to it in one of my later letters.

I have said that necessity taught primitive man painting and sculpture. Let us see, though, what teaching methods she employed in doing so.

To communicate and exchange ideas, the North American

[1] *Vide* reproduction of this in Christol, *op. cit.*, pp. 152-3.

[2] Lubbock, *The Origins of Civilisation* (Paris, 1887, p. 38).

[3] See illustration of these in Grosse, *Anfaenge der Kunst*, pp. 180, 181, 182.

[4] A page is missing here.—Russian Editors.

Indians frequently and readily have recourse to picture-characters or, as Schoolcraft calls it, *picture writing*. The thoughts expressed in this way usually refer to hunting, war and various other aspects of their mode of life. And so they use picture writing[1] first and foremost for purely practical, *utilitarian* aims. Characters of this kind serve the same purpose in Australia, too. In the interior of the Australian mainland Austin found, on rocks near rivers, depictions of kangaroo legs and human arms, made with the obvious aim of showing that men and animals came to drink from this source.[2] The figures previously mentioned that were seen by Grey on the northern shores of Australia, depicting separate members of the human body (arms, legs, etc.), were probably also drawn for the purely utilitarian purpose of communicating some information to absent comrades. Von den Steinen relates how, in Brazil, he once found the drawing of a fish of a variety to be found in that region, made by the natives in the sand by the banks of a river. He ordered the Indians accompanying him to cast nets and they drew out several fish of the same variety as depicted on the sand.[3] It is clear that in drawing his picture the native wanted to bring to the notice of his comrades that a certain kind of fish was to be found at the spot indicated. But the need of the natives for this kind of picture-writing was not, of course, confined to this type of instance. It was frequently felt by them: they must have constantly had recourse to "picture writing," and for this reason their picture-characters must have arisen at an early stage from their hunting mode of life. "It seems to me that the rudiments of written and oral expression of thought and feeling may have had a simultaneous origin," rightly remarks V. I. Jochelson. "Even in the animal world we can see characters in embryo. Tracks lead the wolf to the reindeer. The latter, by his hoofs, communicates to the former the fact that he has passed that way as well as the direction in which he has gone. What animals wrote with their feet had great significance in primitive hunting life, and the track may have been the prototype of the

[1] The term used by Schoolcraft has been adhered to henceforward in translation of Plekhanov's *pis'mena-risunki* (character-drawings).—TRANS.

[2] Waitz-Gerland, *Anthropologie der Naturvoelker*, Vol. VI, p. 760. Depictions of human arms are met with in the artistic monuments of the quaternary era (Mortillet, *op. cit.*, pp. 365, 473–4). Here too these depictions were probably no more than picture-writing.

[3] *Unter den Naturvoelkern Zentral-Brasiliens*, p. 248.

character. The significance of 'tracks' has also been reflected in the language of a hunting tribe like the Yukagirs. In the Yukagir language each verb has three conjugations; one of these, which I have called the *manifest* (*ochevidny*) expresses an action, the completion of which is inferred by the tracks left. For example, if you have discovered from tracks in the forest that such and such a man has been there, in Russian you have to say: *po sledam vidno chto takoi-to byl v lesu* [from the tracks left I can see that such-and-such a man has been in the forest]. But in Yukagir you express this in one word distinguished from the usual form of the verb *byl* (has been) by the simple suffix *jäl*. And so we see that even the form of the language is dependent upon the 'track.' In this way the track was able to serve as a model for the use of conscious signs in intercourse with people at a distance. But these signs were at first the simple depiction of the object they expressed, of the concept, and the accuracy of the drawing was intimately connected with art."[1] Thus, in primitive hunting society writing was, at the same time, too, *pictorial art* and the hunting mode of life must naturally and of necessity have aroused, developed and supported the instincts and talents of the primitive artist.[2] And this is so in actual . . .[3]

. . . talent, he, of course, began to make use of it not merely in the direct struggle for existence alone. The Yukagirs also have recourse to characters for their declarations of love.[4] Luxuries of this kind, of course, still remain inaccessible to the majority of our peasants, but it is a simple and natural consequence of the hunting mode of life. Another equally simple and natural consequence of this life is primitive man's decoration of his weapons

[1] V. I. Jochelson, *ibid.*, pp. 33–4. *Vide* also pp. 34–5, where it can be seen how important such writing was for the Yukagirs when they were on the move: they had to know how to write under pain of failure in hunting.—G. V. Pleckhanov's note. The reference is to Jochelson's book, *Po rekam Yasachnoi i Korkodonu*, which he evidently quoted on the missing pages.—RUSSIAN EDITORS.

[2] Australian children who go to European schools usually display a great ability for drawing. Semon remarks that this is not in the least surprising: "For the adults, too, are expert at reading all marks left by game on the ground, in the grass and on trees, as evidence of their flight. But they are equally skilful, too, at making themselves mutually understood by means of pre-arranged [graphic] signs. . . . There are tribes which, in this respect, accomplish downright wonders." *Im Australischen Busche*, p. 242.

[3] A gap occurs in the manuscript here.

[4] Jochelson, *op. cit.*, p. 34.

and implements of work, and even of his own body,[1] with animal figures. Depictions of this kind lose their original form in so far as they become *stylised*, and often rejoice the heart of the idealist research worker by their apparently abstract character. The intimate connection between primitive ornamentation and the conditions of hunting life has only very recently been clarified, but this very form of ornamentation must now be numbered among the most convincing proofs in support of the materialist view of history.

As Von den Steinen so very aptly remarks, the original association which the art of drawing had in primitive society is clearly revealed in the German word, *zeichnen*. This word has obviously originated from the word *Zeichen*—a sign. Von den Steinen believes that *designation* for the purpose of communicating information is more ancient than *drawing*. I am in complete agreement with him, because—as you are already aware—I am, generally speaking, convinced that the relation to objects (and, of course, also to actions) from the standpoint of their use, was prior to any relation to them from the standpoint of aesthetic pleasure. Von den Steinen adds: In drawing, the pleasure derived from imitation —a conditioning factor of all further development—was in some degree also an operative factor from the very start.[2] In one of my later letters we shall see whether, in fact, "*all*" *further development* of the pictorial art was conditioned by pleasure derived from imitation in drawing. But it goes without saying that if such imitation afforded no pleasure at all pictorial art would never have emerged from the stage of *designation for the purpose of communicating information*. Pleasure, in this event, was quite definitely a necessary factor. The essential question is *why* the pleasure derived from imitation in drawing made itself so strongly felt among the European hunters of the quaternary era, among the Australians and Bushmen, the Eskimos and Yukagirs, and developed a strong inclination for pictorial art among all these peoples, and why this is so little evident, for example, among those

[1] In New Zealand tattooing is called *moko*, which means *lizard*, *snake* (Ratzel, *Voelkerkunde*, Vol. II, p. 137). It is clear that originally tattooing consisted in depicting these creatures. Their stylised depiction was probably what lay behind the "geometrical" figures with which the New Zealanders came to adorn themselves.

[2] Jochelson, *op. cit.*, p. 244.

African negroes who have long been engaged in agriculture? And this question can be satisfactorily answered only by pointing to the difference in character of the productive activity of hunting peoples on the one hand and agricultural peoples on the other.

We have already observed the great significance picture-writing has in the life of primitive hunters. The characters of this writing proved a condition for success in the struggle for existence. But once there, they were bound of necessity to give a definite direction to that tendency to imitation which is rooted in the quality of human nature, but in some way or another develops according to man's environmental conditions. As long as primitive man remains a hunter, his tendency to imitation, amongst other things, makes an artist and a sculptor of him. The reason for this is clear. What does he require *in order to be an artist*? He requires an ability to observe, and manual skill. It is these very same qualities that he needs *in order to be a hunter, too*. His artistic activity is consequently a manifestation of these same qualities which the struggle for existence elaborates in him. When, with the transition to cattle breeding and agriculture, a change occurs in the conditions of the struggle for existence, primitive man in a considerable degree loses the ability and inclination for pictorial art which distinguished him in his hunting period.

"Although agricultural and cattle-rearing peoples are at a considerably higher level than the hunter," says Grosse, "they are considerably inferior to them in the plastic arts, from which incidentally, it is evident that the relationship of art to culture is by no means so simple as certain philosophers think." And it is Grosse again who gives an admirable explanation of this—at first glance—strange artistic backwardness of pastoral and agricultural peoples. "Neither agricultural nor pastoral people," he says, "stand in need of such considerable development of their observational faculties or manual skill; for this reason these faculties of theirs recede into the background, and with them also the talent for faithfully depicting nature."[1] This could not be more fairly stated. We only need to remember that the transition to cattle-rearing and agriculture . . .[2]

[1] *Anfaenge der Kunst*, p. 190.

[2] Here the manuscript breaks off.—RUSSIAN EDITORS.

FRENCH DRAMATIC LITERATURE AND FRENCH EIGHTEENTH CENTURY PAINTING FROM THE SOCIOLOGICAL STANDPOINT

STUDY of the mode of life of primitive peoples is one of the best confirmations of the basic principle of historical materialism, that men's consciousness is determined by their being. Here, to confirm this, it is enough to recall the conclusion which Buecher reached in his brilliant study *Arbeit und Rhythmus*. He wrote:

> "I came to the conclusion that, at the first stage of development, labour, music and poetry were fused together, but that the basic element of the three was labour, while the other two were only of secondary importance."

Buecher states that the origin of poetry is to be sought in labour—"der Ursprung der Poesie ist in der Arbeit zu suchen." And no one familiar with the literature on this subject will accuse him of exaggeration.[1] Objections against his work by competent persons did not concern the essence, but only certain secondary peculiarities of his viewpoint. Fundamentally, Buecher was undoubtedly right.

But his conclusion applies only to the *origin* of poetry. What can be said of its *further development*? What is the situation as regards poetry, and art in general, at a higher level of social development? Is it possible, and at what levels, to observe the existence of causal ties between *being* and *consciousness*, between the technique and the economics of society, on the one hand, and its art on the other?

In seeking to answer this question, we shall, in the present article, base ourselves on the history of French eighteenth-century art. But the following reservation is necessary at the outset.

From the sociological point of view, the first characteristic of French eighteenth-century society is that it was divided into

[1] Moritz Hœrnes writes of primitive ornament that "it could only develop on the basis of industrial activities" and that peoples such as the Ceylon Veddas who are unfamiliar with industrial activities of any kind have no ornaments either (*Urgeschichte der bildenden Kunst in Europa*, Vienna, 1898, p. 38). This conclusion is similar to Buecher's, cited above.

classes. This circumstance could not fail to affect the development of art. Let us take the theatre as an example. In the middle ages, in France as in the whole of western Europe, farce, as it is called, occupied the predominant place in the theatre. Farces were written for the people and played before the people. They always served as an expression of the people's views, their aspirations and —what is important to note here—their dissatisfaction with the upper classes. But farce began to decline from the reign of Louis XIII, when it was classed as an entertainment appropriate only to lackeys and unworthy of people of refined taste: "*Éprouvés des gens sages*," as a French writer said in 1625. In place of farce, tragedy appeared. French tragedy, however, has nothing in common with the views, aspirations and sufferings of the masses of the people. It is the creation of the aristocracy and expresses the outlook, tastes and aspirations of the upper classes. We shall see presently how deep an imprint was left by its class origin on the entire character of French tragedy.

First, however, we would draw the reader's attention to the fact that at the time when tragedy arose in France, the aristocracy of that country did not engage in any productive work; it lived on the products created by the economic activities of the "third estate." It is easy to see that this fact could not fail to influence those works of art which originated in aristocratic circles and which expressed the tastes of those circles.

Consider an example taken from the life of the New Zealanders. Some of their songs are about the growing of sweet potatoes, and these songs are often accompanied by dances, in which are reproduced the movements made by the natives in cultivating these plants. Here may be clearly seen the influence of men's productive activities on their art; and it is no less clear that, since the upper classes do not engage in productive work, art arising in their midst cannot have any direct relation to the social productive process. Does this mean, however, that in a society divided into classes the causal dependence of men's consciousness on their being is weakened? No, it means nothing of the sort, since the division of society into classes is itself conditioned by society's economic development. And if the art created by the upper classes bears no direct relation to the productive process, this also, in the last analysis, is to be explained by economic causes. It becomes evident that here, too, the materialist explanation of history applies;

only in this case, it goes without saying that it is not so easy to discover the unquestionable causal ties between being and consciousness, between the social relations, which arise on the basis of "work," and art. For there are several intermediate links here between "work" on the one hand, and art on the other—and the fact that these often attract the entire attention of investigators renders more difficult a correct understanding of the phenomena.

Having made this necessary reservation, let us now turn to our subject, and deal first of all with tragedy.

> "French tragedy," says Taine in his *Philosophy of Art*, "appears at a time when the well-organised and noble monarchy of Louis XIV is establishing aristocratic elegance, magnificence, court life; it disappears as soon as the nobility and manners of the court fall beneath the blows of the revolution."

This is quite true. But the historical process of the rise, and particularly of the fall, of French classical tragedy was somewhat more complex than is represented by the famous theoretician of art. Let us examine this type of literary production from the point of view of its form and its content.

From the point of view of form, our attention is drawn first of all to the famous *Three Unities*,[1] which later caused so much argument in the period memorable in the annals of French literature, of the struggle between the romantic and the classical schools. The theory of the "unities" had been known in France as far back as the Renaissance, but it only became a law of literature, an undisputed rule of "good taste" in the seventeenth century. "When Corneille[2] wrote his *Mélite* in 1629," writes Lanson, "he knew nothing as yet of the three unities."[3]

It was Mairet who, around 1630, became the propagandist of the three unities. In 1634 his tragedy *Sophonisbe* was staged—the first tragedy written according to the "rules." It aroused con-

[1] *The Three Unities*: a conception borrowed from ancient Greek drama, meaning unity of time, place and action. Unity of time demanded that the events represented in the drama must be confined within a single day; unity of place demanded that the characters must not travel a greater distance than was possible within the time allowed; unity of action demanded the close knitting together of the plot, with no extraneous scenes.—TRANS.

[2] *Pierre Corneille*, 1606–1684: One of the masters of classical French tragedy. His plays include *Le Cid, Horace, Cinna*.—TRANS.

[3] *Histoire de la littérature française*, p. 415. [In the original, Plekhanov wrote *Médée*—to which the remark of Lanson also applies: but the tragedy of *Médée* appeared in 1635. *Mélite* is a comedy.—TRANS.]

troversy in which the enemies of the "rules" advanced arguments which recall, in many respects, the later reasoning of the romantics. The learned admirers of ancient literature ("les érudits") hastened to the defence of the three unities, and won a decisive and lasting victory. To what did they owe their victory, however? Not, certainly, to their "erudition," which interested the public very little; but rather to the growing fastidiousness of the upper class, for whom the naïve theatrical incongruities of the previous epoch were becoming unbearable.

> "Behind the unities lay an idea which was bound to appeal to persons of good breeding" Lanson continues, "the idea of an accurate imitation of reality, capable of evoking the appropriate illusion. The real significance of the unities was that they represented the minimum of convention. . . . Thus the triumph of the unities was in fact the victory of realism over imagination."[1]

In this way what really triumphed was the refinement of aristocratic taste, which developed step by step with the strengthening of the "noble and benevolent monarchy." Later developments of stage technique would have made the accurate imitation of reality possible without observing the unities. But the idea of the unities had meanwhile become associated in the minds of theatre-goers with a whole number of other cherished conceptions; and for this reason it acquired an independent value, as it were, based on what were allegedly the indisputable demands of good taste. Subsequently the rule of the three unities was reinforced, as we shall see below, by other social factors, and for this reason the theory was defended even by those who hated the aristocracy. The battle against the unities became a very hard one: the romantics had to display much ingenuity, steadfastness and an almost revolutionary energy to overthrow them.

With regard to stage technique, there is a further point to be noted.

The aristocratic origin of French tragedy left its imprint, among other things, on the technique of the actor as well. Everyone knows, for example, that French acting technique is distinguished even up to the present time by a certain artificial and even stilted manner, which creates a rather unpleasant impression on the spectator unused to it. No one who has seen Sarah Bernhardt will dispute this. This style of acting was inherited from the time when

[1] *Op. cit.*, p. 416.

classical tragedy dominated the French stage. The aristocratic society of the seventeenth and eighteenth centuries would have been very displeased if tragic actors had conceived the idea of playing their parts with the simplicity and naturalness with which an Eleanora Duse, for example, charms us today. Simple and natural acting was in direct contradiction to all the requirements of aristocratic aesthetics.

"The French do not rely on costume alone to give the actors and the tragedy the nobility and dignity they demand," writes the Abbé Dubos with pride. "We also like our actors to speak in a tone of voice louder, more grave and more sustained than that of everyday speech." This way of speaking is more difficult, but it has greater dignity. Gesture must correspond to tone, Dubos continues, because "we require our tragic actors to assume an air of greatness and superiority in all they do."

But why were actors expected to show greatness and superiority? Because tragedy was the offspring of the court aristocracy and the main characters in the tragedy were kings, "heroes" and, generally speaking, "highly placed" persons whose rank made it necessary for them to seem, if not to be, "great" and "superior." A dramatist whose works lacked the necessary conventional dose of aristocratic "superiority" would never have won the applause of the audience of the day, however great his talent.

This can be best seen from the opinions on Shakespeare expressed at that time in France, and, under French influence, in England too.

Hume found that Shakespeare's genius should not be over-rated. Deformed bodies often appear bigger than they really are. Shakespeare was good for his time, but he was not good enough for a refined audience. Pope expressed regret that Shakespeare wrote for the people and not for "society."

> "Shakespeare would have written better," he said, "if he had enjoyed the patronage of his sovereign and of the court."

Voltaire himself, who in his literary work was the mouthpiece of the new age that was hostile to the "old order," and who gave many of his tragedies a "philosophical" content, paid a tremendous tribute to the aesthetic conceptions of aristocratic society. He considered Shakespeare a genius, but a crude barbarian nevertheless. His opinion of *Hamlet* is highly symptomatic.

"This play," he wrote, "is full of anachronisms and absurdities. Ophelia's burial takes place on the stage, such a monstrous spectacle that the famous Garrick cut the graveyard scene. . . . The play abounds in vulgarities. The watch says in the opening scene, for example, 'not a mouse stirring.' Can one imagine such an incongruity? A soldier may undoubtedly talk like this in the guard-room, but not on the stage, before the first people of the land—personages who speak a noble language, and in whose presence one should express oneself no less nobly. . . . Picture to yourselves, gentlemen, Louis XIV in his Hall of Mirrors at Versailles, surrounded by a brilliant court—and then picture a clown, clad in rags and tatters, pushing his way among the heroes, great men and beauties who make up this court. He suggests that they abandon Corneille, Racine and Molière for a mountebank, who has flashes of talent, but who pulls faces. How do you think this proposal would be received?"

These words of Voltaire's reveal not only the aristocratic source of French classical tragedy, but also the reason for its decline.[1]

Refinement easily turns to affectation, and affectation excludes any serious and penetrating treatment of a theme. And not only its treatment. The range of choice of subjects was bound inevitably to become restricted under the influence of the class prejudices of the aristocracy. Its class conception of what was "correct" clipped the wings of art. In this connection, the demands made of tragedy by Marmontel were extremely characteristic and instructive.

"A nation which is both peaceful and well-bred," he wrote, "in which everyone considers himself obliged to adapt his ideas and feelings to the customs and morals of society, a nation in which the proprieties are law, can only admit characters softened by deference for those around them, and vices which are softened by propriety."

Society manners became the criterion by which works of art were judged. This was sufficient to bring about the decline of classical tragedy. But it does not sufficiently explain the appearance on the French stage of a new kind of dramatic work. Nevertheless, about 1730–40 there did appear a new literary genre—the so-called "*comédie larmoyante*" (sentimental comedy), which for some time enjoyed considerable popularity. If consciousness is to be explained by being, if the so-called spiritual development of mankind is causally dependent on its economic development, then

[1] We may note in passing that it was precisely this aspect of Voltaire's views that repelled Lessing, who was the consistent ideologist of the German burghers, and this is very clearly brought out by F. Mehring in his book *Die Lessingslegende.*

eighteenth century economics should explain for us, among other things, the appearance of the "sentimental comedy." Can it do so?

It not only can, but it has in part already done so—though, it is true, without recourse to any rigorous method. Let us take Hettner, for example, who, in his history of French literature, considers the "sentimental comedy" as a consequence of the growth of the French bourgeoisie. But the growth of the bourgeoisie, as of any other class, can only be explained by the economic development of society. And so, without suspecting or desiring it, Hettner, who is a great enemy of materialism (about which, it may be said in passing, he has the crudest notions) arrives at a materialist explanation of history. And it is not only Hettner who does this. Brunetière, in his book, *Les époques du théatre français*, reveals even better than Hettner the causal dependence which we are seeking.

He writes:

> From the failure of Law's bank onwards—to go no further back—the aristocracy loses ground every day. Everything a class can do to discredit itself, it hastens to do. . . . But above all, it ruins itself while the bourgeoisie, the third estate, enriches itself in proportion, grows in importance and acquires a new consciousness of its rights. Existing inequalities appear ever more abominable, abuses more insupportable. Hearts are 'great with hatred,' as a poet has since expressed it, and 'athirst for justice.' . . . Is it possible that, with such a means of propaganda and action as the theatre at its disposal, the bourgeoisie should not use it? That it should not take as matter for serious treatment, almost for tragedy, those inequalities which only amused the author of *Le bourgeois gentilhomme* and *Georges Dandin*? And above all, could this already triumphant bourgeoisie reconcile itself to the constant portrayal on the stage of emperors and kings, or refrain from spending some of its savings, if one may so express onself, on having its own portrait painted?

Thus the "sentimental comedy" was a portrait of the French bourgeoisie of the eighteenth century. That is quite true. It is, therefore, not surprising that it is also known as bourgeois drama. But Brunetière's opinion, correct as it is, is nevertheless too general and, therefore, too abstract. Let us try to develop the point in somewhat greater detail.

Brunetière writes that the bourgeoisie could not reconcile itself to the constant portrayal only of emperors and kings on the stage.

In the light of the explanations he gives in the excerpts we have quoted this is very probable—but so far only probable. And it will only become indubitable when we have familiarised ourselves with the psychology of at least some of the people who played an active part in the literary life of France at that time. One of these was, undoubtedly, the talented Beaumarchais,[1] the author of several "sentimental comedies." What did Beaumarchais think of the constant portrayal of nothing but emperors and kings?

He was resolutely and passionately opposed to it. He caustically derided the literary custom which made kings and the mighty of this world the heroes of tragedy, while comedy lampooned only people of lower degree.

> Depict middle-class folk in misfortune! *Fi donc!* They should always be laughed at. Comic citizens and a tragic king: that is the entire scope of the theatre. I will take note of that.[2]

This caustic outburst by one of the outstanding ideologists of the third estate seems to confirm the psychological conclusions of Brunetière cited above. But Beaumarchais did not only want to depict middle-class people in "misfortune." He also protested against the convention of choosing the leading characters in "serious" dramatic works from amongst the heroes of the ancient world.

> "What have revolutions in Athens and Rome," he asks, "to do with me—a peaceful subject of an eighteenth century monarchic state? What interest have I got in the death of some Peloponnesian tyrant or the sacrifice of some princess in Aulis? All this is no concern of mine and nothing of the slightest importance to me emerges from it."[3]

The choice of heroes from the ancient world was one of the extremely numerous manifestations of that fascination with the ancient world, which was itself an ideological reflection of the struggle of the new social order, in process of being born, against *feudalism*. This fascination with ancient civilisation was carried over from the Renaissance to the epoch of Louis XIV, whose age, it will be remembered, was readily compared with that of Augustus.

But when the bourgeoisie began to be imbued with opposition sentiments, when "hatred, together with a thirst for justice," was

[1] *Pierre Beaumarchais*, 1732–1799: leading French playwright, satirist of the manners of his day, outstanding in the literary struggles preceding the French bourgeois revolution of 1789.—TRANS.

[2] *Lettre sur la critique du Barbier de Séville.*

[3] *Eugénie, avec un essai sur le genre dramatique sérieux, Oeuvres* I, p. 11.

born in its heart, the fascination with the heroes of antiquity, which had been fully shared by its former representatives, began to appear out of place—and the "events" of ancient history to seem insufficiently instructive. The hero of bourgeois drama became the contemporary "man of middle estate," more or less idealised by the bourgeois ideologists of the day. This characteristic circumstance, of course, could not injure the "portrait" that Brunetière speaks of.

But to continue. The real creator of bourgeois drama in France was Nivelle de la Chaussée. What do we find in his numerous works? Revolt against every aspect of aristocratic psychology, a struggle against the prejudices—or, if you prefer it, the vices—of the nobility. What his contemporaries valued above all in his works was the moral instruction they contained.[1] And from this angle, too, the "sentimental comedy" was true to its origins.

We know that the ideologists of the French bourgeoisie were not very original in their attempts to "portray" this class in their dramatic works. They did not create bourgeois drama—they simply transferred it from England to France. In England this type of dramatic work had arisen at the end of the seventeenth century as a reaction against the terrifying depravity which then held sway on the stage and which reflected the moral decline of the English aristocracy of the day. In its fight against the aristocracy, the bourgeoisie wanted to make comedy "worthy of Christians," and began to preach in it its own morality.

The French literary innovators of the eighteenth century who, by and large, borrowed from English literature everything that was appropriate to the position and the feelings of the French bourgeoisie in opposition, transferred bodily into France this aspect of the English "sentimental comedy." French bourgeois drama is no less successful than the English in preaching the virtues of bourgeois family life. Therein lay one of the secrets of its success, and therein, too, lies the key to what at first sight appears utterly incomprehensible—the fact that French bourgeois drama, which about the middle of the eighteenth century seems to be a firmly established literary form, fairly rapidly recedes into the

[1] d'Alembert writes of Nivelle de la Chaussée: "Both in his literary work and in his private life he held to the rule that that man is wise whose desires and aspirations are in keeping with his means." This is an apologia for equilibrium, moderation and correctness.

background in the face of classical tragedy, instead, as one might have expected, of the other way about. We shall see in a moment how this strange fact is to be explained. But before doing so, it will be as well to add one thing more.

Diderot[1] who, by nature a passionate innovator, could not fail to be carried away by bourgeois drama, and who, as we know, himself tried his hand at the new literary form (his *Le fils naturel* of 1757 and *Le Père de famille* of 1758 come to mind), wished to see on the stage, not character, but situations, and, more precisely, social situations. To this the objection was made that the social situation is not in itself enough to determine personality. "What is a judge in himself?" he was asked (*le juge en soi*). "What is a merchant in himself?" (*le négociant en soi*). Herein lay a great misunderstanding, however. For Diderot did not have in mind the judge or merchant "in himself," but rather the merchant and, particularly, the judge *of that day*. And that celebrated comedy, *Le mariage de Figaro*, proved that the judges of the day contributed a good deal of instructive material for very lively theatrical presentation. Diderot's demand was only a literary reflection of the revolutionary aspirations of the French "middle estate" of the day.

But it was precisely the revolutionary character of these aspirations that prevented French bourgeois drama from finally ousting classical tragedy.

Child of the aristocracy, classical tragedy held unchallenged and undivided sway on the French stage as long as the aristocracy held undivided and unchallenged sway, limited only by the existence of the absolute monarchy, which in its turn was the historical result of a fierce and prolonged class struggle in France. When the rule of the aristocracy began to be questioned, and when the "middle estate" was seized by a mood of opposition, the old literary conceptions began to appear unsatisfactory to them, and the old theatre insufficiently "instructive." At this point bourgeois drama appeared, side by side with classical tragedy which was declining rapidly. In bourgeois drama the French "man of middle estate" contrasted his own domestic virtues with the profound depravity of the aristocracy. Nevertheless, the social contradiction which the France of that day had to solve was

[1] *Denis Diderot*, 1713–84: French materialist philosopher, Encyclopædist and leading bourgeois realist writer.—TRANS.

insoluble merely by preaching morality. The question at issue was not the elimination of aristocratic vices, but the elimination of the aristocracy itself. It is obvious that this could not be done without a bitter struggle, and it is no less understandable that the father of the family (*le père de famille*), despite all the undoubted respectability of his bourgeois morality, could not serve as an example of a tireless and dauntless fighter. The literary "portrait" of the bourgeois did not inspire heroism. Yet the enemies of the old order felt the need of heroism, and recognised the need to develop the *civic* virtues among the third estate. Where at that time could they find examples of such virtues? In the same place where examples of literary taste had formerly been sought—in the ancient world.

And so, once again, the passion for ancient heroes appeared. The enemy of the aristocrat now no longer says, as did Beaumarchais:

> What interest, can I, as a citizen of an eighteenth-century monarchic state, have in revolutions in Athens or Rome?

Athenian and Roman "revolutions" once again began to arouse the liveliest interest in the public. But the interest in them was of a totally different character.

If the young ideologists of the bourgeoisie were now interested in the "sacrifice of the young princess of Aulis," it was because she served, primarily, as material for the unmasking of "superstition." And if their attention could be attracted by the "death of some Peloponnesian tyrant," this was not so much from the psychological as from the political angle. People became interested in the republican heroes of Plutarch, rather than in the imperial epoch of Augustus. Plutarch became the daily reading of the young ideologists of the bourgeoisie, as Mme. Roland's memoirs show. And this passion for republican heroes once again aroused interest in the whole of life in the ancient world. Imitation of antiquity became the fashion and made a deep imprint on the entire French art of the day. Below we shall see what a considerable mark it made on the history of French painting. For the present let us note that it also weakened the interest in bourgeois drama, because of the common-place bourgeois life which the latter portrayed, and put off for a long time the death of classical tragedy.

Historians of French literature have often asked themselves with surprise how to explain the fact that those who prepared and carried out the great French Revolution remained conservative in their literary tastes. And why did the rule of classicism come to an end only a fairly long time after the collapse of the old order? As a matter of fact, the literary conservatism of the innovators of the day was only on the surface. Even if the form of tragedy did not change, its content was changed fundamentally.

Let us take Saurin's tragedy *Spartacus*, which appeared in 1760. Its hero, Spartacus, breathes only the love of liberty. Because of his great ideal he even refuses to marry his beloved, and throughout the play he never ceases to speak of liberty and of love for humanity. A literary conservative would have been the very last either to write such plays or to applaud them. An entirely new, revolutionary, content had been poured into the old literary bottles.

Tragedies like those of Saurin or Lemierre (see his *Guillaume Tell*) embodied one of the most revolutionary demands of Diderot the literary innovator. They took as their theme, not the characters but the social situations and, in particular, the revolutionary social aspirations of the period. And if this new wine was being poured into old bottles, this was because these old bottles had been bequeathed by that same antiquity, universal attraction to which was one of the most outstanding and characteristic symptoms of the new social temper. Beside this new variety of classical tragedy, the bourgeois drama—"morality in action," as Beaumarchais expressed it in what he intended to be praise—seemed, indeed, and could not but seem too colourless, too flat, too conservative in its content.

Bourgeois drama was born of the *opposition* temper of the French bourgeoisie and was no longer of any use in expressing its *revolutionary* aspirations. The literary "portrait" had well reproduced the temporary and ephemeral characteristics of its original: and for this reason, people ceased to care for it when the original had lost those characteristics, and when they had ceased to please. That is the whole point.

Classical tragedy continued to flourish right up to the time when the French bourgeoisie finally triumphed over the defenders of the old order, and when interest in the republican heroes of antiquity lost all social significance for it.[1] And when this time came, bourgeois drama was reborn, and, after undergoing some changes which were appropriate to the peculiar features of the new social situation, but which were by no means fundamental, it became firmly established on the French stage.

Even those who refuse to recognise the close kinship of romantic drama and the bourgeois drama of the nineteenth century, cannot deny that the plays of Alexandre Dumas *fils*, for example, are true nineteenth century bourgeois drama.

Social psychology is expressed in the works of art and literary tastes of a given period; and in the psychology of a class-divided society, much will remain incomprehensible or paradoxical if we continue to ignore the relations between classes and the class struggle, as is being done at the present time by idealist historians, contrary to the best traditions of bourgeois historical science itself.

But we shall now leave the stage and turn our attention to another branch of French art, namely to painting.

Under social influences with which we are already familiar, development here follows parallel lines to those already noted in dramatic literature. This had already been noticed by Hettner, who was quite right when he said that Diderot's "sentimental comedy" was nothing but genre painting transferred to the stage.

In the epoch of Louis XIV, that is, in the heyday of the absolute monarchy, French painting had a good deal in common with classical tragedy. Both were dominated by the idea of "dignity," of "the sublime." And painting, like classical tragedy, chose its heroes from along the mighty of this world. Charles Lebrun, whose word was then law in all matters of taste affecting painting, recognised virtually only one hero—Louis XIV, whom, however, he clothed in classical costume.

His famous "Battles of Alexander," which may be seen today in the Louvre, and are well worth studying, were painted after the Flanders military campaign of 1667, which spread far and

[1] "The ghost of Lycurgus, although he never thought of such a thing, guards the Three Unities," wrote Petit de Julleville *Le théatre en France*, p. 334. This could not have been better expressed. But on the eve of the Great Revolution the ideologists of the bourgeoisie did not see anything conservative about this "ghost." On the contrary, they saw in it only revolutionary civic virtue. This must not be forgotten. (Lycurgus was the famous law-giver of Sparta.—TRANS.)

wide the fame of the French monarchy.[1] The paintings were wholly devoted to glorifying the "Roi Soleil." And they so well corresponded to the feelings of Frenchmen at that time, to their striving towards "greatness," towards glory and victories, that they inevitably made a decisive impression on the social consciousness of the ruling class. Lebrun, perhaps without realising it, responded to the need to speak grandiloquently, to dazzle the eye, to make the brilliance of grand artistic conception be in keeping with the splendour which surrounded the king, writes Genevay. The France of the time was epitomised in the person of its king. It was Louis XIV who was applauded in the image of Alexander.[2]

To give some idea of the profound impression produced by Lebrun's paintings, it is enough to quote Etienne Carneau's exclamation: "Lebrun, with how pure a light dost thou shine!"

But everything moves, everything changes: the summit once reached, the path leads downhill. For the French monarchy the way down had already begun during the lifetime of Louis XIV, and subsequently continued unceasingly right up to the Revolution. The "Sun King" who had declared "I am the State," was nevertheless concerned in his own way for the greatness of France. Louis XV, without renouncing any of the pretensions of absolutism, was interested only in his own pleasures. And the great majority of the aristocratic court which surrounded him were of like mind. His period was a time of insatiable pursuit after pleasure, a period of gay dissipation. Yet, however dirty the diversions to which, at times, aristocratic idlers sank, the tastes of the society of the day were nevertheless distinguished for their undeniable elegance and delicate refinement, which made France "the lawgiver of fashion." And these elegant and refined tastes found expression in the aesthetic concepts of the day.

> When the age of Louis XV succeeded that of Louis XIV, the ideal of art remained artificial and conventional; but it descended from one of majesty to one of pleasure. There spread everywhere a refinement of elegance, a subtlety of sensual pleasure.[3]

[1] The siege of Tournai was successful after two days; the sieges of Furnes, Courtrai, Douai, Armentières were also all of short duration. Lille was captured in nine days, and so on.

[2] See Antoine Genevay, *Charles Lebrun* (Paris, 1886), p. 220.

[3] Goncourt, *L'art au XVIII siècle*, pp. 135–6.

And this artistic ideal was realised at its best and most vivid in the paintings of Boucher.

"Pleasure of the senses," we read in Goncourt, "was Boucher's ideal, the soul of his art. . . . The Venus of whom he dreamed and whom he depicts is wholly a physical Venus."[1]

That is absolutely true, and it was well understood by Boucher's contemporaries. In 1740 his friend Piron, in one of his poems, represented the famous painter as saying to Madame de Pompadour:

> Je ne recherche, pour tout dire,
> Qu' élégance, grâces, beauté,
> Douceur, gentillesse et gaité,
> En un mot, ce qui respire
> Ou badinage, ou volupté;
> Le tout sans trop de liberté,
> Drapé du voile que désire
> La scrupuleuse honneteté.[2]

This was a superb characterisation of Boucher—his muse was the elegant sensuality in which all his paintings are steeped. There are a number of his paintings in the Louvre,[3] and anyone who wants to form an idea of how great a distance separates the aristocratic-monarchic France of Louis XV from the similar France of Louis XIV cannot do better than compare the paintings of Boucher with those of Lebrun. Such a comparison will be more instructive than whole volumes of abstract historical commentaries.

The success of Boucher's painting was as great as Lebrun's had been in the earlier period. His influence was truly immense. It was justly said that the young French painters of the day who went to Rome to finish their artistic education, left France with their minds full of his paintings, and brought back with them, not impressions received from the great masters of the Renaissance, but only their memories of Boucher. But his supremacy and influence were not lasting. Under the influence of the emancipation movement of the French bourgeoisie, the advanced criticism of the day adopted a negative attitude towards him.

[1] Goncourt, *L'art au XVIII siècle*, p. 145.

[2] I seek, after all, only for elegance, grace, beauty, sweetness, charm and gaiety; in a word, for whatever breathes either badinage or pleasure; all without too much license, veiled as scrupulous chastity would desire.

[3] And also in the National Gallery, London.—TRANS.

Already in 1753, Grimm was severely criticising him in his *Correspondance Litteraire*. "There is little masculine strength in Boucher," he writes. And, in point of fact, the male sex is represented in Boucher's paintings mainly by cupids, who obviously bore not the slightest relation to the aspirations for liberty of that epoch. Diderot in his *Salons* attacked Boucher even more sharply than Grimm.

"Degradation of taste, colour and composition, of characters, conception and drawing," wrote Diderot in 1765, "accompanied in him the corruption of morals step by step." In Diderot's opinion, Boucher ceased to be an artist, "and it was precisely at this moment that he was appointed painter to the King." But it is Boucher's cupids, mentioned above, that particularly aroused Diderot's wrath. The impassioned Encyclopædist rather unexpectedly remarks that there is not a single child among all this crowd of cupids who would be of any use whatsoever in real life—"to learn his lessons, read, write or crush hemp." This reproach, which in some ways recalls our own Pisarev's criticisms of Pushkin's *Evgeny Onegin*, makes many present-day French critics shrug their shoulders contemptuously. They say that "crushing hemp" is not the job of cupids, and they are right. What they fail to see, is that Diderot's naïve indignation with these "debauched little satyrs" expressed the class hatred of the then industrious bourgeoisie for the frivolous delights of the aristocratic idlers.

Nor was Diderot any more pleased with what was undoubtedly Boucher's strength, his femininity. "Was there not a time when he had a passion for painting young maidens?" he says. "What sort of girls were they? Pretty little sluts."

These elegant demi-mondaines were beautiful enough in their way. But their beauty only revolted, instead of attracting, the ideologists of the third estate. It was admired only by the aristocracy and those members of the third estate who, under the influence of aristocrats, had acquired aristocratic tastes.

"The painter for you and me," writes Diderot, addressing the reader, "is Greuze. Greuze was the first to make art moral." This praise is as characteristic of Diderot's state of mind—and, at the same time, of the state of mind of all the thinking bourgeois of the day—as the angry reproaches addressed by him to the hateful Boucher.

As a matter of fact Greuze was indeed a moral painter in the highest degree. If the bourgeois plays of Nivelle de la Chaussée, Beaumarchais and others were "moralities in action," Greuze's paintings may be called "moralities on canvas." The "father of the family" holds the place of honour in his work; he stands in the foreground; he is to be found in the most varied, but always touching, situations; and is distinguished by the same respected domestic virtues which adorn him in bourgeois drama. But while this patriarch undoubtedly deserves all due respect, he is entirely devoid of political interest. He stands, "a reproach incarnate," before the dissolute and degenerate aristocracy—and his "reproach" goes no further. This is not in the least surprising, since the painter who created him also confines himself to "reproach." Greuze is far from being a revolutionary. He is striving, not for the abolition of the old order but only for its improvement in a spirit of morality. For him the French clergy were "the guardians of religion and morality, the spiritual fathers of every citizen."[1]

Nevertheless, the spirit of revolutionary dissatisfaction was already penetrating into French artistic circles. In the 1750's a pupil who had refused to observe fast days was expelled from the French Academy of Fine Arts in Rome. In 1767, another pupil of the same academy, the architect Adrien Mouton, suffered the same punishment for the same misdemeanour. The sculptor Claude Monot, who took Mouton's part, was also expelled from the institution. Public opinion in Paris decisively supported Mouton, who instituted legal proceedings against the Director of the Rome Academy; the court of the Chatelet found the latter guilty, and ordered him to pay Mouton 20,000 *livres* damages. The social atmosphere became more and more heated and, as the revolutionary mood took hold of the third estate, interest in genre painting—sentimental comedy painted in oils—faded away. Changes in the mood of the advanced people of the day led to a change in their aesthetic tastes—just as it led to a change in literary conceptions—and genre painting in the manner of Greuze, which had so recently called forth general enthusiasm,[2] was eclipsed by the revolutionary painting of David and his school.

[1] See his "Lettre à Messieurs les curés" in the *Journal de Paris* of December 5, 1786.

[2] Such enthusiasm was evoked, for example, in 1735 by his painting, shown at the Salon, *Le Père de famille* and in 1761 by his *L'accordée du village*.

Afterwards, when David was a member of the Convention, he said, in a speech to that assembly:

> There was not a form of art but served the tastes and whims of a handful of sybarites with pockets stuffed with gold. The corporations (David's name for the Academies) persecuted men of genius and, in fact, all who came to them with pure ideas of morality and philosophy.

In David's opinion art should serve the people of the Republic. But this same David was a determined partisan of classicism. More than that: by his own artistic activities he brought declining classicism to life again, and prolonged its reign for several decades. The example of David shows better than anything else that French classicism at the end of the eighteenth century was conservative (or, if you prefer it, reactionary, since after all it was striving to return from modern imitators to the antique models) only in *form*. Its *content* was entirely steeped in the most revolutionary spirit.

In this respect one of the most characteristic and remarkable works by David was his *Brutus*. The lictors are bringing to Brutus the bodies of his children, who have just been executed for participation in monarchist activities; his wife and daughter are in tears; but Brutus himself sits grim and unyielding, and one realises that for this man the good of the republic is, indeed, the supreme law. Brutus too, is "father of a family." But this is the father of a family who has become a citizen. His virtue is the political virtue of a revolutionary. He shows us how far bourgeois France had moved from the period when Diderot praised Greuze for the moral character of his painting.[1]

Exhibited in 1789, in the year when the great revolutionary upheaval began, *Brutus* was astoundingly successful. The painting brought to consciousness that which had become the very core, the most essential demand of being—that is, of the social life of the France of the day. Ernest Chesneau is quite justified when he writes, in his book on the French schools of painting:

> David accurately reflected the feeling of the nation, which, in applauding his paintings, applauded its own portrait. He depicted those same heroes which the public was taking as its model; admiring his pictures, it confirmed its own

[1] "Brutus" hangs to-day in the Louvre. The Russian who may find himself in Paris has the bounden duty to go and pay it his respects. [Plekhanov was thinking of many Russian families who lost their young people in Tsarist days, for political reasons—though different from those mentioned.—TRANS.].

"What have revolutions in Athens and Rome," he asks, "to do with me—a peaceful subject of an eighteenth century monarchic state? What interest have I got in the death of some Peloponnesian tyrant or the sacrifice of some princess in Aulis? All this is no concern of mine and nothing of the slightest importance to me emerges from it."[9]

The choice of heroes from the ancient world was one of the extremely numerous manifestations of that fascination with the ancient world, which was itself an ideological reflection of the struggle of the new social order, in process of being born, against *feudalism.* This fascination with ancient civilisation was carried over from the Renaissance to the epoch of Louis XIV, whose age, it will be remembered, was readily compared with that of Augustus.

But when the bourgeoisie began to be imbued with opposition sentiments, when "hatred, together with a thirst for justice," was born in its heart, the fascination with the heroes of antiquity, which had been fully shared by its former representatives, began to appear out of place—and the "events" of ancient history to seem insufficiently instructive. The hero of bourgeois drama became the contemporary "man of middle estate," more or less idealised by the bourgeois ideologists of the day. This characteristic circumstance, of course, could not injure the "portrait" that Brunetière speaks of.

But to continue. The real creator of bourgeois drama in France was Nivelle de la Chaussée. What do we find in his numerous works? Revolt against every aspect of aristocratic psychology, a struggle against the prejudices—or, if you prefer it, the vices—of the nobility. What his contemporaries valued above all in his works was the moral instruction they contained.[10] And from this angle, too, the "sentimental comedy" was true to its origins.

We know that the ideologists of the French bourgeoisie were not very original in their attempts to "portray" this class in their dramatic works. They did not create bourgeois

[9] *Eugénie, avec un essai sur le genre dramatique sérièux, Oeuvres* I, p. 11.

[10] d'Alembert writes of Nivelle de la Chaussée: "Both in his literary work and in his private life he held to the rule that that man is wise whose desires and aspirations are in keeping with his means." This is an apologia for equilibrium, moderation and correctness.

drama—they simply transferred it from England to France. In England this type of dramatic work had arisen at the end of the seventeenth century as a reaction against the terrifying depravity which then held sway on the stage and which reflected the moral decline of the English aristocracy of the day. In its fight against the aristocracy, the bourgeoisie wanted to make comedy "worthy of Christians," and began to preach in it its own morality.

The French literary innovators of the eighteenth century who, by and large, borrowed from English literature everything that was appropriate to the position and the feelings of the French bourgeoisie in opposition, transferred bodily into France this aspect of the English "sentimental comedy." French bourgeois drama is no less successful than the English in preaching the virtues of bourgeois family life. Therein lay one of the secrets of its success, and therein, too, lies the key to what at first sight appears utterly incomprehensible—the fact that French bourgeois drama, which about the middle of the eighteenth century seems to be a firmly established literary form, fairly rapidly recedes into the background in the face of classical tragedy, instead, as one might have expected, of the other way about. We shall see in a moment how this strange fact is to be explained. But before doing so, it will be as well to add one thing more.

Diderot[11] who, by nature a passionate innovator, could not fail to be carried away by bourgeois drama, and who, as we know, himself tried his hand at the new literary form (his *Le fils naturel* of 1757 and *Le Père de famille* of 1758 come to mind), wished to see on the stage, not character, but situations, and, more precisely, social situations. To this the objection was made that the social situation is not in itself enough to determine personality. "What is a judge in himself?" he was asked (*le juge en soi*). "What is a merchant in himself?" (*le négociant en soi*). Herein lay a great misunderstanding, however. For Diderot did not have in mind the judge or merchant "in himself," but rather the merchant and, particularly, the judge *of that day*. And that celebrated comedy, *Le mariage de Figaro*, proved that the

[11] *Denis Diderot*, 1713-84: French materialist philosopher, Encyclopaedist and leading bourgeois realist writer.—TRANS.

We should never take off our hats except when our heads feel too hot, or when we wish to speak at a meeting, as a way of showing that we have a resolution to propose. In the same way the habit of bowing must be given up, because it is a relic of the days of slavery.

It was also necessary to forget and to exclude from one's vocabulary phrases and expressions like: "I have the honour," "You will do me the honour," and so on. At the end of a letter one should never write "Your most obedient servant," "Your most humble servant." All such expressions were relics of the old order, unworthy of free men. One should write, "I remain, your fellow citizen," "Your brother," "Your comrade" or, finally, "Your equal."

Citizen Chalier prepared and presented to the Convention a whole dissertation on manners, in which he sharply criticised old aristocratic politeness and asserted that any special care about cleanliness in dress was ridiculous because aristocratic. Elegant clothes were nothing short of a crime, a theft from the State. Chalier considered that everyone should use "thou," the familiar form of address: "By saying 'thou' to one another, we complete the collapse of the old system of insolence and tyranny." And it seems that Chalier's dissertation created an impression. On November 8, 1793, the Convention prescribed that all civil servants should use the familiar form of address in their dealings with one another. A certain Lebon, a convinced democrat and ardent revolutionary, received an expensive suit as a gift from his mother. Not wishing to offend the old lady, he accepted it; but his conscience began to try him sorely, and he wrote to his brother:

I have not slept for ten days now because of this accursed suit. I, a philosopher, the friend of mankind, dressing so lavishly while thousands of my fellow-men are dying of hunger and wearing pitiable rags! How can I enter their humble dwellings to comfort them in their adversity? How can I continue to plead the cause of the poor? How can I protest against the robberies of the rich, when I myself imitate their luxury and elegance? These thoughts pursue me mercilessly and give me no peace.

And this was by no means a unique occurrence. The question of dress became at the time a question of conscience, just as it did with us in our so-called "nihilist" period.[1] And for the same reasons. In January, 1793, the journal *Le courrier de l'égalité*

[1] The period of democratic-revolutionary Narodnik activities among the educated Russian youth in the '60s and '70s.—TRANS.

declared that it was shameful to have two suits while soldiers defending the independence of the Republic at the frontiers went in rags. At the same time, the famous *Père Duchêne* demands that fashion shops be turned into workshops, that skilled carriage-makers should make only baggage-waggons, that goldsmiths should become ironsmiths, while the cafés, instead of being meeting places for the idle, should be handed over to the workers for their meetings.

When such was the condition of "manners," it is quite understandable that art should go to the extreme limit in its rejection of all the old aesthetic traditions of the aristocratic epoch.

The theatre, which, as we have seen, had already served the third estate as a spiritual weapon in its struggle against the old order in the pre-revolutionary epoch, now ridiculed the clergy and the nobility without the slightest restraint. In 1790 a drama entitled *La liberté conquise, ou le despotisme renversé* (Liberty Triumphant, or Tyranny Overthrown) enjoyed a great success. The audience chanted in chorus, "Aristocrats, you are defeated!" The defeated aristocracy, on the other hand, flocked to see tragedies, which reminded them of the good old times—*Cinna, Athalie* and so on. In 1793 people danced the *carmagnole* on the stage and ridiculed kings and emigrés. As Goncourt, from whom we have learned the facts concerning this period, puts it, "The theatre was taken over by the *sans-culottes*."[1] Actors mocked at the bombastic mannerisms of the old-timers. They behaved with the utmost lack of constraint, climbing in through the windows, for example, instead of entering by the door. Goncourt describes how on one occasion, during a performance of the play *Le faux savant*, an actor came down the chimney instead of in through the door. *Se non è vero, è ben trovato.*[2]

It is not in the least surprising that the theatre was "*sans-culottisé*" by the revolution, since for a short time the revolution put power into the hands of the *sans-culottes*. But it is important for us here to record the fact that even during the revolution—as in all previous epochs—the theatre served as a true reflection of

[1] *Sans-culottes*: literally, "without breeches," a derisory term applied to the common people during the French Revolution—who wore trousers, convenient for work, rather than the tight breeches which were the wear of the gentry. The epithet was taken up by the revolutionaries and used with pride.—TRANS.

[2] If not the truth, a good idea.

social life, with its contradictions and with the class struggle to which they gave rise. If, in the good old days, when manners served as laws—to use the expression of Marmontel quoted above—the theatre expressed the aristocratic view of men's mutual relations, now, under the rule of the *sans-culottes*, there was realised the ideal of M. J. Chenier, who said that the theatre should instil in citizens contempt for superstitions, hatred of oppressors and love of liberty.

The ideals of the time demanded of the citizen such intensive and unceasing work for the general good that there was little room left for purely aesthetic requirements in the sum-total of his spiritual needs. The citizen of this great epoch delighted above all in the poetry of action, and the beauty of civic achievement. And this circumstance at times gave a somewhat original character to the aesthetic judgments of the French "patriots." Goncourt writes that one of the members of the jury chosen to judge works exhibited in the Salon of 1793, a certain Fleuriot, regretted that the bas-reliefs submitted for award failed to express clearly enough the great principles of the revolution:

> What sort of men are these, anyway, occupying themselves with sculpture, at a time when their brothers are shedding their blood for the fatherland? In my opinion, there should be no prizes!

Another member of the jury, Hassenfratz, said:

> I will speak frankly—in my opinion, the talent of an artist is in his heart, not in his hand; what the hand can master is comparatively unimportant.

A certain Neveu having been bold enough to declare: "I must tell Hassenfratz that regard must be paid to craftsmanship and expression" (don't forget that sculpture was under discussion), Hassenfratz answered: "Citizen Neveu, skill of the hand is nothing—you shouldn't base your judgment on skill of hand." It was decided not to award any prizes for sculpture.

During the discussion on painting the same Hassenfratz ardently sought to prove that the citizens fighting for freedom on the frontiers were the best painters. In his enthusiasm he even said that "everything in painting ought to be done with a ruler and compass." When architecture came up for judgment, a certain Dufourny asserted that all buildings "should be as plain as a citizen's virtues." "What end is served by superfluous decoration?" he added. "Architecture must be regenerated by geometry."

It goes without saying that we are dealing here with a most gross exaggeration, and have reached the limits beyond which reason could not go, even at that time of pressing to the limit logical conclusions from premises accepted as indubitable. And it is not difficult to ridicule—as Goncourt does—opinions of this sort. But to conclude from such opinions that the revolutionary period was altogether unfavourable to the development of art, would be quite wrong. We repeat, the bitter fight then being waged—not only "on the frontier," but throughout French territory from end to end—left citizens little time for peaceful pursuit of the arts. But it far from stifled the aesthetic requirements of the people. Quite the contrary. The great social movement which made the people clearly aware of their worth gave a strong and unprecedented impetus to the development of these requirements.

To be convinced of this one has only to visit the Paris "Musée Carnavalet." The material in this interesting museum, devoted to the revolutionary period, shows irrefutably that, in becoming *sans-culottisé*, art certainly did not perish, nor cease to be art. It simply became steeped in an entirely new spirit. As the virtue of the French "patriot" of the day was primarily political virtue, so was his art primarily political. Dear reader, don't be alarmed. It simply means that the citizen of that time—i.e. a citizen of course, worthy of the name—could not be moved, or was almost unmoved, by an art which was not based upon some cherished political idea.[1]

And let it not be said that such art must be barren. That is a mistake. The inimitable art of the ancient Greeks was, to a very large degree and in the same sense, political art. And is it alone in this? French art of the age of Louis XIV was also in the service of certain political ideas, but this did not prevent it from flourishing. As for French art of the revolutionary period, the *sans-culottes* made it something which the art of the upper classes could never be: art became the affair of the whole people.

The numerous civic holidays, processions and celebrations of that time were the best and most convincing evidence in favour of the aesthetics of the *sans-culottes*. Not everybody takes this evidence into account, however.

But because of the historical circumstances of that epoch, art

[1] We are using the word "political" in the same broad sense in which it has been said that every class struggle is a political struggle.

for the whole people lacked any firm social foundation. The cruel Thermidor[1] reaction soon put an end to the rule of the *sans-culottes* and, opening up a new era in politics, opened up also a new era in art—an era expressing the aspirations and tastes of a new upper class, the bourgeoisie which had won power. We shall not say anything here of this new era: it deserves detailed analysis, and it is time we finished.

What follows from all we have said? The following conclusions may be drawn:—

First: even if it is correct to say that art—like literature—is a reflection of life, it is nevertheless still a very vague statement. To understand in what manner art reflects life, one must understand the mechanism of the latter. Among civilised peoples the class struggle constitutes one of the mainsprings in this mechanism. And only if we examine this mainspring, take into account the class struggle and study its many and various aspects, shall we be able to explain to ourselves at all satisfactorily the "spiritual" history of civilised society. The "march" of its ideas is a reflection of the history of its classes and of their struggle one with the other.

Second: Kant wrote that the feeling of pleasure which determines the judgment of taste must be free of all interest, and that any judgment of beauty into which the slightest interest enters, is very partisan and far from a pure judgment of taste.[2] This is quite true as applied to a single individual. If I like a picture only because I can make money by selling it, then my judgment is, of course, not a pure judgment of taste. But it is a different matter when we take the standpoint of society. Study of the art of primitive tribes has shown that social man looks at objects and phenomena in the first instance from the utilitarian standpoint, and only subsequently changes, in his attitude to some of them, to an aesthetic viewpoint. This throws fresh light on the history of art. Naturally, not every useful object appears beautiful to social man. But undoubtedly only that which is useful—that is to say, of importance in his struggle for existence, with nature or with

[1] *Thermidor*: name given by the French revolutionaries to the period covering July 19 to August 18, when the months were renamed for a short period. Also applied to the counter-revolutionary upheaval of July 27/8, 1794, which put an end to the dictatorship of the Jacobins or radical petty bourgeoisie during the French Revolution.—TRANS.

[2] *Critique of the Capacity of Judgment* (1790).

other social men—can seem beautiful to him. This does not mean that for social man the utilitarian viewpoint coincides with the aesthetic. Not at all! Usefulness is perceived by reason: beauty by the contemplative faculty. The sphere of the first is calculation, the sphere of the second is instinct. Moreover—and it is necessary to remember this—the field of the contemplative faculty is incomparably broader than the field of reason; enjoying what appears to him beautiful, social man hardly ever takes into account the utility of the object concerned.[1] In the vast majority of cases this utility can only be discovered by scientific analysis. The main distinguishing feature of aesthetic pleasure is its *directness.* But the utility exists nevertheless: it still lies at the basis of aesthetic enjoyment (let us recall that we are speaking of social man, not of the individual), and if it were non-existent, the object would not appear beautiful.

It may be objected that an object's colour pleases us independently of the significance which this object could have, or may have, in the struggle for existence. Without entering into any lengthy argument, allow me to recall an observation by Fechner. We like red when we see it on the cheeks of a young and beautiful woman, for example. But what effect would this colour have on us if we saw it on the nose, instead of on the cheeks, of our beauty?

Here there is to be observed a complete parallel with morality. Not everything which is good for social man is moral. But only that which is useful to his life and his development can assume moral significance for him: not man for morality, but morality for man. In exactly the same way it may be said that man is not made for beauty, but beauty is made for man. And this may, indeed, be called utilitarianism, understood in its real, that is to say in its broadest sense: as being useful not for individual man but for society—the tribe, the whole clan, the class.

But precisely because we are thinking, not of the individual, but of society (tribe, people, class) we can find room also for the Kantian view of this question: judgments of taste undoubtedly presuppose the absence of any utilitarian considerations whatever in the individual who expresses them. Here also one can draw an exact parallel with moral judgment. If I pronounce a given action to be moral only because it is useful to *me*, then I have no moral instinct.

[1] By "object" we must here understand not only material things but also natural phenomena, human feelings and relations between people.

ART AND SOCIAL LIFE[1]

I

THE question of the relationship of art to social life has always played a very important part in all literature that has reached a certain level of development. More often than not the question has been resolved in two ways which are directly contradictory to each other.

Some have said and still say: Man is not made for the Sabbath, but the Sabbath for man. Society is not made for the artist, but the artist for society. Art must promote the development of human consciousness and the improvement of the social order.

Others decisively reject this viewpoint. In their opinion, art is an end in itself, and to turn it into a means of achieving some other end, however noble, is to lower the dignity of a work of art.

The first of these two views was clearly expressed in our advanced literature of the '60s. Even if we leave out Pisarev, who, in his extreme one-sidedness, carried it almost to the point of caricature, we may cite Chernyshevsky and Dobrolyubov as the most well-grounded defenders of this viewpoint among the critics of that day. In one of his first critical essays, Chernyshevsky wrote,

> Art for art's sake—such an idea is as strange now-a-days as "wealth for wealth's sake," "science for science's sake" and so on. All human activities should serve a useful purpose for man, if they are not to be empty, frivolous occupations. Wealth exists so that man may use it, science so that she may be man's guide, and art also must serve some essential purpose and not be an idle amusement.

In Chernyshevsky's opinion, the importance of the arts and, in particular, of "the most serious among them," poetry, is determined

[1] The work here offered to the reader's attention is a revision of a paper which I read in Russian in November 1912, at Liége and Paris. That is why it has to some extent retained a form suitable to the spoken word. At the end of its second part the objections raised publicly with me in Paris by Mr. Lunacharsky on the question of a criterion for beauty, will be examined. Having answered them verbally at the time, I consider it useful to dwell on them in print.

by the mass of knowledge they disseminate in society. He writes:

> Art, or rather, poetry (and only poetry, since the other arts do very little in this respect) disseminates among the mass of readers a vast quantity of knowledge and, what is still more important, familiarity with concepts elaborated by science —herein lies the great importance of poetry for life.[1]

He expresses the same idea in his famous dissertation *The Aesthetic Relationship of Art to Reality*. According to its seventeenth thesis, art not only reproduces life but also explains it; and works of art often "have the significance of a judgment on the phenomena of life."

In the eyes of Chernyshevsky, and of his pupil Dobrolyubov, the main importance of art lay precisely in its reproduction of life and its passing of judgment on the phenomena of life.[2]

Not only literary critics and theoreticians of art regarded the matter in this light. It is not surprising that Nekrassov called his muse a muse of "sorrow and revenge." In one of his poems, the citizen, addressing the poet, says:

> And thou, poet, art chosen of the skies,
> Voice of truths eternal.
> Think not the hungry mortal's cries
> Unworthy of prophetic song.
> Think not that men have fallen quite,
> God is not dead in man,
> The cry of a believing heart
> Will ever reach man's spirit.
> Become a citizen! In serving art.
> Live for the good of fellow-men,
> Submitting genius to the sense
> Of all-embracing love.

In these words, "citizen" Nekrassov expressed his own conception of the tasks of art. The same viewpoint was shared at that

[1] N. G. Chernyshevsky, *Collected Works*, Vol. I, 1906, pp. 33–4.

[2] This view was partly a repetition, and partly a further development, of the views worked out by Belinsky in the last years of his life. In his article *A glance at Russian literature in 1847*—Belinsky wrote: "The highest and most sacred interest of society is its own well-being, equally distributed among all its members. The road to this well-being is consciousness, and art can help consciousness as much as science. Science and art are equally necessary: science cannot take the place of art, nor art of science." But art can only contribute to the development of consciousness when it "passes judgment on the phenomena of life." And thus Chernyshevsky's dissertation is linked with Belinsky's final views on Russian literature.

time by the most outstanding personalities in the plastic arts, for example, in painting. In serving art, Perov and Kramskoy strove, like Nekrassov, to be "citizens." And like him, they passed judgment in their works on the phenomena of life.[1]

A contrary viewpoint on the task of artistic creation had a mighty defender in the Pushkin of the time of Nicholas I. Everyone knows such poems of his as *The Rabble* and *To the Poet*. To the people, demanding that the poet should by his songs improve social morality, he replies scornfully—one might almost say, brutally:

> Away then! May the peaceful poet own
> a common lot with you? Go, struck to stone,
> on your remorseless course of wickedness!
> No song of mine will ease your souls and bless;
> the spirit shrinks from you like open graves.
> Aye, when your madness or your malice raves,
> you've found upon your backs
> the whip, the dungeon-cell, the axe,
> enough for you, enough, insensate slaves.

Pushkin expressed his idea of the poet's task in the following, so often-quoted lines:

> Not for the world, ambition-torn,
> rage of war and profit's cares,
> for inspiration we were born,
> sweetness of harmony, and prayers.

Here we meet the so-called theory of art for art's sake in its sharpest formulation. It was not without good grounds that the opponents of the literary movement of the '60s so readily and often quoted Pushkin.

Which of these two flatly contradictory opinions on the task of art should we take to be right?

In setting out to solve this question, it is essential to note, in the first place, that it is badly formulated. Neither this nor any similar question can be examined from the standpoint of "duty."

[1] A letter from Kramskoy to V. V. Stasov from Mentone (April 30, 1884) is proof of the influence on him of the views of Belinsky, Gogol, Fedotov, Ivanov, Chernyshevsky, Dobrolyubov and Perov (*Ivan Nikolayevich Kramskoy, his life, correspondence and art criticism*, St. Petersburg, 1888, p. 487). It is worth while noting, however, that the judgments passed on the phenomena of life in I. N. Kramskoy's critical essays, are far from being as clear as those passed, for example, by G. I. Uspensky, not to mention those of Chernyshevsky and Dobrolyubov.

If in a particular country and at a particular time the artist finds that worldly "agitation" and "battles" are no concern of his, while at another time, on the contrary, he eagerly seeks for battles and for the agitation which inevitably goes with them, this happens, not because some outside authority imposes on him different obligations ("duties") at different times, but because in different social conditions he is swayed by different feelings. Therefore, a correct approach to the subject requires that we examine it, not from the standpoint of what ought to have been, but from the standpoint of what was and is.

We will therefore pose the question as follows:

What are the principal social conditions in which, in artists and in people taking a lively interest in art, the tendency to "art for art's sake" arises and is strengthened?

When we approach the answer to this question, it will not be difficult to solve another equally interesting question, which is closely related to it:—

What are the principal social conditions in which, in artists and people taking a lively interest in art, there arises and is strengthened the so-called "utilitarian" conception of art, that is, the tendency to accord to works of art "the significance of judgments on the phenomena of life?"

The first of these two questions leads us back again to Pushkin.

There was a time when he did not support the theory of art for art's sake. There was a time when he did not avoid battles, but sought them out. This was during the reign of Alexander I. At that time he did not think that "the people" should be satisfied with whips, dungeons and axes. On the contrary, he exclaimed with indignation, in his *Ode to Liberty*—

> Alas, where'er I look there loom
> whips and chains in serried doom,
> laws broken with no shames or fears,
> slaves with powerless tears
> and power unjust in its distorting gloom.

But later his mood changed radically. In the epoch of Nicholas I, he adopted the theory of art for art's sake. What brought about this tremendous change in his mood?

The beginning of Nicholas I's rule, was marked by the catastrophe of December 14,[1] which had a tremendous influence not

[1] The "Decembrist" rising of revolutionary noblemen against Tsar Nicholas I in December 1825, brutally suppressed.—TRANS.

only on the further development of our "society" but also on Pushkin's personal fate. The defeat of the "Decembrists" meant the disappearance of the most educated and advanced representatives of the society of the time, and inevitably resulted in a considerable lowering of its moral and intellectual level.

> "Although I was so young at the time," writes Herzen, "I can yet remember how visibly high society sank and became foul and servile when Nicholas I ascended the throne. The aristocratic independence and military daring of Alexander's reign, vanished in 1826."

It was hard for an intelligent and sensitive person to live in such a society. "All about one was a wilderness, silence," wrote the same Herzen in another essay. "All was pusillanimous, inhuman, hopeless, and, what is more, utterly flat, stupid and petty. Appeals for sympathy were met by servile threats or fear; men either turned away from them or answered with insults." In Pushkin's letters, written during the period when he was composing *The Rabble* and *To the Poet*, one constantly meets with complaints about the boredom and vulgarity of both our capitals. But Pushkin did not only suffer from the vulgarity of the society that surrounded him; his relations with the "ruling circles" also caused him a good deal of unpleasantness.

There is a touching and widely spread legend that in 1826 Nicholas I magnanimously "pardoned" Pushkin for the political "mistakes of his youth," and even became his generous patron. But the facts were very different. Nicholas and his right-hand man in affairs of this sort, Chief of Police A. K. Benckendorf, "forgave" Pushkin nothing; and their "patronage" was expressed in a long series of unbearable humiliations. In 1827, Benckendorf reported to Nicholas:

> After meeting me Pushkin spoke enthusiastically about your Majesty at the English Club and made the people dining with him drink your Majesty's health. He's altogether pretty much of a scapegrace, but *it would be an advantage* to be able to guide his pen and his speeches.

The last words reveal the secret of the "patronage" accorded Pushkin. They wanted to make him sing the praises of the existing order. Nicholas and Benckendorf set themselves the task of directing his previously turbulent muse into the path of official morality. When Field-Marshal Paskevich wrote to Nicholas after Pushkin's death, Nicholas replied: "I am sorry about Pushkin, as a writer. I entirely subscribe to your opinion and it may be justly said that in him we mourn the future, not the past."[1]

This means that the unforgettable Emperor prized the dead poet, not for the great works he had written in his short life, but for what he might have written under appropriate police surveillance and guidance. Nicholas expected of him "patriotic" works like Kukolnik's play, *The Hand of the Almighty saved the Fatherland*. Even V. A. Zhukovsky, that "other-worldly" poet, who was a first-rate courtier, tried to bring Pushkin to his senses and to inculcate in him a respect for morality. In a letter of April 12, 1826, he wrote:

> Our young people (that is, the whole rising generation), whose bad education leaves them without any support in life, have become familiar with your turbulent thoughts, clothed in exquisite verse. You have already done incalculable harm to many—and that should make you tremble. Talent means nothing. The main thing is moral greatness. . . .[2]

It must be admitted that, in *such* a situation, shackled by *such* a patronage, and having to listen to *such* edifying exhortations, Pushkin was quite justified in hating "moral greatness," in feeling the most profound disgust for all the "benefits" which art might produce, and in exclaiming to his advisors and patrons:—

> Away then! May the peaceful poet own a common lot with you?

In other words, in the circumstances in which he found himself it was natural for Pushkin to become an advocate of the theory of art for art's sake, and to say to the poet, in his own person:

> You're king, so dwell alone. Your free path tread
> Wherever your free mind your steps may lead;
> Perfect the fruits your secret thoughts have bred,
> And for your high achievement ask no meed.[3]

D. I. Pisarev would have objected that Pushkin was addressing these sharp words, not to his protectors, but to "the people." But at that time the people, in the real sense of the word, were completely excluded from the literary field of vision. For Pushkin, the word "people" had the same meaning as the word "crowd," which he frequently used. And this latter word, of course, had

[1] Shchegolev, *Pushkin*, St. Petersburg, 1912, p. 357.
[2] Shchegolev, *op. cit.*, p. 241.

nothing to do with the working mass. In his *Gypsies*, describing the inhabitants of stuffy towns, Pushkin says:

> Ashamed of love, they chase away
> all thought, and their own souls they sell.
> Bowing to idols and their spell,
> for money and for chains they pray.

It can hardly be supposed that he was here thinking of the town artisans.

If all this is correct, then we seem to be arriving at the following conclusion:—

The tendency towards art for art's sake arises where the artist is in disaccord with his social environment.

It may be said that the single example of Pushkin is not by itself enough to support such a conclusion. I do not dispute it. But I will cite other examples from the history of French literature—that is, from the literature of a country whose intellectual trends met with the widest sympathy throughout Europe, at least until the middle of the last century.

The French Romantics, Pushkin's contemporaries, were, with few exceptions, fervent supporters of art for art's sake. Théophile Gautier, probably the most consistent of them, launched the following diatribe against the defenders of the utilitarian view of art.

> No, you idiots, no, you cretins, you can't make soup out of a book or a pair of boots out of a novel. . . . I swear by the guts of all past, present and future Popes—no, a thousand times, no! I am one of those who consider the superfluous essential; my love for things and people is in inverse proportion to their utility.[1]

The same Gautier, in a biographical note on Baudelaire, highly praised the author of the *Fleurs du mal* because he had defended the "absolute autonomy of art and would not allow poetry to have any other purpose than itself, or any task than that of arousing in the reader's heart a sense of the beautiful in the absolute meaning of this word."

How little the "sense of the beautiful" was connected in Gautier's mind with any social and political considerations, may be gathered from the following declaration:—

> I will most gladly renounce my rights as a Frenchman and a citizen, in order to see an original by Raphael or a beautiful woman in the nude.

[1] Foreword to the novel, *Mademoiselle de Maupin*.

It would be impossible to go further than this. Yet all the Parnassians[1] would probably have agreed with Gautier even if some of them might have expressed certain reservations about the excessively paradoxical form in which, especially in his youth, he expressed his demand for the "absolute autonomy of art."

Whence came this mood among the French romantics and Parnassians? Were they, too, out of tune with the society about them?

In 1857, in an article on the revival at the Théâtre-Français of de Vigny's play *Chatterton*, Théophile Gautier recalled its first presentation on February 12, 1835, and told the following story:

> The pit before which *Chatterton* was being played was filled with pale, long-haired youths, who firmly believed that there was no more worthy profession than the writing of verses or the painting of pictures, and who regarded the "bourgeois" with a scorn surpassing beyond compare that of the Heidelberg or Jena undergraduate for the "philistine."[2]

And who were these despised "bourgeois"?

> "The bourgeois," replied Gautier, "comprised nearly everyone—bankers, stockbrokers, lawyers, merchants, shopkeepers and so on—everyone, in a word, who did not belong to the secret *cenacle* (that is, to the romantic circle—G. V. P.), and who got his living in a commonplace way."[3]

And here is another witness. In the commentary to one of his *Odes funambulesques*, Théodore de Banville admits that he, too, lived through this phase of hatred for the "bourgeois." At the same time he explains whom precisely the Romantics called by this name.

> In the language of the Romantics, a "bourgeois" is a man whose only religion is that of the five-franc piece, whose only ideal is to save his own skin, who in poetry enjoys sentimental ballads and in the plastic arts—coloured lithographs.[4]

In view of this, de Banville asked his readers not to be surprised if, in his *Odes funambulesques*—which, by the way, were published during the last period of romanticism—people whose only crime was that they led a bourgeois life and did not worship Romantic heroes, were treated as the greatest blackguards.

[1] A group of French poets initiated and led by Théophile Gautier, Leconte de Lisle and others after the defeat of the 1848 Revolution. They believed in "art for art's sake," and at the same time advocated clarity of imagery and objectivity of content in poetry.—TRANS.

[2] *Histoire du romantisme*, pp. 153–4.

[3] *Ibid.*, p. 154.

[4] *Les Odes funambulesques*, Paris, 1858, pp. 294–5.

This evidence shows convincingly enough that the Romantics did in fact find themselves out of tune with the bourgeois society round them. True, their disaccord held no threat to bourgeois social relationships. The romantic circles were composed of young bourgeois who had no objection to these relationships, but inveighed against the dirt, boredom and vulgarity of bourgeois existence. The new art which so much attracted them was their refuge from this dirt, boredom and vulgarity. In the last years of the Restoration and the first half of the reign of Louis Philippe—that is, in the best period of romanticism—the youth of France found it all the harder to become accustomed to the prosaic dirt and boredom of bourgeois life, since not so long before France had passed through the fearful storms of the great Revolution and of the Napoleonic era, both of which had profoundly stirred every human passion.[1] When the bourgeoisie had assumed a leading position in society and was no longer fired by the struggle for emancipation, there was only one thing left for the new art to do—*to idealise the renunciation of the bourgeois mode of life*. Romantic art was such an idealisation. The Romantics sought to express their hostility to bourgeois moderation and punctiliousness not only in their works of art, but also in their appearance. We have already heard from Gautier that the young men who filled the theatre at the first performance of *Chatterton*, wore their hair long. Who has not heard of the red waistcoat sported by Gautier himself, which horrified "respectable people?" Fantastic dress, like long hair, served the young Romantics as a means of counterposing themselves to the hated bourgeois. A pale face served the same purpose. It was like a protest against the well-fed bourgeois. Gautier wrote:

> It was then the fashion for the Romantics to look as pale as possible, with even a green and almost corpse-like pallor. This gave a man a fateful, Byronic

[1] Alfred de Musset described this disaccord as follows: "From this moment one might say that two camps were created. On the one hand were the exalted and suffering spirits, all the expansive souls yearning after the infinite. Bathed in tears, they bowed their heads, wrapped themselves in sickly visions and all that could be seen were frail reeds quivering in a sea of bitterness. On the other hand, the men of flesh and blood stood upright and unbending, thoroughly enjoying themselves, and untroubled by any thought save that of counting their money. There remained nothing but a sob and a guffaw—the one coming from the soul, the other from the body" (*La confession d'un enfant du siècle*, p. 10).

aspect, as though he were torn asunder by passions and tortured by pangs of conscience, and it made him interesting to women.[1]

Gautier also tells us that the Romantics found it hard to forgive Victor Hugo his respectable outward appearance:

> Behind closed doors, when no strangers were present, they used to deplore this weakness of a great genius, which linked him with mankind and even with the bourgeoisie.[2]

It is worth while noting, by the way, that in the efforts of people to give themselves some particular external appearance or another are always reflected the social relationships of the epoch concerned. An interesting sociological study could be written on this subject.

With such an attitude towards the bourgeoisie, the young Romantics inevitably waxed indignant at the thought of "utilitarian art." To make art useful meant, in their eyes, forcing it to serve the very bourgeois they so deeply despised. This explains Gautier's outbursts against the protagonists of utilitarian art, quoted above, whom he described as idiots, cretins, and so on. It also explains his paradoxical idea that the value of people and things was in inverse proportion to their use. All these outbursts and paradoxes are equivalent in their content to Pushkin's:—

> Away then! May the peaceful poet own a common lot with you?

The Parnassians and the first French realists (Goncourt, Flaubert and others) were also filled with limitless scorn for the bourgeois society around them. They, too, unceasingly abused the hateful "bourgeois." If they published their works, it was done, so they said, not at all for the broad public, but for the chosen few, for "unknown friends," as Flaubert expressed it in one of his letters. In their opinion, only second-rate writers could appeal to any broad reading public. Leconte de Lisle, considered that, for a writer, a great success was a sign of intellectual inferiority. It is hardly necessary to add that the Parnassians, like the Romantics, were unquestioning supporters of the theory of art for art's sake.

Many such similar examples could be cited. But there is no need. It is already clear enough that the tendency of the artist to accept the theory of art for art's sake arises when he finds himself in disaccord with the society in which he lives. It will be as

[1] *Op. cit.*, p. 31.

[2] *Op. cit.*, p. 32.

well, however, to define the nature of this disaccord more precisely.

At the end of the eighteenth century, in the period immediately preceding the great Revolution, leading French artists also found themselves in disaccord with the ruling "society" of the day. David and his friends were opponents of the "old order." And this disaccord was, of course, quite insoluble, in the sense that any reconciliation between themselves and the old order was impossible. More than that, the differences of David and his friends with the old order went incomparably deeper than those of the Romantics with bourgeois society. David and his friends were striving to put an end to the old order, while Théophile Gautier and those who thought like him had nothing against bourgeois social relationships, as I have said more than once, but wished only that the bourgeois system should cease to give rise to vulgar bourgeois habits.[1]

Nevertheless, in protesting against the old order, David and his friends knew very well that behind them in serried ranks marched that third estate which was soon to become everything —as the Abbé Sieyès had expressed it. And so the sense of disaccord with the prevailing order was supplemented in their case by sympathy for the new society which was taking shape within the womb of the old and preparing to supplant it. With the Romantics and the Parnassians it was a very different matter. They neither expected nor desired a change in the social order of France. And for that reason, their disagreement with society was without hope and without issue.[2]

[1] Théodore de Banville said frankly that the attacks of the Romantics on the "bourgeois" did not have in view the "bourgeoisie" as a social class. (*Les Odes funambulesques*, Paris 1858, p. 294.) This conservative revolt against the "bourgeois," peculiar to the Romantics, which was far from assailing the basis of bourgeois society, has been understood by some Russian would-be theoreticians at the present time (like Mr. Ivanov-Razumnik, for example), as a struggle against philistinism which far exceeds in its scope the social and political struggle of the proletariat against the bourgeoisie. I leave it to the reader to judge the profundity of this conception. In point of fact it shows that people who discuss the history of Russian social thought have, unfortunately, not always given themselves the trouble of making a preliminary acquaintance with the history of thought in Western Europe.

[2] A similar hopeless disaccord with their social environment marked the temper of the German Romantics, as has been well demonstrated by Brandes in his book *Die romantische schule in Deutschland*, Vol. II of his work, *Die Hauptströmungen der Litteratur des 19—ten Jahrhunderts.*

Nor did Pushkin expect any changes in the Russia of his day. One might even say that in the reign of Nicholas he had probably ceased to desire them. That is why his attitude to social life too was coloured with pessimism.

It seems to me that I can now add a word to my first conclusion and say:

The tendency of artists, and of those who have a lively interest in art, towards art for art's sake, arises when they are in hopeless disaccord with the social environment in which they live.

Nor is this all. The example of the Russian "men of the sixties" who firmly believed in the approaching triumph of reason, and the example also of David and his friends, who were no less firmly of the same opinion, shows us *that the so called utilitarian view of art, that is to say, the inclination to attribute to works of art the significance of judgment on the phenomena of life, and its constant accompaniment of glad readiness to participate in social struggles, arises and becomes stronger wherever a mutual sympathy exists between the individuals more or less actively interested in artistic creation and some considerable part of society.*

How true this is, is conclusively proved by the following:

When the refreshing storm of the 1848 Revolution burst, many French artists who had previously subscribed to the theory of art for art's sake, decisively rejected this theory. Even Baudelaire, whom Gautier later cited as an example of an artist unshakably convinced of the need for the unconditional autonomy of art, at once began the publication of a revolutionary journal, *Le Salut Public*. True, the journal soon ceased publication, but as late as 1852, in the foreword to the *Chansons* of Pierre Dupont, Baudelaire called the theory of art for art's sake puerile and proclaimed that art must serve social ends. Only the victory of the counter-revolution finally turned Baudelaire and other artists, whose temper was similar to his own, back to the "puerile" theory of art for art's sake. One of the future lights of Parnassus, Leconte de Lisle, revealed very clearly the psychological significance of this about-turn, in the foreword to his *Poèmes antiques*, a first edition of which appeared in 1852. Here we read that—

> poetry can no longer give birth to heroic deeds, it can no longer inspire social virtues, because at the present stage, as in all periods of literary decadence, its sacred tongue can express only petty personal experiences . . . and is no longer capable of teaching mankind.[1]

[1] *Poèmes antiques*, Paris, 1852, Préface, p. vii.

Addressing himself to the poets, he continues: "Poets, what would you say, what would you teach? Teachers, the time has come when your pupil instinctively knows more than you."[1] In the words of the future Parnassian, the task of poetry is to "give an ideal life to those who no longer have a real one."[2] In these profound words the entire psychological secret of the tendency towards art for art's sake is revealed. Later on, we shall have occasion more than once to refer to this foreword of Leconte de Lisle.

To finish with this side of the question, I will add that any given political power, in so far as it is interested in art at all, always favours the utilitarian view of art. And this is quite understandable: it is in its interests to make all ideologies serve the cause to which it is itself devoted. And since political power, which is sometimes revolutionary, is more often conservative or even entirely reactionary, it would be a mistake to assume that the utilitarian view of art is peculiar to revolutionaries, or to people with advanced ideas. The history of Russian literature graphically shows that even our imperial "guardians" were far from antagonistic to this view of art. Here are several examples:

In 1814 there appeared the first three parts of a novel by V. T. Narezhny, *The Russian Gil Blas, or the Adventures of Count Gavril Semonovich Christyakov*. This novel was at once banned by order of Razumovsky, Minister of Education, who on this occasion expressed himself on the connection between literature and life in the following terms:

> It often happens that novelists, while apparently combating vices, nevertheless paint them in such colours or describe them in such detail that they attract young people to such vices, which it would be better not to mention at all. Whatever the literary merits of a novel, it should only be published if it has a moral aim.

As you see, Razumovsky considered that art could not be an end in itself.

Similar views were held by all those servants of Nicholas I whose official position required them to have some sort of outlook on art. Benckendorf, it will be remembered, sought to direct Pushkin along the path of "truth." Nor did Ostrovsky escape the care of the authorities. When his comedy *Blood is thicker than water* appeared in March 1850, and certain enlightened pillars of

[1] *Op. cit.*, p. ix. [2] *Op. cit.*, p. xi.

literature (and of trade) were afraid it might offend the merchants, the Minister of Education, Count P. A. Shirinsky-Shikhmatov, ordered the warden of the Moscow Education District to summon the rising dramatist into his presence and—

inform him that talent should set itself the noble and useful aim not only of depicting vice and folly in lively colours, but also of justly condemning them—and that not only by caricature, but also by inculcating the loftiest moral sentiments. Consequently, virtue should be counterposed to vice; and in contrast to what is ridiculous or criminal, he should depict ideas and actions capable of elevating the soul. Finally, the author should reaffirm the belief, so important for both public and private life, that evil-doing reaps its punishment here on earth.

Even the Emperor Nicholas I himself regarded art primarily from the "moral" standpoint. As we have already seen, he shared Benckendorf's opinion as to the value of taming Pushkin. Nicholas I wrote in praise of Ostrovsky's *Don't sit in other people's sledges*: "This isn't a play, it's a lesson." This edifying play was written at the time when Ostrovsky was under the influence of the Slavophils, and used to announce at dinner parties that, with the aid of some of his friends, he would "turn back all the work of Peter."[1]

In order not to multiply examples, I will limit myself to only two more facts.

N. Polevoy's *Moscow Telegraph* was finally damned in the eyes of Nicholas' government, and was suppressed, when it published an unfavourable review of Kukolnik's "patriotic" play *The Hand of the Almighty saved the Fatherland*. Yet when N. Polevoy himself wrote two patriotic plays, *The Grand Old Man of the Russian Fleet* and *Merchant Igolkin*, the Tsar, so Polevoy's brother tells us, became enthusiastic over Polevoy's own dramatic gifts. " 'This author is exceptionally gifted,' he said, 'he must write and write and write!' . . . 'He should write,' the Tsar added with a smile, 'and not publish a journal.' "[2]

The rulers of Russia did not stand alone in this respect. In France, that typical representative of absolutism, Louis XIV, was no less firmly convinced that art cannot be an end in itself, but should assist in moral education. And the whole of the literature

[1] I.e. undo the reforms instituted by Peter the Great.—TRANS.

[2] *Diaries of Xenofont Polevoy*, St. Petersburg, published by Suvorin, 1888, p. 445.

and art of his famous era was steeped in this conviction. Similarly, Napoleon I regarded the theory of art for art's sake as one of the harmful inventions of noxious "ideologists." He also wanted literature and art to serve moral ends. And he so far succeeded that the majority of the paintings exhibited during his reign at the *Salons* depicted the military exploits of the Consulate and the Empire.

His "little" nephew, Napoleon III, followed in this respect in his footsteps, although much less successfully. He also wanted to make literature and art serve what he called morality. In November, 1852, a Lyons Professor, V. de Laprade, mercilessly ridiculed these Bonapartist attempts at edifying art in a satire called *State Muses.* In it he prophesied that the time would soon come when the State Muses would subject human wisdom to military discipline, after which order would reign and not a single writer would dare express disapproval of any kind:

> *Il faut etre content, s'il pleut, s'il fait soleil,*
> *S'il fait chaud, s'il fait froid: "Ayez le teint vermeil,*
> *Je déteste les gens maigres, à face pale";*
> *Celui qui ne rit pas merite qu'on l'empale. . . .*[1]

Let us note in passing that this witty satire cost Laprade his chair. The government of Napoleon III could not allow such liberties to be taken with the "State Muses."

II

But let us leave governmental "spheres."

Among the French writers of the Second Empire were to be found men who rejected the theory of art for art's sake by no means from progressive motives. Alexandre Dumas *fils* categorically stated, for example, that the expression "art for art's sake" was nothing but "three words strung together without sense." In his plays *Le fils naturel* and *Le père prodigue,* he pursued definite social aims, believing it to be his duty to support the "old society," which, as he asserted, was everywhere crumbling.

In 1857, after the death of Alfred de Musset, Lamartine, summing up his work, regretted that it had not served as an

[1] You must be content whether it is rain or sunshine, hot or cold. "Your cheeks must be pink—I loathe thin people with pale faces." Whoever doesn't laugh deserves to be impaled. . . .

expression of religious, social, political or patriotic faith, and reproached contemporary poets for "forgetting the meaning of their work and concerning themselves only with metres and rhymes." Finally, to cite a much lesser literary figure, Maxime du Camp condemned the exclusive concern with form, exclaiming:

> *La forme est belle, soit! quand l'idée est au fond*
> *Qu'est ce donc qu'un beau front, qui n'a pas de cervelle?*[1]

It was he, too, who attacked the leader of the romantic school in painting:

> Like so many writers who create art for art's sake, M. Delacroix has produced *colour for colour's sake.* History and mankind serve him only as an excuse for the combination of well selected shades.

In the opinion of this same writer, "the days of art for art's sake have gone for ever."[2]

Lamartine and Maxime du Camp can no more be suspected of subversive tendencies than the younger Dumas. They rejected this theory of art, not because they wanted to replace the bourgeois social order by anything else, but because they wanted to strengthen bourgeois social relations, considerably disturbed by the struggle of the proletariat for its emancipation. In this respect, they differed from the Romantics, and particularly from the Parnassians and early realists, simply in that they were incomparably more successful in making their peace with the bourgeois way of life. They were optimistic conservatives, whereas the others were pessimistic conservatives.

From this it follows that the utilitarian view of art is as much the expression of a conservative as of a revolutionary frame of mind. Such a standpoint requires only one condition—a lively and active interest in some social order or social ideal—no matter what; and it perishes wherever this interest vanishes, for whatever reason.

Let us now go further and inquire which of these two contradictory views is the more favourable to the development of art. Like all questions of social life and social thought, this question

[1] Form is beautiful—yes, when it is based on an idea. What is a beautiful face, without intelligence?

[2] In connection with this, see the brilliant book by M. Cassagne, *La théorie de l'art pour l'art en France chez les derniers romantiques et les premiers réalistes,* Paris, 1906, pp. 96–105.

cannot be solved categorically. Everything depends on the conditions of time and place. Remember Nicholas I and his servants. They wanted to make Pushkin, Ostrovsky and other contemporary artists preachers of morality, as it was understood by the gendarmerie. Let us imagine for a moment that they had succeeded. What would have happened? The answer is not far to seek. The muses of these artists, having come under police supervision and been converted into "State Muses," would have begun to display the most obvious signs of decline, and would have lost a great deal of their truth, of their strength and of their appeal.

Pushkin's poem *To the Slanderers of Russia* is far from being one of his best poetical works. Ostrovsky's play *Don't sit in other people's sledges*, which was graciously welcomed as a "useful lesson," is also, God knows, no great achievement. But yet, in this play, Ostrovsky had barely taken a few steps towards the ideal which the Benckendorfs, Shirinsky-Shikhmatovs and the like advocates of utilitarian art were striving to achieve.

Let us further assume that Théophile Gautier, Théodore de Banville, Leconte de Lisle, Baudelaire, the brothers Goncourt, Flaubert—in short, all the Romantics, Parnassians and the first French realists—had made their peace with the bourgeois world about them, and had devoted their talents to the service of those who, in Banville's words, "had no religion but that of the five-franc piece." What would have come of it? Again it is not difficult to give the answer. The Romantics, the Parnassians and the first French realists would have fallen very low. Their works would have lost much of their power, their truth and their appeal.

Which is of greater artistic merit, Flaubert's *Madame Bovary* or Augier's *Le gendre de Monsieur Poirier*? The question is hardly worth asking. And it is not only a matter of talent. The dramatic vulgarity of Augier, which represents the true apotheosis of bourgeois moderation and respectability, necessarily pre-supposes quite different creative methods from those of Flaubert, Goncourt and the other realists who scornfully turned their backs upon this moderation and respectability. Finally, it was no accident, after all, that the one literary trend attracted to itself far more talents than the other.

What does this prove? Something with which the Romantics of the stamp of Théophile Gautier could in no wise agree: to wit, that the value of a work of art is determined, in the last analysis by its content. Théophile Gautier maintained not only that poetry does not prove anything, but also that it does not say anything, and that the beauty of a poem depends upon its music and rhythm. But this is a profound mistake. Exactly the contrary is true. Poetry and art in general, always have something to say, because they always express something. Of course, the arts "say" things in their own special way. The painter expresses his ideas in images, while the pamphleteer drives home his points by logical arguments. If instead of depicting character the writer makes use of logical arguments, or if his characters are invented only to drive home an argument, then he is not an artist but a pamphleteer, even if he does not write treatises and articles, but novels, short stories and plays. All this is true. But it by no means follows that ideas have no significance in a work of art. I will go further: there can be no work of art devoid of ideas. Even those works in which the authors are concerned only with form, and ignore content, express some idea, in one way or another.

Gautier, despite his indifference to the ideological content of his poetry, nevertheless asserted, as we have seen, that he was prepared to sacrifice his political rights as a French citizen for the pleasure of seeing "an original by Raphael or a beautiful woman in the nude." The one attitude was closely linked with the other: exclusive attention to form was determined by social and political indifference.

Works in which the authors value only form always express a particular attitude—as I explained earlier, a hopelessly negative attitude—on the part of their authors to the surroundings in which they live. And herein lies the idea common to them all, and expressed by each of them individually in different ways. But if there is no work of art entirely devoid of ideas in its content, nevertheless not every idea can be expressed in a work of art. Ruskin put it excellently: A young woman can sing about her lost love, but a miser cannot sing about his lost money. And he also justly observes that the value of a work of art is determined by the loftiness of the mood it expresses. He says that we can ask of every strong feeling whether it can be sung by a poet, whether it can truly inspire him. If it can, then it is a noble feeling. If it cannot, or if it can arouse only ridicule, then it is a base feeling.

And it cannot be otherwise. Art is one of the means of spiritual communion between people. And the deeper the feeling expressed in a work of art, the more that work facilitates such intercourse, other things being equal. Why cannot a miser sing about his lost money? Quite simply because, if he did so, nobody would be moved by his song, it could not serve as a means of communion between him and other people.

But what about war songs, it may be asked. Does war bring men closer together? To this I will answer that war poetry, though it expresses hatred of the enemy, at the same time expresses the selflessness of the warrior, ready to die for his country, his State, and so forth. Just in so far as it expresses such readiness, it does bring men closer together, within those limits (the tribe, the community, the State) the extent of which is determined by the level of cultural development achieved by mankind, or, rather, by the part of mankind in question.

Turgenev, who had little liking for the zealots of utilitarian art, once said: "The Venus de Milo is more incontestable than the principles of 1789." He was quite right. But what follows? Something quite different from what Turgenev sought to prove.

There are a great many people in the world who not only "contest" the principles of 1789, but know absolutely nothing about them. Ask a Hottentot, who has not been to a European school, what he thinks about these principles, and you will find that he has not even heard of them. But the Hottentot not only knows nothing of the principles of 1789: he is equally ignorant of the existence of the Venus de Milo. And if he saw her, he would undoubtedly "have his doubts" about her. He has his own ideal of beauty, the so-called Hottentot Venus, reproductions of which are frequently to be found in anthropological works. The appeal of the Venus de Milo is "incontestably" attractive only for a part of the white race. And for this part of humanity she may be said to be more incontestable than the principles of 1789. Why? For the simple reason that these principles are the expression of social relations which correspond only to a particular phase in the development of the white race, the period when the bourgeois order was consolidating itself in its struggle with feudalism,[1]

[1] The second article of the *Declaration of the Rights of Man and of the Citizen*, adopted by the French Constituent Assembly at its meetings from August 20–26, 1789, says: "The end of all political association is the conservation of the natural and indefeasible rights of man. These rights are: liberty, property, security and resistance to oppression." The concern for property demonstrated

whereas the Venus de Milo is an ideal of feminine beauty which corresponds to *many* phases of that development. Many—but not all. The Christians had their own ideal of feminine beauty. It is to be found in the Byzantine icons. And it is common knowledge that those who worshipped these icons very strongly "contested" the Melian and all other Venuses. They denounced them as she-devils and destroyed them wherever they could. But then came an age when the she-devils of antiquity once again began to appeal to people of the white race. The way was prepared for this age by the emancipation movement among the Western European townsfolk, that is, by precisely the movement which was expressed most clearly in the principles of 1789. That is why we can say, despite Turgenev, that the more the European population grew ripe for the proclamation of the principles of 1789, the more "incontestable" became the Venus de Milo in the new Europe. This is no paradox. It is a stark historical fact.

The whole history of art during the Renaissance—if one studies it from the standpoint of the conception of beauty—is dominated by the fact that the Christian, monastic ideal of the human form was gradually pushed into the background by an earthly ideal, whose appearance was bound up with the urban struggle for emancipation; and its realisation facilitated by memories of the she-devils of antiquity.

Belinsky, who, in the later period of his literary work, rightly maintained that "pure" art, art in the abstract, or what the philosophers call "*absolute art*," had never existed anywhere, nevertheless considered that the paintings of the Italian school of the sixteenth century approached in some measure the ideal of absolute art, since they were products of a period when "art was the main interest, the exclusive pre-occupation of the educated section of society." And he cites as an example Raphael's Sistine Madonna, "that masterpiece of Italian sixteenth century painting." The Italian sixteenth-century schools of painting, however, marked the conclusion of the long struggle between the profane and Christian-monastic ideals. And however exceptional the

the bourgeois character of the revolution which was taking place, and recognition of the right of "resistance to oppression" demonstrated that the revolution was still in progress and not completed, since it met with powerful resistance from the temporal and spiritual aristocracy. In June, 1848, the French bourgeoisie no longer proclaimed the right of the citizen to resist oppression.

artistic interest of the educated section of sixteenth-century society,[1] it is indisputable that Raphael's Madonnas represent one of the most characteristic artistic expressions of the victory of the profane over the Christian-monastic ideal. This can be said, without exaggeration, even of the Madonnas which Raphael painted while he was still under the influence of his teacher Perugino, whose Madonnas seem to reflect a purely religious emotion. This religious appearance is transfused with such healthy enjoyment of a purely earthly existence, that they no longer have anything in common with the pious Virgins of the Byzantine masters.[2]

The works of the sixteenth-century Italian masters were no more examples of "absolute art" than were the paintings of the earlier masters, beginning with Cimabue and Duccio di Buoninsegna. In point of fact, nowhere and at no time has such art existed. And if Turgenev regarded the Venus de Milo as a product of such art, this was only because, like all idealists, he was mistaken in his views on the actual course of mankind's aesthetic development.

The ideal of beauty that obtains at a given time, in a given society and in a given class of society, has its roots partly in the biological conditions of development of the human species, which account, amongst other things, for certain racial peculiarities; and partly in the historical conditions in which this society or class arose and existed. And precisely because of this the ideal is always very rich in a content which is quite definite and not at all absolute, i.e. unconditioned. The worshipper of "pure beauty" does not in any way make himself independent of the biological, social and historical conditions which determine his aesthetic tastes: he merely shuts his eyes, more or less consciously, to these conditions. This was the case with the Romantics too, like Gautier. I have already pointed out that his exclusive preoccupation with poetic form was intimately and causally bound up with his indifference to social and political questions.

[1] Its exceptional character, which cannot be denied, only means that in the sixteenth century there existed a hopeless disaccord between lovers of art and their social environment. It was this disaccord which gave rise to the tendency to pure art, i.e. art for art's sake. In the preceding periods, in Giotto's time, for example, neither this disaccord nor this tendency existed.

[2] It is interesting that Perugino himself was suspected by his contemporaries of being an atheist. *Sovremennik*, 1912, Vol. XII.

This indifference enhanced the value of his poetry in so far as it preserved it from bourgeois vulgarity, narrowness and respectability. But at the same time, by limiting Gautier's range of vision and preventing him from accepting the progressive ideas of his time, it diminished the value of his poetry. Consider once more the preface to *Mademoiselle de Maupin*, with its almost childishly vehement attack on the defenders of the utilitarian view of art.

> "How idiotic is this pretended perfectibility of mankind, which is always being dinned into our ears!" Gautier exclaims. "What they are telling us, indeed, is that man is a machine susceptible of improvement, and that by replacing some cog or rearranging some counterweight he can be made to function better."[1]

To prove that such improvement was impossible, Gautier cited Marshal de Bassompierre, who could empty a whole top-boot full of wine to the health of the thirteen cantons. Gautier remarks that it would be as difficult to improve on this Marshal in respect of drinking as for a modern man to outdo Milo of Crotona, who could eat a whole ox at a sitting.

These remarks, true enough in themselves, are characteristic of the art for art's sake theory, in the form given it by the consistent Romantics. But it may be asked, who was it that "dinned into" Gautier's ears this pretended perfectibility of mankind? The Socialists, and particularly the Saint-Simonists, who had attained a considerable success in France shortly before the publication of *Mademoiselle de Maupin*. It was against the Saint-Simonists that he was directing his arguments about the difficulty of surpassing Marshal de Bassompierre as a drinker or Milo of Crotona as a glutton. But these arguments, however correct in themselves, become pointless when directed against the Saint-Simonists. The perfectibility of mankind which the Saint-Simonists were talking about had nothing to do with increasing the capacity of the stomach. What they had in mind was the improvement of social organisation in the interests of the majority of the people, that is, of the productive workers. To speak of such an ideal as "idiotic," and to ask whether its realisation would lead to an increase in the human ability to tipple wine or gorge meat, was simply a revelation of the same bourgeois vulgarity that aroused such fiery indignation amongst the young Romantics.

[1] *Mademoiselle de Maupin*, Preface, p. 23.

How, then, did this come about? How did this bourgeois vulgarity infect the judgment of that very writer who considered it his main aim in life to wage a relentless struggle against it?

I have more than once answered this question, it is true, only in passing, by contrasting the outlook of the Romantics with that of David and his friends. For I pointed out that, while revolting against bourgeois tastes and manners, the Romantics had no objection to bourgeois social organisation. We must now analyse this more carefully.

Some of the Romantics—Georges Sand, for example, at the time of her association with Pierre Leroux—were in sympathy with socialism. But these were exceptions. As a general rule, whilst protesting against bourgeois vulgarity, the Romantics adopted a more or less hostile attitude towards the socialist philosophies which were pointing to the necessity of a social reform. The Romantics wanted to change social manners without changing anything in the social order. But this obviously was impossible. For this reason, the romantic revolt against the "bourgeois" was just as barren of consequences as the contempt of the Göttingen or Jena undergraduates for the "philistines."

The Romantic revolt against the "bourgeois" was quite sterile in the practical sense. But its practical sterility had very important effects on literature. It gave the Romantic heroes that stilted and conventionalised character which finally brought about the school's downfall. A stilted and conventionalised character in one's heroes is certainly no asset in a work of art. Against the *plus* we referred to above, we must now put the following *minus*: *While the art of the Romantics gained much from their revolt against the "bourgeois," on the other hand, it also lost a great deal because this revolt had no practical meaning.*

The first French realists already strove to do away with the principal weakness of the Romantics: the artificial and conventionalised character of their heroes. In Flaubert's novels there is no trace of this stilted artificiality (except perhaps in *Salambo* and *Les Contes*). These early realists are still in revolt against the "bourgeois," but in a different way. They no longer pit imaginary heroes against the bourgeois vulgarians. They rather attempt to make the latter the subject of faithful artistic portrayal. Flaubert considered it his duty to describe the social scene as objectively as a scientist describes nature.

"One must regard people in the same way that one regards mastodons or crocodiles," he said. "Can one possibly get worked up over the horns of the former or the jaws of the latter? Display them, stuff them, pickle them in spirits —that is all. But do not pass moral judgments on them. For if it comes to that, what are you yourselves, you little frogs?"

And in so far as Flaubert succeeded in remaining objective, the characters in his works assumed the importance of "documents," providing essential material for anyone concerned with the scientific study of social psychology. Objectivity was the strongest feature of his method.

Yet despite his artistic objectivity, Flaubert remained extremely subjective in his attitude towards contemporary social movements. As with Théophile Gautier, his savage contempt for the "bourgeois" was accompanied by a most marked hostility towards those who in any way threatened the structure of capitalist society. And with Flaubert this hostility went deeper than with Gautier. He was a determined opponent of universal suffrage, which he described as "a disgrace to the spirit of man." With universal suffrage, he wrote to Georges Sand, "number prevails over intelligence, over education, over breeding and even over money, which is worth more than number."

And in another letter he says that universal suffrage is even sillier than the principle of divine right. He looked upon socialism as some horrible monster which would swallow up all individual initiative, all personality, all thought in a single unified control. In his hostility towards democracy and socialism, this enemy of the "bourgeois" was completely at one with the most narrow-minded of bourgeois ideologists. And this is characteristic of all his contemporaries who were supporters of art for art's sake.

In a biographical sketch of Edgar Allen Poe, Baudelaire, who had long since forgotten his revolutionary journal, *Le Salut Public*, wrote: "For a people that has no artistocracy, the cult of beauty inevitably becomes corrupted, shrinks and disappears." And elsewhere he asserts that only "the priest, the warrior and the poet" are worthy of respect. This is no longer simply conservatism, it is full reaction. Equally reactionary was Barbey d'Aurevilly. In his book, *Les poètes*, speaking of the poetry of Laurent Pichat, he says that the latter could have been a great poet "if only he had been willing to join in stamping out atheism and democracy, these two disgraces to his thinking."

Much water had flowed under the bridge since May, 1835, when Théophile Gautier was writing his Preface to *Mademoiselle de Maupin*. The Saint-Simonists, who had, it seemed, "dinned into his ears" the supposed perfectibility of mankind, had loudly proclaimed the necessity for social reform. But, like most Utopian Socialists, they were convinced supporters of peaceful social evolution, and, for that reason, no less convinced opponents of the class struggle. Moreover, they addressed themselves mainly to the propertied classes. They did not believe in the independent action of the proletariat. The events of 1848, however, had shown that its independent action could become very terrible. After 1848 it was no longer a question of whether the propertied classes would do something to improve the lot of the propertyless. It was a question of who would win the upper hand in the struggle, the possessors or the dispossessed. Relations between classes in latter-day society had become greatly simplified. By this time all the bourgeois ideologists understood that the question at issue was whether the capitalists would succeed in keeping the working masses in economic enslavement. And the realisation of this situation also penetrated into the minds of the protagonists of art for the well-to-do. One of the most remarkable among them, Ernest Renan, in his essay on *Intellectual and Moral Reform*, called for a strong government, "which would compel the sturdy country folk to do our work for us, while we give ourselves up to reflections."[1]

The bourgeois ideologists were coming to understand far more clearly the meaning of the struggle between the bourgeoisie and the proletariat—a fact which could not but exert considerable influence on their "reflections." Ecclesiastes rightly says: "Surely oppression maketh a wise man mad." (*Eccl.* 7, 7.) The discovery by the bourgeois ideologists of the secret of the struggle between their class and the proletariat led to them gradually losing the capacity to study social phenomena with scientific detachment. And this considerably reduced the intrinsic value of their more or less scientific work. Whereas in an earlier period bourgeois political economy could produce such a giant of scientific thought as David Ricardo, the tone was now set in its ranks by chattering dwarfs like Frédéric Bastiat. In philosophy a form of idealist reaction was rapidly gaining strength, the essence of which was the

[1] Quoted by Cassagne, *op. cit.*, pp. 194–5.

conservative tendency to reconcile the latest achievements of natural science with ancient religious traditions, or, to put it more succinctly, to reconcile the oratory with the laboratory.[1]

Nor did art escape this common fate. We shall see later to what ridiculous absurdities the influence of present-day idealist reaction has driven certain modern painters. All I would say for the moment, however, is this: the conservative, and in part even reactionary outlook of the earliest realists did not prevent them from observing the society in which they lived with close attention, or from producing works of great artistic value. It did beyond doubt, however, greatly limit their field of vision. By turning away with hostility from the great contemporary struggle for emancipation, they excluded from their collection of "mastodons" and "crocodiles" the most interesting specimens, those possessed of the richest inner life. Their objective attitude in respect of the social environment they were studying was a mark of complete lack of sympathy on their part. For, obviously, they could not sympathise with what, thanks to their conservatism, formed the unique subject matter of their observation—the "mean and petty passions and ideas" born of the "unclean slime" of everyday middle class existence. And this lack of sympathy for what they were observing and describing was bound before long to lead also to a loss of interest in it—and fairly rapidly did so. Naturalism, for which their brilliant works had laid the foundation, soon found itself, as Huysmans said, in a "blind alley, a tunnel from which the way out was blocked." According to him, naturalism could make everything, down to and including syphilis, the object of its observation.[2]

But the contemporary working-class movement remained

[1] "One can quite consistently go straight from the laboratory to the oratory," remarked Grasset, Professor of Clinical Medicine at Montpelier, some ten years ago. This opinion was enthusiastically echoed by theorists like Jules Soury, author of a book entitled *Bréviaire de l'histoire du matérialisme*, written in the spirit of the well-known work on the same subject by Lange. (See the article, *Oratoire et laboratoire*, in the collection, *Campagnes nationalistes*, Paris, 1902, pp. 233–66 and 267.) See also, in the same collection, an article entitled *Science et réligion*, the dominant theme of which is summed up in the well-known words of du Bois-Raymond: "*Ignoramus et ignoramibus*"—"we neither know nor shall we ever know."

[2] In saying this, Huysmans had in mind the novel by the Belgian writer, Tabarant, *Les Virus d'amour*.

inaccessible. True, Zola wrote *Germinal*. But apart from the weaknesses of this novel, it should not be forgotten that, even though Zola began, as he himself said, to incline towards socialism, nevertheless his so-called experimental method never enabled him to study and portray great social movements artistically. His method was closely connected with what Marx called the outlook of "naturalist-scientific materialism," which fails to understand that the actions, desires, tastes and habits of mind of social man cannot be adequately explained in terms of *physiology* or *pathology*, since they are always conditioned by social relationships. By sticking to this method, the artist could study and depict his "mastodons" and "crocodiles" as individuals, but not as members of a great social unity. And this is what Huysmans felt, when he said that naturalism had landed in a blind alley, and that nothing was left for it but to describe once again "the love affair of the grocer's wife with the wine-merchant on the corner."[1] Such themes could only be of interest if they threw light on some aspect of social relations, as was the case with Russian realism. But the French realists were completely devoid of social interests. And as a result, the portrayal of "the love affair between the grocer's wife and the wine-merchant on the corner" finally lost all interest, became boring and even disgusting.

In his early works—for example, in the novel *Les Soeurs Vatard*—Huysmans himself was a pure naturalist. But he grew tired of depicting the "seven deadly sins" (his own words again), and rejecting naturalism, ended by throwing (as the Germans put it) the baby out with the bath-water. His curious, and in parts extremely boring novel, *A rebours*, is instructive in its very shortcomings. Here, in the character of Des Esseintes, Huysmans presented, or perhaps we should say in the old manner, "composed," the portrait of an original type of superman—in fact, an utterly degenerate aristocrat—whose mode of life was intended to be the absolute antithesis of that of the "wine-merchant" and "the grocer's wife."

A creation of this kind underlines once again the truth of Leconte de Lisle's observation that, where there is no longer any real life, it is the function of poetry to create an ideal life. But the ideal life of Des Esseintes is so lacking in any human content

1 See Jules Huret, *Enquête sur l'évolution littéraire*, conversation with Huysmans, pp. 176–7.

that creating it offered not the least way of escape from the blind alley. Huysmans therefore turned to mysticism, which offered an "ideal" way out of a situation from which "reality" offered no escape. And, in the circumstances, this was the natural way out. Yet what was the result?

The artist who turns mystic does not reject ideological content, but simply gives it a particular character. Mysticism is also an idea, but an obscure idea, formless as the mists, and mortally opposed to reason. The mystic is not averse either to telling a story or even to proving something. But his story is of "something that never was," the basis of his proof is the negation of commonsense. The example of Huysmans proves once again that a work of art cannot manage without ideological content. But when the artist becomes blind to the most important social trends of his day, the ideas expressed in his works lose much of their value. And, as a result, the works themselves inevitably suffer.

This fact is so important for the history of art and literature that it must be examined from all sides. But before attempting this, we will sum up the conclusions so far reached:

The tendency towards art for art's sake arises and becomes established wherever insoluble disaccord is to be found between those engaged in art and the social environment in which they live. This disaccord has a beneficial influence on artistic work in so far as it helps artists to rise above their social milieu. This was the case with Pushkin under Nicholas I. It was the case with the Romantics, the Parnassians and the early realists in France. And, by taking further examples, it would be possible to prove that this has always been the case whenever such a disaccord has existed.

But at the same time, although in revolt against the vulgarities of the society they lived in, the Romantics, Parnassians and realists in no way rebelled against the social relations in which these vulgarities were rooted. On the contrary, whilst denouncing the "bourgeois," they approved of bourgeois society—at first instinctively, and later, quite consciously. And the more the emancipation struggle against the bourgeois social system developed, the more conscious became the attachment to this system of the French adherents of art for art's sake. And the more conscious this attachment became, the less were they able to remain indifferent to the ideological content of their own work.

But their blindness towards the new trend, which was seeking to regenerate the whole of social life, made their ideas mistaken, narrow and bigoted. It depreciated the quality of the ideas expressed in their works. As the natural result of all this, French realism found itself at a dead-end, out of which were to develop, in writers who had at one time belonged to the naturalist school, decadent and mystical tendencies.

I shall return to this conclusion in my next article. But it is time to end; and I will merely add a further word about Pushkin.

When his "poet" thunders against "the rabble," his words are full of anger, but they have no trace of triviality, whatever D. I. Pisarev may say. The poet reproaches the society rabble—and not, be it noted, the real people, who at that time stood right outside the field of vision of Russian literature—because they prized a "mess of pottage" more highly than the Apollo Belvedere. It is this earthbound vulgarity that he finds intolerable. And that is all. If he refuses to try to teach "the rabble," it is because he is entirely without hope for it. There is no trace of reaction here. And this constitutes Pushkin's immense superiority over the defenders of art for art's sake such as Gautier. But at the same time this superiority is of a relative character. Pushkin did not jeer at the Saint-Simonists; but he had probably never heard of them. He was an honest and generous man, but despite his honesty and generosity, he had been imbued from childhood with certain class prejudices. The ending of the exploitation of one class by another would have seemed to him an unattainable, even an absurd Utopia. Had he heard of any practical plans to end exploitation, and especially if they had caused such a stir in Russia as the Saint-Simonists had caused in France, it is probable that he would have fulminated against them with biting polemical articles and ironical epigrams. Some of his remarks—in his article *Thoughts Whilst Travelling*—on the advantages enjoyed by the Russian peasant serf in comparison with the West European worker, lead one to think that in such circumstances the intellectually gifted Pushkin might sometimes have reasoned little better than the much less gifted Gautier. Russia's economic backwardness saved Pushkin from this possible failing.

It is an old, but ever new, story. When a class lives by exploiting another at a lower level on the economic ladder, then once the former has achieved full mastery over society, for it to *go forward* means that it must *go down*. And herein lies the explanation of a phenomenon at first sight incomprehensible and possibly even incredible, that the ideological level of the ruling classes is often much higher in economically backward than in economically advanced countries.

Today even Russia has reached that level of economic development at which the adherents of art for art's sake are becoming conscious defenders of a social order based on the exploitation of one class by another. That is why we find not a little reactionary nonsense being talked at present about the "absolute autonomy of art." But in Pushkin's day it was quite different. And in this he was fortunate.

III

I have said that there is no such thing as a work of art entirely devoid of ideological content. To this I added that not every idea is capable of constituting the foundation of a work of art. Only those which promote communion between men can give true inspiration to the artist. And the possible limits of such communion are determined, not by the artist, but by the level of culture achieved by the society to which he belongs. In a society divided into classes, moreover, it also depends on the nature of the class relationships and on the stage of development which each of the classes has attained. When the bourgeoisie was still fighting to throw off the yoke of the aristocracy, spiritual and temporal, that is, when it was itself a revolutionary class, it led in its train all the working people, and constituted, together with them, a single "third estate." At that time the advanced ideologists of the bourgeoisie were also the advanced ideologists of "the entire nation, with the exception of the privileged classes." In other words, the limits of the communion between men which could be forwarded by artists who took the bourgeois side were very extensive. But when the interests of the bourgeoisie ceased to be those of all the working people, and especially when they came into conflict with the interests of the proletariat, then the limits of this communion sharply contracted. Ruskin had said that a miser cannot make a poem about his lost money. A time had now arrived when the temper of the bourgeoisie was beginning to approach that of a miser lamenting his gold—with this difference, that Ruskin's miser lamented what had already happened, whereas the bourgeoisie was losing its peace of mind over a loss which threatened it in the future. "Surely oppression maketh a wise man mad," said Ecclesiastes. The same effect is produced on a wise man (even a wise man!) by the fear that he may lose the possibility of oppressing others. The ideologies of a ruling class lose their intrinsic value in the same measure as the class ripens for its doom. The art produced by its experiences declines. The purpose of the present article is to develop what has already been said on this subject in the last article, by examining some of the most outstanding signs of the present decline of bourgeois art.

We have seen how mysticism made its appearance in the contemporary literature of France. This happened because writers who were conscious of the impossibility of limiting themselves to form without content, i.e. without idea, were at the same time unable to rise to an understanding of the great liberating ideas of our time. This very consciousness and inability had many other consequences which, no less than mysticism, spoiled their work.

Mysticism is the irreconcilable enemy of reason. But it is not only the convert to mysticism who is at enmity with reason. Whoever defends a false idea, on whatever grounds or by whatever means, is also at enmity with reason. And when a work of art is founded upon a false idea, this produces so many internal inconsistencies that its aesthetic value inevitably suffers.

I once examined Knut Hamsun's play, *At the King's Gates*, as an example of a work of art that suffers from falsity of fundamental conception.[1] But I hope I may be excused if I repeat myself.

The hero of this play is the young writer Ivar Kareno, who makes up by conceit what he lacks in talent. In his own opinion, he is a man with "thoughts as free as a bird." What does this thinker, free as a bird, write about? About "resistance."

[1] See my article, *The Son of Dr. Stockman*, in my collection *From Defence to Attack*.

Knut Hamsun, prominent Norwegian writer (1859), worked in his youth as docker, stonemason and lumberjack, and afterwards spent a number of years in dire poverty in the United States. He began writing in 1877, and his first success came with the publication of extracts from his novel, *Hunger*, in a Copenhagen journal in 1888. Later, during the rise of German fascism, he became a supporter of the Nazis, and enthusiastically continued this support during the Nazi occupation of his country.—TRANS.

About "hatred." Whom does he call on us to resist? Whom does he teach us to hate? He calls for resistance to the proletariat. Is this not, indeed, a new type of hero? Certainly we have met very few, if any, such heroes in literature—in fact, we have not hitherto met any at all. Whatever else he may be, a man who preaches resistance to the proletariat is certainly a bourgeois ideologist. But the bourgeois ideologist Ivar Kareno appears, both to himself and to his creator, Knut Hamsun, as a great revolutionary.

We have already met such "revolutionary" frames of mind in the early French Romantics, and have seen that their most distinctive feature is their conservatism. Théophile Gautier hated the "bourgeois," and at the same time denounced those who said it was time to do away with bourgeois social relations. Ivar Kareno is evidently one of the spiritual heirs of this celebrated French Romantic. But he goes much further than his master. His hostility is deliberate, where his forerunner's was only instinctive.[1]

[1] I am speaking of the time when Gautier had not yet worn out his famous red waistcoat. Subsequently, at the time of the Paris Commune, for example, he had become a conscious enemy—and what a fire-eater!—of working-class aspirations to liberty. It should be noted, by the way, that Flaubert may also, and with even greater justification, be called an ideological forerunner of Knut Hamsun. The following remarkable passage occurs in one of his note-books: "It is not against God that Prometheus would have to rise at the present time, but against the people, the new god. The place of the old priestly, feudal and monarchic tyrannies has been taken by a new one, more subtle, infrangible, imperious, which in time will not have left free a single corner of the earth." See *Les carnets de Gustave Flaubert* in Louis Bertrand's book, *Gustave Flaubert*, Paris, 1912, p. 255.

This is precisely the thought, free as a bird, which inspires Ivar Kareno. In a letter to Georges Sand dated September 8, 1871, Flaubert wrote: "I think that the mob, the herd, will always be hateful. What counts is only the small group of kindred spirits, ever the same, who hand on the torch from one to another." It is in this same letter that the words which I quoted earlier on universal suffrage occur, where he states that it was a disgrace to human reason that numbers should prevail even over money! (See Flaubert, *Correspondance, quatrième série* (1869–1880), huitième mille, Paris, 1910.)

In these views Ivar Kareno would certainly have recognised his own thoughts, free as a bird. But such views had not yet found *direct* expression in Flaubert's novels. A further development of the class struggle in modern society was necessary before the ideologists of the ruling class were to feel the need for directly expressing in literature their hatred for the emancipation movement of the "people." But then they could no longer defend the "absolute autonomy" of art. On the contrary, they imposed upon art the conscious aim of serving as a spiritual weapon in the struggle against the proletariat. But of this more later.

If the Romantics were conservatives, then Ivar Kareno is a diehard reactionary of the purest water: and, in addition, a utopian of a similar type to Schedrin's[1] eccentric squire. Kareno wants to destroy the proletariat, just as the squire wanted to destroy the peasant. With them, utopia reaches the utmost limits of absurdity. But, in general, all Ivar Kareno's bird-free thoughts are inane in the extreme, the most wrong-headed of them all being that the proletariat appears in his eyes as a class exploiting the other classes of society. And the trouble is that Knut Hamsun himself obviously shares the mistaken notions of his hero. Ivar Kareno meets with all kinds of misadventures simply because he "resists" the hated proletariat. For this reason he loses a job as a professor and cannot even get his book published. In short, he is victimised time after time by the "bourgeois" who surrounded him. But where in the world, in what utopia, is to be found the bourgeoisie which would so ruthlessly victimise anyone for resisting the proletariat? Such a bourgeoisie never has and never can exist. Knut Hamsun bases his play on an idea which is quite contrary to reality. And as a result, incidents which he evidently intended to be tragic, turn out to be merely comical, seriously injuring the play itself.

Knut Hamsun has great talent. But no talent can make truth out of its direct opposite. The failure of his play, *At the King's Gates*, is the inevitable result of the complete bankruptcy of its fundamental idea. And this bankruptcy is caused by his inability to understand the nature of that class struggle in present-day society, of which his play is a literary echo.

Knut Hamsun is not a Frenchman. But that makes no difference. *The Communist Manifesto* long ago made the penetrating observation that, in civilised countries, thanks to the development of capitalism, "national one-sidedness and narrow-mindedness become more and more impossible, and from the numerous national and local literatures there arises a world literature." True, Hamsun was born and brought up in one of those West European countries which is far from being among the most developed economically. And this, of course, explains his naïve conception of the militant proletariat in present-day society. But the economic backwardness of his own country has not saved him from becoming imbued with that hostility to the working class, and

[1] Nineteenth-century Russian playwright and satirist.—TRANS.

sympathy for the struggle against it, which is now taking hold of bourgeois intellectuals in the most advanced countries. Ivar Kareno is a variation on the Nietzschean theme. And what is Nietzscheanism? It is a new version, revised and enlarged, of the struggle against "the bourgeois" with which we have already become familiar, which goes hand in hand with an unshakeable sympathy for bourgeois society—a version altered in accordance with the requirements of the most modern capitalism. The example of Hamsun, moreover, can easily be paralleled by another, this time from contemporary French literature.

One of the most talented and, what is here even more important, one of the most thoughtful dramatists of present-day France, is undoubtedly François de Curel. And, equally undoubtedly, the most outstanding of his plays is *Le repas du Lion*,[1] which, as far as I know, has been little noticed by Russian critics. The leading character in this play, Jean de Sancy, had once, under certain exceptional childhood influences, been interested in Christian Socialism. But later he makes a complete break with it, and comes forth as an eloquent defender of large-scale capitalist enterprise. In Act IV, Scene 3, he sets out in a long speech to prove to the workers that "the egoism which promotes production is, for the mass of the workers, the same as charity is for the destitute—a source of benefits." And when his hearers express dissent, he becomes more and more heated, explaining to them the role of the capitalist and his workers in present-day production in a picturesque simile.

> They say (he thunders) that whole flocks of jackals follow the lion into the wilderness to eat what remains of his prey. Too weak to attack buffaloes, not fleet enough to catch gazelles, all their hopes are pinned on the claws of the king of beasts. You hear me—on his claws! At dusk he leaves his lair and seeks a victim. He finds it. He takes a mighty leap, a fierce struggle ensues, a mortal encounter takes place, and the earth becomes covered with blood—not always the blood of the victim. Then follows the royal feast, which is watched by the jackals with attentive respect. When the lion has eaten his fill, the jackals dine. Do you think that the jackals would be better fed if the lion divided his prey equally with all of them, leaving himself only a small piece? Not in the least! Such a nice kind lion would be a lion no longer, hardly a blind man's dog. I can see him giving up the kill at the first groan, and licking his victim's wounds. But give me a ferocious animal, avid for booty, thinking only of killing and butchery. When such a lion roars, the jackals lick their chops.

[1] *The Lion's Feast.*

The eloquent orator rubs in the meaning of this parable, clear enough in all conscience, in the following brief but expressive words:

> The employer discovers those nourishing waters of which the spray besprinkles the workers.

I am well aware that the artist is not necessarily committed to the views expressed by his heroes. But we can often ascertain his own views from the hints he gives us as to his attitude to these speeches. The whole subsequent course of the play, *Le repas du Lion*, shows that the author himself wholeheartedly agrees with Jean de Sancy's comparison of the employer with a lion, and of the workers with jackals. It is obvious that he himself would be prepared to repeat with complete conviction the words of his hero: "I believe in the lion; I respect the rights which his claws confer on him." He himself is ready to call the workers jackals, feeding themselves on the scraps of what the capitalist has secured by his labour. The struggle of the workers against the employers seems to him, as to Jean de Sancy, a struggle between envious jackals and the mighty lion. This comparison is the underlying idea of the play, determining the fate of his principal character. But there is not a grain of truth in it. It falsifies the true character of contemporary social relations far more than even the economic sophisms of Bastia and all his numerous followers up to Böhm-Bawerck in our own day. The jackals do absolutely nothing to provide that which the lion feeds on, and which partially assuages their own hunger. And yet who will dare to say that the workers employed in a factory do nothing towards making its products? Surely, all economic sophistries notwithstanding, it is clear that these articles are precisely the product of their labour? Of course, the employer himself participates in the production process as its organiser. And, as an organiser, he himself must be numbered among those who work. But, once again, it is common knowledge that the salary of the factory director is one thing, and the manufacturer's profit another. After deducting this salary, there still remains a profit, which goes to swell the fund of capital. The whole question is: Why does capital receive this surplus? And there is not a hint as to the solution of this question in the eloquent speeches of Jean de Sancy. Moreover, it should be pointed out that he does not even suspect that his own income, as one of the shareholders in the undertaking, would in no way be justified, even if the quite baseless comparison of the employer with the lion and the workers with jackals were a sound one. He himself does nothing for the business beyond accepting each year a handsome income from it. If anyone does resemble a jackal, feeding on what has been won by other people's efforts, it is precisely the shareholder, whose sole "work" consists in keeping an eye on his shares—and the bourgeois ideologist, who himself takes no part in production, but picks up what is left over from the lavishly-spread tables of capital. Unfortunately, the talented de Curel is himself such an ideologist. In the struggle between the wage-workers and the capitalists, he has ranged himself firmly on the side of the latter, drawing an utterly false picture of their real relations with those whom they exploit.

And what is Bourget's play, *La Barricade*, but a call to the bourgeoisie by this well-known, and also undoubtedly talented, author, summoning them to close their ranks for the struggle against the proletariat? Bourgeois art is beginning to grow bellicose. Its representatives are no longer justified in speaking of themselves as not born "for trouble or strife." No! They are eager for battle, and are anything but fearful of the emotions associated with it. But in the name of what are the battles being fought? Alas, in the name of "greed." True, not their own personal greed. It would be strange to maintain that people like de Curel or Bourget are acting as defenders of capital from motives of personal gain. The "greed" for whose sake they are ready to sustain these stirring "emotions," and for which they are eager to do battle, is the greed of an entire class. But since it is not, on this account, any the less greed, it may be seen what a pass we have come to.

What once made the Romantics despise the "bourgeois"? We already know what it was: "the bourgeois" as Théodore de Banville said, valued the five-franc piece above everything else. But what is it that artists like de Curel, Bourget and Hamsun are defending? The social relations which guarantee to the bourgeois his source of a large number of five-franc pieces. How far these artists have travelled from the romanticism of earlier days! What has come between them and the early romantics? Nothing less than the inexorable course of social development. And the sharper grow the internal contradictions inherent in the capitalist mode of production—the more difficult is it for artists who remain true to bourgeois ways of thinking to uphold the theory of art for art's sake, and to continue to live in their ivory towers.

I do not think there is a single country in the contemporary civilised world where bourgeois youth does not sympathise with the ideas of Friedrich Nietzsche. Friedrich Nietzsche despised his "sleepy" (*schläfrigen*) contemporaries even more, perhaps, than Théophile Gautier despised the "bourgeois" of his time. But what, in Nietzsche's eyes, were his "sleepy" contemporaries guilty of? What was their fundamental fault, the well-spring of all others? The fact that they could neither think, nor feel, nor, what is even more important, act in a manner suitable for those occupying the ruling position in society. In present historical conditions, to say this is to accuse them of not displaying sufficient energy and consistency in defending the capitalist order against the revolutionary onslaughts of the proletariat. No wonder Nietzsche speaks with such venom of the Socialists!

But let us consider once more what follows from this. Whereas Pushkin and the Romantics contemporary with him reproached the "rabble" with setting too much store by its bread and butter, those who inspire the present-day neo-Romantics reproach it with not defending its bread and butter with sufficient determination, i.e. with not setting sufficient store by it. Nevertheless, like the early Romantics, the neo-Romantics still proclaim the "absolute autonomy" of art. But can we seriously talk of the autonomy of art, when it consciously sets itself the aim of defending definite social relations? Of course not! Art of this kind is obviously utilitarian. And if its representatives profess to despise all utilitarian art, this is simply a misunderstanding. Of course, there is no question here of personal interest, which can never be decisive for men sincerely devoted to art; but in point of fact their sole objection is against anything which would be to the advantage of the exploited majority. It is the advantage of the exploiting minority which is, to them, the supreme law. Thus, the attitude of a Knut Hamsun or a François de Curel to utilitarianism in art is, in fact, directly opposed to the attitude of Théophile Gautier or Flaubert, even though as far as we know, Gautier and Flaubert themselves were by no means free from conservative prejudices. But in the meantime, as a result of sharpening of social contradictions, these prejudices have become so deeply entrenched among artists who have taken the bourgeois side that it has become incomparably more difficult for them to maintain the theory of art for art's sake consistently. Of course, it would be a great mistake to imagine that no artist any longer consistently adheres to this theory. But, as we shall see in a moment, they now have to pay a heavy price for this kind of consistency.

The neo-Romantics, once again under Nietzsche's influence, like to think of themselves as being "beyond good and evil." But what does being "beyond good and evil" mean? It means to be engaged in an historical cause so great that it cannot be judged in terms of the ideas of good and evil which have arisen on the basis of a particular social order. The French revolutionaries of 1793 were undoubtedly "beyond good and evil" in their struggle against reaction, in the sense that their actions contradicted the ideas of good and evil rooted in the old, decaying order. Such contradictions, which always have their very tragic aspect, are vindicated solely by the fact that the actions of the revolutionaries, forced for a time to go "beyond good and evil," finally result in evil retreating before good in social life. To take the Bastille it was necessary to fight its defenders. And he who carries on such a fight puts himself "beyond good and evil" for the time being. But because the taking of the Bastille curbed the arbitrary power of the absolute monarchy, whereby anyone could be imprisoned "at the king's pleasure," it resulted in evil retreating before good in the social life of France. And this was the vindication of those who had temporarily placed themselves "beyond good and evil" in the fight against despotism.

But not all who claim to be "beyond good and evil" can find such a vindication. Ivar Kareno, for example, would have had no scruples in placing himself "beyond good and evil" in order to realise his "bird-free thoughts." Yet as we have seen, the position he took up was one of irreconcilable struggle against the proletarian movement for emancipation. Therefore, in his case, to go "beyond good and evil" meant to cease to be restrained by even those few rights which the working class has succeeded in winning in bourgeois society. And so the victory of his cause would not bring about any lessening of evil in social life, but rather its increase. His temporary departure "beyond good and evil" could not possibly be justified; nor can it ever be justified when it serves reactionary purposes. Someone may object that though Ivar Kareno cannot be vindicated from the standpoint of the proletariat, he can certainly be vindicated from the point of view of the bourgeoisie. I agree. But the bourgeois standpoint is, in this instance, that of a privileged minority, seeking to perpetuate its privileges. The proletarian standpoint, on the other hand, is that of the majority, demanding the abolition of all privileges. That is why actions which are vindicated from the bourgeois standpoint must be condemned from the standpoint of all those who are not inclined to defend the interests of the exploiters. But that is all I require; the irresistible course of economic development itself ensures that the latter will continually increase in number.

The neo-Romantics, who loathe "sleepiness" from the bottom of their hearts, want a movement. But the movement they desire is a conservative movement, opposed to the emancipation movement of our time. This is the key to their whole psychology. And this is why even the best of them cannot produce the fine work of which they might have been capable had their social sympathies and way of thinking been different.

We have already seen how false was the idea on which de Curel based his play, *Le repas du Lion*. And a false idea at its basis inevitably spoils a work of art, since it brings a lie into the psychology of the characters. It is easy to see how false is the psychology of Jean de Sancy, the main character of this play. But to deal further with this character would mean a long digression. I shall take another example which can be discussed more briefly.

The basic idea in *La Barricade* is that each individual must take the side of his own class in the class struggle of his day. Yet whom does Bourget consider "the most likeable character" in his play?[1] The old worker Gaucheron, who takes the side of the employers, and not of the workers. Everything this working man is made to do belies the fundamental idea of the play, and no one not completely blinded by sympathy for the bourgeoisie could admire him. Gaucheron's sentiments are those of a slave who reveres his chains. But Count Alexei Tolstoy proved long ago how hard it is to arouse sympathy for a loyal slave, among those who have not been educated in the spirit of slavery. We need only remember his Vasili Shibanov, who so surprisingly well maintained his "slavish loyalty" that he died a martyr, despite frightful tortures:

'Tis ever, Tsar, the selfsame word:
He glorifies his sovereign lord,

[1] These are his own words. See *La Barricade*, Paris, 1910, Preface, p. xix.

The present-day reader, however, is left unmoved by this servile heroism. Generally speaking, he finds it hard to understand how a "machine endowed with speech" can be so selflessly devoted to its owner. Yet the old man Gaucheron, in Bourget's play, is, after all, not unlike Shibanov, changed from a serf into a modern proletarian. One's eyesight must indeed be defective if one finds him "the most likeable character" in the play. In any case, if Gaucheron is likeable, then, whatever Bourget may say, this implies that we should side, not necessarily with our own class, but with the class whose cause we consider most just.

In creating this character, Bourget contradicted his own conception. And this is once more because, in oppressing others, a wise man becomes a fool. When a talented artist is inspired by a false idea he spoils his own work. And no modern artist can be inspired by true ideas if he is seeking to defend the bourgeoisie in its struggle against the proletariat.

I have already observed that it has now become far more difficult than it was in the past for an artist who takes his stand on the side of the bourgeoisie to follow through consistently the theory of "art for art's sake."

Bourget, by the way, admits this. In fact he himself puts it even more bluntly:

> No one who thinks and feels can remain a mere impartial chronicler of the frightful civil strife in which perhaps, the whole future of our country and of civilisation itself is at stake.[1]

But we must qualify this statement. No one who thinks and feels can look on indifferently at the civil war being waged in modern society. If his field of vision is narrowed by bourgeois prejudices, he will find himself on one side of the "barricade," if he is not infected by these prejudices, on the other. That is true. But not all the sons of the bourgeoisie—or of any other class, for that matter—are capable of thought. Nor are all those who think capable of feeling. Such people can easily, even today, remain consistent supporters of the theory of art for art's sake. For no theory could be better adapted to indifference to social interests—even if only to narrow class interests. And the bourgeois social system, perhaps more than any other, fosters such indifference. When entire generations are brought up in the spirit of that

[1] *La Barricade*, Preface, p. xxiv.

notorious principle, "every man for himself and the devil take the hindmost," this inevitably breeds egoists who think only of themselves, and are interested only in themselves. Indeed, there are more individualists among the bourgeoisie of today than ever before in history. As witness we may cite one of the most outstanding ideologists of the bourgeoisie, Maurice Barrès.

> Our morals, our religion, our national feelings, all have broken down. They can give us no guidance. And until some teacher arises who can re-establish the certainties for us, we must hold fast to the sole reality—to our ego.[1]

When he finds that everything has "broken down" except his own ego, why should not a man play the part of "impartial chronicler" of that great war which is being fought out in the very heart of modern society? Yet something still remains to hinder him, namely, the complete absence of all social interest which is so apparent in the lines I have cited from Barrès. How can he become a chronicler of the social struggle, when he has no interest either in it or in society? To him it must all be unbearably tedious. And so, if he is an artist, he will not so much as hint at it in his work. He will rather occupy himself, there too, with the "sole reality"—that is, his own ego. And since his "ego" may, all the same, grow weary with no other company than itself, he will invent for its benefit a fantastic "other world," elevated far above this earth and above all earthly "questions."

And that is just what many contemporary artists are doing. I am not slandering them. They admit it themselves. This is what our compatriot, Zinaida Hippius, has to say, for example:

> I consider the natural and most essential need of mankind to be prayer. Every man undoubtedly prays or wants to pray, no matter whether or not he is conscious of this need, no matter what the form in which his prayer is poured forth, nor to what God it is addressed. Its form depends on the capabilities and inclinations of the individual. Poetic art as a whole, and verse composition in particular, verbal music—these are but one of the forms that prayer takes in our souls.[2]

[1] *Sous l'œil des barbares*, ed. 1901, p. 18.

Needless to say, this identification of "verbal music" with prayer is without foundation. There have been very long periods in the history of poetry during which it has had absolutely no connection whatever with prayer. But I need not labour this point. I merely wished to familiarise the reader with Mme. Hippius's terminology, without some knowledge of which he might have been puzzled by the following extracts, which are nevertheless essential.

Mme. Hippius continues:

> Are we to blame for the fact that every "ego" has to-day become an individual, solitary "ego," cut off from all other "egos" and therefore incomprehensible to and unwanted by them? Each one of us is passionately in need of prayer and finds in it something we can understand and treasure. We need our poetry—the reflection of the momentary fullness of our heart. But to another, who has his "own" cherished need, my prayer is alien and incomprehensible. Consciousness of solitude separates men still further from each other, isolates them and forces them to become locked up in themselves. We are ashamed of our prayers and, knowing that we cannot in any case join in them with anyone else, we speak them in half-tones to ourselves, hinting at things which only we ourselves can understand.[1]

When individualism reaches such extremes as this, then indeed, the "possibility of communion in prayer itself, as well as community of devotional (i.e. poetic—G. V. P.) impulse," does in fact disappear, as Mme. Hippius so rightly says. But poetry, and art in general, inevitably suffer as a result, since they serve as one of the means of communion between men. Long ago the Old Testament Jehovah justly proclaimed that man cannot live by himself. And this is confirmed in the person of Mme. Hippius. In one of her poems we read:—

> Merciless is my road
> Leading me on unto death,
> But I love myself as the Lord,
> And love will save my soul.

This is open to doubt. Who loves "himself as the Lord"? Only an illimitable egoist. And it is unlikely that such an egoist would be capable of saving anybody's soul.

But it is no concern of our's whether Mme. Hippius's soul, or the souls of those who, like her, love "themselves as the Lord," will be saved. The point is that poets who love themselves as the

[1] *Collected Poems*, Foreword, p. iii.

Lord can have no interest in what is going on in society around them. Their aspirations must remain extremely nebulous.

In her poem entitled *Song*, Mme. Hippius "sings":

> Alas, I die in senseless melancholy,
> I die
> Striving for I know not what,
> Know not what. . . .
> And whence this striving came I know not
> Whence it came.
> But the heart wants and asks a miracle,
> A miracle!
> O, that something may happen
> Which never happens!
> The wan sky promises me wonders,
> It promises. . . .
> Yet I weep without tears of a vow without faith,
> Vow without faith . . .
> I need that which does not exist in this world,
> Which does not exist in this world.

This is not badly put, perhaps. To anyone who "loves himself as the Lord," and has lost the ability to communicate with other people, there is nothing left but to "ask for a miracle" and aspire to something "which does not exist in the world." What does exist in this world cannot be of interest to him. Cornet Babayev, in Sergeyev-Tsensky's tale, says that "art is the product of green sickness."[1] This philosophising son of Mars is gravely mistaken when he supposes that *all* art is the product of green-sickness. But undoubtedly the art which aspires to "what does not exist in the world" is the creation of "green-sickness." It marks the collapse of a whole system of social relations, and is therefore very well named "decadent."

True, the system of social relations the collapse of which is marked by this art, i.e. the system of capitalist production, is far from collapse in our own country. Capitalism in Russia has not yet finally settled its score with the old order. But Russian literature, since the time of Peter I, has been strongly influenced by that of Western Europe. For this reason certain currents, which fully correspond to West European social relations, have made themselves felt in Russian literature, although they correspond much less to the comparatively backward conditions in

[1] *Stories*, Vol. II, p. 128.

Russia. There was a time when some of our aristocrats were attracted by the teachings of the Encyclopaedists,[1] which were related to one of the final stages of the struggle of the third estate with the aristocracy in France. Many of our "intellectuals" to-day are embracing social, philosophical and aesthetic theories which are products of the age of decline of the West European bourgeoisie. This infatuation anticipates the course of our own social development just as much as did the interest of the men of the eighteenth century in the French Encyclopaedists.[2]

But the nature of the decadent tendencies in Russia is unaltered by the fact that such tendencies are not entirely home produced, so to speak. Imported from the West, decadent art remains what it was at its birthplace—a product of the "green-sickness" accompanying the decay of the class which to-day rules Western Europe.

Mme. Hippius will perhaps object that I have arbitrarily accused her of indifference to social questions. But in the first place, I have accused her of nothing. I have simply given an account of her own lyrical effusions, confining myself to a definition of their meaning. The reader can judge whether or not I have correctly understood these effusions. In the second place, I am aware of course, that Mme. Hippius is not unwilling, nowadays, to say a few words about the social movement. Here, for example, is a book she has written in collaboration with Messrs. D. Merezhkovsky and D Filosofov, and published in Germany in 1908. It convincingly demonstrates her interest in the Russian social movement. But one needs only read the preface to realise how exclusively the authors are striving after "they know not what." The preface states that Europe knows the facts of the

[1] It is known, for example, that Helvetius' *De l'homme* was published at The Hague in 1772 by a Prince Golitzyn.

[2] The passion of certain Russian aristocrats for the French Encylopaedists had, in actual fact, no practical consequences. Nevertheless it was *useful*, in the sense that it cleared some aristocratic heads of a few aristocratic prejudices. On the other hand, the present infatuation of a certain section of our intelligentsia for the philosophical and aesthetic theories of the declining bourgeoisie is *harmful*, because it fills our intellectuals' heads with bourgeois prejudices, which could not have arisen independently, since Russian social development had not yet itself prepared the ground for them. These prejudices even penetrate the minds of many Russian sympathisers with the proletarian movement, in whose heads there results an amazing hotch-potch of socialism and modernism, born of the decay of the bourgeoisie. This confusion does a great deal of harm in practical matters too.

Russian revolution, but not its soul. And doubtless to make known to Europe the soul of the Russian revolution, the authors inform the Europeans of the following:

> We are as like you as the left hand is like the right. . . . But we are equal to you only in the sense that we are opposite. . . . Kant would say that our spirit dwells in the transcendental, while yours dwells in the phenomenal. Nietzsche would say:—Apollo rules with you and Dionysus with us. Your genius lies in moderation, ours in impulsiveness. You know how to stop in time; if you come up against a wall you either stop or go round it, while we rush at it head on. It is difficult for us to let ourselves go, but once we do we cannot stop. Instead of walking we run. Instead of running we fly, and when we fly we crash. You prefer the golden mean, we prefer extremes. You are just, for us there are no laws. You know how to maintain your spiritual equilibrium, while we are always striving to lose it. You rule the kingdom of the present, we seek the kingdom of the future. In the last resort you always place State power higher than all the freedoms you have been able to win. But we remain rebels and anarchists even when we are chained in slavery. Reason and emotion lead us to the utmost bounds of negation and, despite this, we remain mystics to the very depths of our being.[1]

The Europeans further learn that the Russian revolution is as absolute as the State against which it is directed, and that while the empirical conscious aim of this revolution is socialism, its subconscious mystic aim is anarchism.[2] In conclusion our authors state that they are addressing, not the European bourgeoisie, but . . . the proletariat, you think, dear reader? You're mistaken! "Only the single minds of universal culture, those who share Nietzsche's view that the State is the coldest of all cold monsters" —and so on.[3]

I have not made these quotations for polemical purposes. I am not, in fact, engaged in polemics, but am merely seeking to characterise and explain certain attitudes sometimes found among certain social strata. The passages cited have shown, I hope, that when Mme. Hippius does (at last!) become interested in social questions she remains the same as she was before: an extreme individualist of the decadent variety, thirsting for a "miracle" precisely because she has no serious ties with real social life. The reader will not have forgotten Leconte de Lisle's view that poetry to-day provides an ideal life for those who no longer have a real

[1] D. Mereschkowsky, Zinaida Hippius, Dmitri Philosophoff *Der Zar und die Revolution*, München, K. Piper und C-o Verlag, 1908, Seite 1–2.

[2] *Ibid.*, p. 5.

[3] *Ibid.*, p. 6.

one. But when a man loses all spiritual contact with his fellows, his ideal life loses all contact with the earth. And then his fantasy carries him off into the skies, and he becomes a mystic. Mme. Hippius' interest in social questions, steeped in mysticism as it is, remains quite unproductive.[1] But she and her collaborators are wrong in thinking that their thirst for a "miracle," and her "mystic" rejection of politics "as a science," constitute a distinctive feature of the Russian decadents.[2] The "sober" West produced, before ever "drunken" Russia, men who rebelled against reason in the name of irrational cravings. Erik Falk, in Pryzbyszewski's book, denounced social-democrats and "drawing-room anarchists" like John Henry Mackay, simply because they set too much store by reason.

"They all of them," declares this non-Russian decadent, "preach a peaceful revolution, the changing of a broken wheel for a new one while the wagon is in motion. Their whole dogmatic structure is absurd just because it is so logical, for it is founded on the omnipotence of reason. Everything that has taken place up till now, however, has come about, not by reason, but by stupidity and meaningless accident."[3]

Falk's recourse to "stupidity" and "meaningless accident" is essentially the same thing as the quest for a "miracle" which we find in the German book by Mme. Hippius and Messrs. Merezhkovsky and Filosofov. It is the same idea under a different name.

[1] Merezhkovsky, Hippius and Filosofov do not at all reject in their book the term "decadents." They confine themselves to modestly informing Europe that the Russian decadents "have reached the highest peaks of world culture." ("Haben die höchsten Gipfel der Weltkultur erreicht.") *Ibid.*, p. 151.

[2] It stands to reason that her mystic anarchism will frighten no one. Anarchism, generally speaking, is nothing but the final outcome, the logical conclusion, from the basic premises of bourgeois idealism. That is why we often find sympathy for anarchism among bourgeois ideologists in the period of decadence. Maurice Barrès also sympathised with anarchism at the period in his development when he was asserting that there was no reality other than the "ego." It is probable that today he has no *conscious* sympathy for anarchism, since all the sham stormy passions of Barrès' individualism have long since died down. Those "certainties" which he once declared to be "destroyed" he now regards as "restored." The process of their restoration was concluded by Barrès taking up a nationalistic attitude of the most blatant sort. And there is nothing surprising in this change-over. It is only a stone's throw from extreme bourgeois idealism to the most reactionary "certainties." *Avis à* Mme. Hippius and for Messrs. Merezhkovsky and Filosofov.

[3] Stanislas Przybyszewski, *Homo Sapiens*, t. III, p. 181.

It arises from the extreme subjectivism of so many bourgeois intellectuals today. When a man considers his own "ego" to be the "sole reality," then he can find no objective connection, "rational" in the sense of being determined by definite laws, between his "ego" on the one hand and the external world on the other. The external world must appear to him as either altogether unreal or as real only in part—in so far, namely, as its existence is based on the only true reality, that is to say, on the "ego."

If such a person has a philosophical bent he may assert that when the "ego" creates the external world, it introduces into that world something at least of the ego's rationality. No philosopher can completely banish reason from the world, even if he limits its rights for one consideration or another—in the interests of religion, for example.[1]

If, however, someone who is not philosophically inclined, comes to consider his own "ego" to be the sole reality, he will certainly not bother to ask himself how this "ego" created the external world. And so he will not be prepared to admit the least measure of reason, i.e. of conformity to law, in the external world. On the contrary, the world will appear to him a realm of "meaningless chance." And if he comes to sympathise with any great social movement, then he will believe, like Falk, that no laws of social development can assure its success, but that its future is in the hands only of human "stupidity" or—what amounts to the same thing—of "meaningless" historical "accident." But I have already pointed out that the mystical views of Mme. Hippius and her two adherents with regard to the Russian emancipation movement are in essence no different from those of Falk on the "meaningless" causes of great historical events. In their attempt to amaze Europe with the unprecedented boundlessness of Russian aspirations to freedom, these authors remain decadents of the purest water. They can sympathise only with that "which never happens" and "does not exist"; they are incapable of any sympathy with what is really going on. And so there is nothing in their mystical anarchism to modify the conclusions I reached on the basis of Mme. Hippius' lyrical effusions.

1 Kant may be cited as an example of a thinker of this sort, who has limited the rights of reason in the interests of religion. "I have therefore found it necessary to deny *knowledge,* in order to make room for *faith.*" (*Critique of Pure Reason,* Preface to 2nd Edition.)

Having touched on this point, I will be entirely frank. The events of 1905–6 made a strong impression on the Russian decadents, just as the events of 1848–9 did on the French Romantics. They were roused to take an interest in social affairs. But this interest was even less suited to the psychology of the decadents than it had been to the psychology of the romantics: with the result that their concern with social questions was even more superficial. There are no grounds for taking it seriously.

To return to contemporary art. An individual who considers his "ego" to be the sole reality is bound to "love himself as the Lord," just like Mme. Hippius. This is perfectly comprehensible and quite inevitable. And when he "loves himself as the Lord," he can be concerned in his artistic work with nothing but himself. The external world will only interest him in so far as it affects his precious "ego," that "sole reality."

In Sudermann's very interesting play, *Das Blumenboot*,[1] the Baroness Erfflingen says to her daughter Thea:

> The business of people of our class is to create for ourselves, out of the things of this world, a kind of gay panorama which is always passing before our eyes—or rather, seems to, for really it is we who are moving. I have no doubt at all about this. And for this reason we want nothing that weighs us down. (Act II, Scene i.)

These words admirably express the outlook of the class to which the Baroness Erfflingen belongs. Such people can repeat to themselves with full conviction the words of Maurice Barrès—"Our ego is the sole reality." When it comes to art, people pursuing such an aim in life can see it as nothing but a means of embellishing the panorama which "seems" to pass before their eyes. And so with art, too, they will try not to burden it with "anything that weighs us down." They will either despise any idea which may be contained in works of art, or they will adapt them to the requirements of their own capricious and fickle subjectivism.

Let us now turn to painting. The impressionists were already completely indifferent to the ideas contained in their work. One of them well expressed their common conviction when he said: "Lght is the principal personage in a picture." But the sensation of light is precisely a sensation, i.e. it is not yet an emotion, not yet a thought. The artist who limits himself to the sphere of sensations remains unmoved either by feelings or thoughts. He may paint a

[1] *The Flower Boat.*

good landscape. Indeed, the impressionists have painted many outstanding landscapes. But landscape does not comprise the whole art of painting.[1]

Let us recall "The Last Supper" by Leonardo da Vinci and ask ourselves:—Was light the principal personage in this famous fresco? As we know, its subject was that moment, full of thrilling drama, in the story of Jesus and his disciples, when he said to them: "Verily, verily, I say unto you, one of you shall betray me." Leonardo da Vinci's task was to depict both Jesus' own state of mind, his deep grief at his fearful discovery, and also that of his disciples, unable to believe that treachery had wormed its way into the midst of their little family. If the artist had felt that light was the principal personage in painting, he would not even have attempted to paint this drama. And if he had nevertheless done so, his main artistic interest would not have been focused on what was passing in the minds of Jesus and his disciples, but on what was happening on the walls of the room in which they had gathered, on the table at which they were sitting and on their own skins—in a word, on the variety of light effects. He would have given us, not a moving spiritual drama, but a complex of well-depicted light effects—one patch of light, let us say, on the wall of the room, another on the tablecloth, a third on Judas' crooked nose, a fourth on Jesus' cheek, and so on and so forth. This would have vastly enfeebled the impression created by the fresco; the specific importance of Leonardo da Vinci's work would have suffered greatly.

Certain French critics have compared impressionism to realism in literature: and the comparison is not without foundation. But

[1] There were very talented people among the first impressionists. But it is noteworthy that among these very talented people there were no first-rate portrait painters. And this is understandable. In portrait painting light can no longer play the main role. In the same way again, the landscapes of the outstanding impressionist masters are good because they successfully convey a capricious and varied play of light, but there is little "wood" about them. Feuerbach wrote brilliantly: "To think means to read the gospel of the senses in their interdependence." Not forgetting that by "senses" and "sensuality," Feuerbach meant everything connected with the sphere of sensations, we can say that the impressionists could not, and did not want to, read the "gospel of the senses." This was the main failing of their school. And it soon led to its degeneration. While the landscapes of the earliest and chief of the impressionist masters were good, a great many of the landscapes of their great many followers look like caricatures.

even if the impressionists were realists, their realism was entirely superficial; it never went below "the surface of things." And when this style of realism had won wide recognition in modern art—and it undoubtedly did so—the painters brought up under its influence were left with one of two alternatives: they could either concern themselves with "the surface of things," inventing ever new and more and more sensational and artificial light effects; or they could seek to penetrate below the outer crust of phenomena, having understood the mistake of the impressionists, and realised that the principal personage in a painting is not light but man, with his great variety of experience. Both trends are in fact to be met with in present-day painting. Concentration of interest on "the surface of things" is producing those paradoxical canvases before which even the most indulgent critics wring their hands in despair and admit that present day painting is passing through a "crisis of ugliness."[1]

On the other hand, the realisation that it is impossible to limit art to "the surface of things" leads artists to seek some idea in their work, i.e. to pay their respects to what was only recently being consigned to the flames. But it is not so easy as it sounds for an artist to instil an idea into his work. An idea has no existence apart from the real world. The stock of ideas of any individual is determined and enriched by his relationship with that world. And he whose relationship with the world has so developed that he considers his own "ego" the "sole reality," can be nothing but a pauper when it comes to ideas. Not only does he possess none, but, what is more, he has no means of thinking any out. And just as, for want of bread, men will eat pigweed, so for want of clear ideas they content themselves with vague hints of ideas, substitutes culled from mysticism, symbolism and other similar "isms" characteristic of the period of decay.

In brief, what we have already observed in literature is repeated in painting. Realism collapses as a result of its own lack of content. Idealist reaction triumphs.

Subjective idealism has always based itself on the idea that the sole reality is our "ego." But it needed the boundless individualism of the period of bourgeois decline to turn this idea, not only into a principle of egoism determining the mutual relations

[1] See article by Camille Mauclair, *La crise de la laideur en peinture*, in his interesting collection entitled *Trois crises de l'art actuel*, Paris, 1906.

between men, each "loving himself as the Lord"—the bourgeoisie has never been distinguished for an excess of altruism—but also into the theoretical basis for a new aesthetics.

The reader has heard, of course, of the so-called cubists. And if he has ever looked at their handiwork, I doubt if they aroused in him any enthusiasm. In me, at all events, they fail to arouse anything comparable with aesthetic pleasure. "Rubbish cubed!" —these are the words that spontaneously come to mind on seeing these allegedly artistic exercises. And yet there is a reason for "cubism." To call it rubbish raised to the third degree does not explain its origin. Of course, this is not the place to enter into a lengthy explanation of the origin of cubism. But at least one may indicate the direction in which an explanation is to be sought.

Before me is an interesting book by Albert Gleizes and Jean Metzinger, entitled *Du cubisme.* Both the authors are painters and both belong to the "cubist" school. Let us turn to them, in accordance with the rule *audiatur et altera pars.*[1] How do they justify their extraordinary methods of work?

> "Nothing outside us is real," they say. ". . . We do not intend to cast doubt on the existence of objects which act on our external senses: but the only thing we can be reasonably sure about is the image evoked by them in our minds."

From this the authors conclude that we do not know what forms objects have in themselves. And because we do not know these forms, they consider that they have the right to depict them according to their own arbitrary conceptions. They also make the reservation, which is worth noting, that they do not wish to limit themselves, like the impressionists, to the sphere of sensation.

> "We are seeking the essential," they declare, "but we seek it in our personality, and not in any realm of eternities industriously laid out by mathematicians and philosophers."

In these arguments we meet again, as the reader will see, the already familiar idea that the "ego" is the "sole reality." True, its form has been modified. Gleizes and Metzinger say that doubts about the existence of external objects are entirely foreign to them. But, admitting that the external world exists, our authors

[1] Let the other side also be heard—the motto which Plekhanov put on the title page of his famous book, *The Monist View of History* (published in English as *In Defence of Materialism*).—TRANS.

immediately proclaim it unknowable. And this means that for them, too, nothing is real except their "ego."

If images of objects arise in our minds as the result of the action of those objects on our external senses, then we clearly cannot say the external world is unknowable. We know about it precisely by means of this action. Gleizes and Metzinger are mistaken. And their argument about "forms in themselves" is also unsound. We cannot blame them overmuch for their mistakes; similar mistakes have been made by men infinitely better versed in philosophy. But we are bound to draw attention to the following:

Because of our supposed inability to know the external world, our authors conclude that we must seek the essential in "our personality." This conclusion can be understood in two ways. By "personality" may be meant, firstly, something which is the common possession of all mankind, or, secondly, the personality of each separate individual. The first interpretation leads us to the transcendental idealism of Kant, the second to the sophistical conception that each individual is "the measure of all things." It is towards the sophistical interpretation that our authors incline.

And once this sophistical conception has been accepted, then in painting, as in everything else, absolutely anything becomes permissible. If, instead of "The Woman in Blue" (this was the title of a painting by F. Léger exhibited at the *Salon* last autumn), I draw a number of geometrical figures, who has the right to tell me that my picture is not a good one? Women constitute a part of the external world in which I live. The external world is not knowable. To depict a woman I can only appeal to my own "personality," and my "personality" gives the woman the form of several carelessly scattered cubes or, rather, parallelopipeds. The visitors to the "Salon" may laugh. But that does not matter. The "rabble" only laughs because it does not understand the language of the artist. The artist must on no account make concessions to the "rabble."

> The artist who makes no concession, explains nothing and says nothing, accumulates an inner strength which lights up everything around him.[1]

And while waiting for this strength to accumulate there is nothing left but to draw geometrical figures.

[1] Albert Gleizer and Jean Metzinger, *Du cubisme*, p. 42.

And so we have a kind of comic parody on Pushkin's poem, *To the Poet*

> Can you your own sharp criticism meet?
> You can? Then let the mob besmirch your name,
> Spit on the altar that enshrines your flame,
> In childish horse-play shake your tripod's feet.[1]

What is comic about this parody is that the "exacting artist" is now satisfied with the most patent rubbish. This demonstrates, incidentally, that the inner dialectic of social life has today reduced the theory of art for art's sake to complete absurdity.

It is not good for man to be alone. The present-day "innovators" in art are not satisfied with what their predecessors created. There is no harm in that; on the contrary, the search for novelty is often a source of progress. But not everyone who looks for something new succeeds in finding it. We need to know where to look. He who is blind to the lessons of social life, who knows no reality other than his own "ego," will not find anything new, search as he may, except new rubbish. It is not good for man to be alone.

It turns out that in present social conditions, art for art's sake produces not very sweet fruit. Extreme individualism in the period of bourgeois decay shuts off the artist from all sources of real inspiration. It makes him quite unaware of what is going on in society, and condemns him to barren preoccupation with his own private and empty experiences and sickly, fantastic inventions. In the final count, the results not only bear no sort of relation to any kind of beauty, but constitute an obvious absurdity which can only be defended by a sophistical distortion of the idealist theory of knowledge.

In Pushkin, the "cold and haughty people" listen "without understanding" to the singing poet. I have already pointed out that Pushkin's opposition between poet and people is to be explained by special historical circumstances. To understand him, we need only remember that the epithets "cold and haughty" were certainly not applicable to the Russian serfs. But they were very apt as a description of that worldly "rabble" which, unheeding as it was, destroyed our great poet. The people who made up this "rabble" might well say of themselves, without the least exaggeration, as the "mob" say in Pushkin's lines:

[1] Translated by Walter Morison (*Pushkin's Poems*, Allen and Unwin, 1946).

We are timid and treacherous tools
whom shameless cruelty rules,
eunuchs with icy hearts,
malicious and fettered fools,
playing our sin-rotted parts.

Pushkin realised that it would be senseless to give "bold" lessons to this soulless society rabble, who would not have understood a word. He was right in proudly turning his back on them. Indeed, he was wrong in not spurning them sufficiently, to the great misfortune of Russian literature. In advanced capitalist countries today, however, the poet's attitude towards the people, and generally speaking, the attitude of the artist who cannot discard his old bourgeois self, is the direct opposite of Pushkin's. It is not the "people" who are stupid; and it is certainly not the real people, the advanced part of which is becoming more and more conscious, but the artists, who now listen to noble words "without understanding." At the very best, these artists are to blame for their clocks being about eighty years behind the times. Rejecting the finest aspirations of their epoch, they naïvely imagine themselves to be continuing the struggle against philistinism in which the Romantics engaged.

The Western European aesthetes, with our own Russians tagging along behind them, are fond of dilating on the philistine nature of the contemporary proletarian movement. This is absurd. Richard Wagner pointed out long ago how baseless is the accusation of philistinism which such aesthetes make against the working class movement. As Wagner rightly says, if one pays attention to the facts (*Genau betrachtet*), it is evident that the working class movement is not heading towards philistinism but away from it to a free life, towards "artistic humanism" (*zum künstlerischen Menschentum*). "It is an effort towards a life of dignified enjoyment, a life in which man will no longer have to expend all his vital energies in finding the means of subsistence." The expenditure of all one's vital energies in acquiring the means of subsistence is, today, precisely what gives rise to "philistine" sentiments. Constant worry over the means of livelihood—

makes man weak, submissive, dull-witted and pitiable, and turns him into a creature incapable either of loving or of hating, into a citizen capable at any moment of sacrificing the last remnants of his free will simply in order to be relieved of his cares.

The goal of the working-class movement is the elimination of this degrading and corrupting care. Wagner came to the conclusion that only with its elimination, only with the fulfilment of the emancipating mission of the proletariat, would the words of Jesus be realised: "Take no thought for your life, what ye shall eat" (Luke xii. 22).[1]

He might have added, that only the realisation of the above conditions would leave no more basis for the opposition of aesthetics to morality, which we find among adherents of art for art's sake such as Flaubert. Flaubert considered that "virtuous books are tedious and false."[2] He was right. But only because the virtue of present-day society, bourgeois virtue, is tedious and false. The "virtue" of antiquity, in the eyes of the same Flaubert, seemed neither tedious nor false. And yet the only difference between it and bourgeois virtue is that it was free of bourgeois individualism.

Shirinsky-Shikhmatov, in his capacity as Minister of Education under Nicholas I, saw the task of art as being the—

> affirmation of the belief, so important for both public and private life—that evil-doing reaps its punishment here on earth

i.e. in the society so zealously guarded by Shirinsky-Shikhmatov. This, of course, was a great lie and tedious vulgarity. Artists are well advised to ignore such stuff. And when we read Flaubert's words that, *in a certain sense*, "there is nothing more poetic than vice,"[3] we understand that the real sense of this comparison lies in the opposition of vice to the vulgar, tedious and false virtue of bourgeois moralists like the Shirinsky-Shikhmatovs. But with the elimination of the social order which gave rise to this vulgar, tedious and false virtue, the *moral* need to idealise vice will also be removed. Let me repeat—the ancient virtues did not seem vulgar, tedious or false to Flaubert, although, as a result of his extremely undeveloped social and political understanding, he could, while respecting these virtues, delight in such a monstrous negation of them as the behaviour of a Nero. In socialist society, interest in art for art's sake will quite logically become impossible in the same measure as the vulgarisation of social morality, which is today an

[1] *Die Kunst und die Revolution*, R. Wagner, Gesammete Schriften, II B. Leipzig, 1872, pp. 40–1.

[2] *Les carnets de Gustave Flaubert*, L. Bertrand, *Gustave Flaubert*, p. 260.

[3] *Ibid.*, same page.

unavoidable consequence of the desire of the ruling class to maintain its privileges, comes to an end.

Flaubert remarked: "*L'art, c'est la recherche de l'inutile*" (art is the quest for the useless). It is not difficult to recognise in these words the basic concept of Pushkin's poem *The Rabble*. But such an approach merely means that the artist is in revolt against the narrow utilitarianism of a particular ruling class or caste. The abolition of classes will also put an end to this narrow utilitarianism, first cousin to self-interest. Self-interest has nothing in common with aesthetics: a judgment of taste always implies the absence of considerations of personal advantage on the part of the person expressing it. But personal advantage and *social* advantage are two quite different things. The desire to serve the community which lay at the basis of ancient virtue is a source of selflessness, and selflessness can very easily become, and in fact has become—as the history of art shows—the subject of works of art. One need only recall the songs of primitive peoples or, not to go back so far, the statues to Harmodius and Aristogeiton in Athens.

The ancient philosophers—Plato and Aristotle, for example—clearly understood how degraded a man becomes when all his energies are absorbed in care for his own material existence. Present-day bourgeois ideologists realise this, too. They, too, see the need to relieve man of the degrading burden of constant economic cares. But the man they have in mind is the man of the upper classes, who lives by exploiting the workers. They see the solution of the problem exactly as it was seen by the thinkers of antiquity—in the enslavement of the producers by a chosen happy few, who approach more or less to the ideal of "the superman." But if such a solution was already conservative in the days of Plato and Aristotle, it has now become ultra-reactionary. And while the Greek conservatives, the slave-owners of Aristotle's day, could hope to preserve their ruling position by relying on their own "valour," those who advocate the enslavement of the mass of the people today are extremely sceptical as to the valour of the exploiter of bourgeois origin. Therefore they very willingly dream of some superman of genius at the head of the State, who by the force of his iron will can strengthen the now tottering edifice of class domination. Those decadents who are not strangers to political interest are often ardent admirers of Napoleon I.

If Renan needed a strong government, to force the "sturdy rustic" to work for him while he devoted himself to reflection, what the present-day aesthetes need is a social order that will force the proletariat to work while they give themselves up to elevated pleasures . . . such as the drawing and colouring of cubes and other geometrical figures. Constitutionally incapable of serious work, they are filled with most sincere indignation at the thought of a social order in which there will be no idlers.

When in Rome, do as Rome does. Whilst fighting in words against the philistine, our bourgeois aesthetes worship the golden calf just like the most commonplace philistines. "It is thought there is an artistic movement," writes Mauclair. "It is really a movement in the picture sales rooms, where bids are also made for unpublished geniuses."[1] I would add in passing that this speculation in "unpublished genius" explains incidentally the feverish pursuit of "new" forms to which the majority of present-day artists abandon themselves. Men always aspire to the "new" because the old does not satisfy them. But the question is, *why* does it not satisfy them? For a great many contemporary artists, the only reason is that so long as the public approves the old, the work of their own genius remains "unpublished." They are pushed into revolt against the old by that same "sole reality," that same beloved "ego," and not by love of any new idea. But love of this kind does not inspire the artist: it only prompts him to regard everything, even the Apollo Belvedere, from the standpoint of profit or loss.

"The question of money has become so inextricably mixed up with the question of art," Mauclair continues, "that the art critic is caught in a vice. The best critics cannot say what they think, and the remainder only say what they think is opportune, since, after all, they have to make a living. I do not say there is anything wrong in this, but there is no harm in realising the complexity of the problem."[2]

Art for art's sake, we see, has become *art for money's sake*. And the whole problem which interests Mauclair is the problem as to why this has taken place. It is not difficult to find the answer.

There was a time, as in the Middle Ages, when only the superfluity, the excess of production over consumption, was exchanged.

There was again a time, when not only the superfluity, but all products, all

[1] Camille Mauclair, *Trois Crises de l'art actuel*, Paris, 1906, pp. 319–20.

[2] *Op. cit.*, p. 321.

industrial existence, had passed into commerce, when the whole of production depended on exchange. . . .

Finally, there came a time when everything that men had considered as inalienable became an object of exchange, of traffic and could be alienated. This is the time when the very things which till then had been communicated, but never exchanged; given, but never sold; acquired, but never bought—virtue, love, conviction, knowledge, conscience, etc.—when everything, in short, passed into commerce. It is the time of general corruption, of universal venality or, to speak in terms of political economy, the time when everything, moral or physical, having become a marketable value, is brought to the market to be assessed at its truest value.[1]

Is it in the least surprising that, in a generally mercenary age, art too has become mercenary?

Mauclair does not want to commit himself as to whether there is "anything wrong" in this. I, too, have no desire to consider it from the moral standpoint. I am trying, not to condemn nor to approve, but to understand. I do not say: artists "ought" today to be inspired by the working-class emancipation movement. No. Just as an apple tree *must* produce apples and a pear tree pears, so must the artist who adopts the bourgeois standpoint be against the working-class movement. Art, in periods of decadence, "*must*" itself be decadent. That is inevitable. And there would be no point in saying it is "wrong." But, as *The Communist Manifesto* rightly points out:

In times when the class struggle nears the decisive hour, the process of dissolution going on within the ruling class, in fact within the whole range of the old society, assumes such a violent glaring character, that a small section of the ruling class cuts itself adrift, and joins the revolutionary class, the class that holds the future in its hands. Just as, therefore, at an earlier period, a section of the nobility went over to the bourgeoisie, so now a portion of the bourgeoisie goes over to the proletariat, and in particular, a portion of the bourgeois ideologists who have raised themselves to the level of comprehending theoretically the historical movement as a whole.

Among the bourgeois ideologists who have come over to the side of the proletariat, we find very few artists. This is probably because only thinking people "can raise themselves to the level of comprehending theoretically the historical movement as a whole," while contemporary artists, however—unlike the great masters of the Renaissance—think very little.[2]

[1] Karl Marx, *The Poverty of Philosophy*, Chapter 1, Section 1.

[2] "We touch here on a defect in general culture amongst the greater part of the younger artists. Acquaintance with them will quickly show that they are

But however this may be, one can confidently state that the powers of any true artist today are greatly enhanced if he identifies himself with the great emancipatory ideas of our time. But these ideas need to become part of his flesh and blood, so that he can indeed express them as an artist.[1]

He must also be able to judge at its true worth the artistic modernism of the present-day bourgeois ideologists. The ruling class is today in a position where its further advance means its decline. And all its ideologists share this pitiable fate. The most advanced among them are precisely those who have fallen lower than any of their predecessors.

* * *

When I expressed the views expounded here, Mr. Lunacharsky[2] raised several objections, the most important of which I will examine.

(1) He was surprised that I should, as he put it, recognise an absolute criterion of beauty, for there is no such criterion. Everything is in movement, everything is changing. And men's conceptions of beauty change too. That is why, according to him, we cannot say that present day art is in fact experiencing "a crisis of ugliness."

To this I objected and object, that I have all along denied that

generally very ignorant. . . . Helpless or indifferent in face of conflicting ideas and real dramatic situations, they work in painful remoteness from all intellectual and social agitation . . . concerned only with questions of technique, absorbed by the material appearance of a painting rather than by its general meaning and its intellectual influence." Holl, *Le Jeune Peinture Contemporaine*, Paris, 1912, pp. 14–15.

[1] Here I am glad to quote Flaubert. "I believe in form and content," he wrote to Georges Sand, "two things which can never exist the one without the other." *Correspondance*, quatrième serie, p. 225.

Anyone who thinks it possible to sacrifice form "for an idea" ceases to be an artist, if he ever was one.

[2] At a public lecture in Paris in November, 1912. *V. Lunacharsky*, Marxist literary critic, dramatist, journalist. First People's Commissar for Education after the 1917 October Socialist Revolution. He was at one time severely criticised by Lenin (see Lenin's *Materialism and Empirio-Criticism*) as well as by Plekhanov for turning away from Marxist materialism to idealism.—TRANS.

there is or can be any absolute criterion of beauty.[1] Men's conceptions of beauty undoubtedly change in the course of history. But while there is no *absolute* criterion of beauty, and while all criteria are relative, this is far from implying that we have no *objective* possibility of judging whether or not a given artistic conception is well realised.

Let us assume that the artist wants to paint "a woman in blue." If what he depicts in his painting does in fact look like such a woman, we say that he has succeeded in painting a good picture. If, on the other hand, instead of a woman in a blue dress, we see on his canvas a group of assorted geometrical figures, more or less thickly coated in blue paint in different places, then we shall say that he has painted anything you like, but not a good picture. The more the realisation of a concept—or to put it in more general terms—the more the form of a work of art, corresponds to its idea, the more successful it is. There is your objective criterion. And only because such a criterion exists, have we the right to assert that the drawings of Leonardo da Vinci, for example, are superior to the drawings of some petty Themistoclus, who daubs paper for his own amusement. When Leonardo da Vinci drew an old man with a beard, for example, it did turn out an old man with a beard. And how well he succeeded! So much so that when we see it we say—how alive! But when Themistoclus draws a similar old man, the best thing to do to avoid misunderstanding, is to write underneath it, "This is an old man with a beard, and nothing else."

In asserting that there can be no objective criterion of beauty, Mr. Lunacharsky has fallen into the error committed by so many

[1] "It is not the subconscious whim of fastidious taste which prompts in us the desire to find original aesthetic values, not subject to vainglorious fashion and imitation of the crowd. The creative dream of a unique, imperishable beauty, the living image of which 'will save the world' and illumine and revive the lost and the fallen, is nurtured by the ineradicable need of the human spirit to penetrate the creative secrets of the absolute." V. N. Speransky, *The Social Role of Philosophy*, Introduction, p. xi, 1st edition, St. Petersburg, published by "Shipovnik," dated 1913.

People who talk like this are forced by logic to recognise an absolute criterion of beauty. But those who talk like this are pure-blooded idealists and I consider myself a no less pure-blooded materialist. I not only do not recognise the existence of a "unique, imperishable beauty," but do not even understand what sense can be attached to these words. What is more, I am sure the idealist gentlemen concerned do not understand either. All argument about such beauty is so much "word-spinning."

bourgeois ideologists, including the cubists—the error of extreme subjectivity. I entirely fail to understand how a man who calls himself a Marxist can make such a mistake.

It should be added, however, that I am here using the term "beauty" in a very broad sense—in too broad a sense, if you like. To draw an old man with a beard *beautifully* does not mean to draw something which is beautiful, i.e. a *handsome* old man. The field of art is far wider than the sphere of "the beautiful." The criterion I have given, that of the correspondence of the form to the idea, may be used with equal facility throughout this broad field. Mr. Lunacharsky asserted (if I understood him aright) that form can also fully correspond to a false idea. With this I cannot agree. Let us recall de Curel's play *Le repas du lion*. The basis of this play is, as we have seen, the false idea that the employer bears the same relation to his workers as the lion does to the jackals, who feed themselves on the scraps left over from his royal table. I ask you—could de Curel express this false idea correctly in his drama? No! The reason why the idea is false, is precisely that it contradicts the real relations between the employer and his workers. To express this idea in a work of art means to distort reality. And when a work of art distorts reality, it is a failure. That is why *Le repas du lion* falls far short of de Curel's talent; and for the same reason the play, *At the King's Gates*, falls far short of Hamsun's talent.

(2) Mr. Lunacharsky reproached me with "excessive objectivism" in my exposition. He evidently agreed that an apple tree must produce apples and a pear tree pears. But he pointed out that among artists taking the bourgeois point of view there are also waverers, who need to be convinced and not left to the mercy of bourgeois influences.

I must admit that I find this criticism even less comprehensible than the other. I said and (I would like to think) demonstrated in my lecture that contemporary art was in decline.[1] I gave as the

[1] I am afraid that there may be a misunderstanding here too. By the word "decline" I mean, *comme de raison*, the whole process, and not any particular episodes. This process is not yet complete, just as the social process of the collapse of the bourgeois order is not yet complete. It would be strange to think, therefore, that present-day bourgeois ideologists are utterly incapable of producing any kind of outstanding work at all. It stands to reason that, even at this stage, such works are possible. But the chances of their appearance are being drastically reduced. What is more, even outstanding works bear the imprint of the period of decadence. We have only to take the already mentioned Russian trinity: while Mr. Filosofov is devoid of talent of any kind in any

reason for this phenomenon, concerning which no one who genuinely loves art can remain indifferent, the fact that the majority of present-day artists have a bourgeois outlook and remain entirely inaccessible to the great emancipatory ideas of our time. I ask, how can it influence the waverers to point this out? If it is convincing, then it must rouse them to go over to the proletarian standpoint. And this is all that can be demanded of a lecture devoted to an analysis of the question of art, and not to the exposition and defence of the principles of socialism.

(3) Last, but not least. Mr. Lunacharsky, who considers it impossible to prove that bourgeois art is decadent, considers that I could have approached the matter more rationally had I opposed to bourgeois ideas an "orderly system"—that, so far as I can remember, is how he expressed it—of principles which are opposed to them. And he added that such a system would be worked out in due course. But such an objection is utterly beyond my comprehension. If this system has *yet* to be worked out, it is clear that it does not yet exist. And if that is the case, how could I counterpose it to bourgeois views? And what sort of orderly system of concepts is this? Modern scientific socialism is undoubtedly a fully organised theory. And it has the advantage of *already* existing. But, as I have said, it would be very strange if, in setting out to speak on "art and social life," I began to expound the doctrine of contemporary scientific socialism, for example, the theory of surplus value. There is a time and place for everything.

It is possible, however, that, in mentioning this orderly system of concepts, Mr. Lunacharsky had in mind the considerations on "proletarian culture" recently advanced in the press by Mr. Bogdanov[1]

sphere, Mme. Hippius has some artistic talent, and Mr. Merezhkovsky can even be said to be a very talented artist. But it is easy to see that his last novel (*Alexander I*), for example, is irrevocably spoilt by his religious mania, which is in its turn a phenomenon peculiar to a period of decadence. In such periods even very great talents do not by any means contribute all that they might.

[1] A. A. Bogdanov (1873–1928), once a Bolshevik, who under the influence of defeatism after the 1905 revolution turned away from Marxist materialism to a variety of idealism which he called "empiriomonism"—completely exposed by Lenin in his *Materialism and Empirio-Criticism* (1909)—and from Marxist economics (*A Short Course of Economic Science*) to various "mechanistic" theories. His theory of an entirely fresh "proletarian culture" was popularised by him for a time after the October Revolution of 1917. He was Director of the State Institute of Blood Transfusion when he died.—TRANS.

(his closest ideological colleague). In this case, his last criticism implies that I would have been far more proficient had I learned a little from Mr. Bogdanov. I return thanks for the advice; but I do not intend to make use of it. And for anyone who, through lack of experience, may be interested in Mr. Bogdanov's pamphlet *On Proletarian Culture*, I would recall that this pamphlet was fairly successfully laughed out of court in *The Contemporary World* by another of Mr. Lunacharsky's fellow-thinkers—Mr. Alexinsky.[1]

[1] G. A. Alexinsky (1879–), formerly a Bolshevik, broke away in 1908–9 for the same reasons as Bogdanov, but became a jingo, supporter of monarchism and (after 1917) a counter-revolutionary.—TRANS.

WORKS BY PLEKHANOV TRANSLATED INTO ENGLISH

Anarchism and Socialism, translated by Eleanor Marx Aveling (Twentieth Century Press).

Fundamental Problems of Marxism, translated by E. and C. Paul (Martin Lawrence).

Essays on the History of Materialism, translated by Ralph Fox (John Lane The Bodley Head).

The Materialist Conception of History (Lawrence & Wishart).

The Role of the Individual in History (Lawrence & Wishart).

In Defence of Materialism (The Development of the Marxist View of History), translated by Andrew Rothstein (Lawrence & Wishart).

INDEX